asfa presents

108 drawin

by

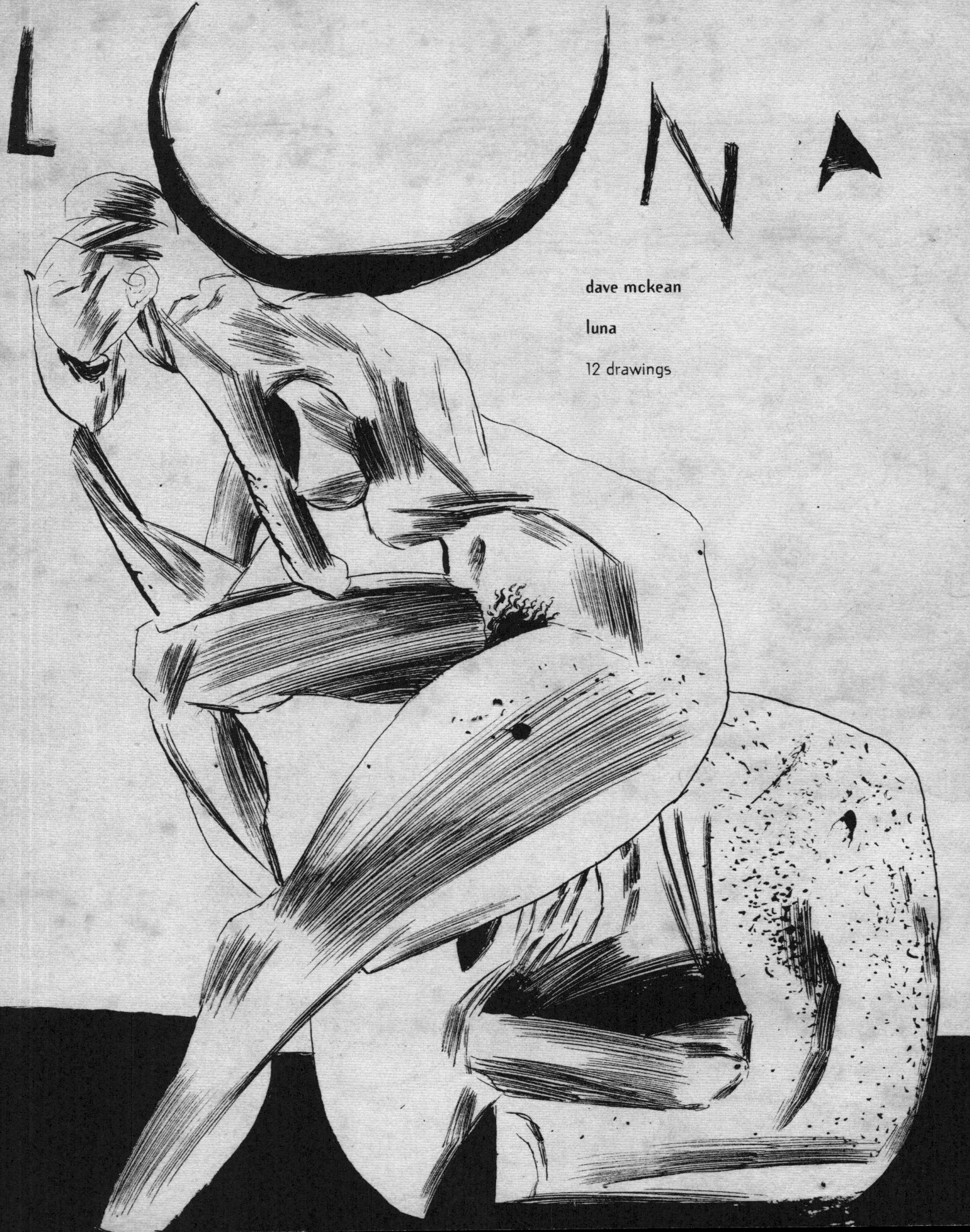

dave mckean

luna

12 drawings

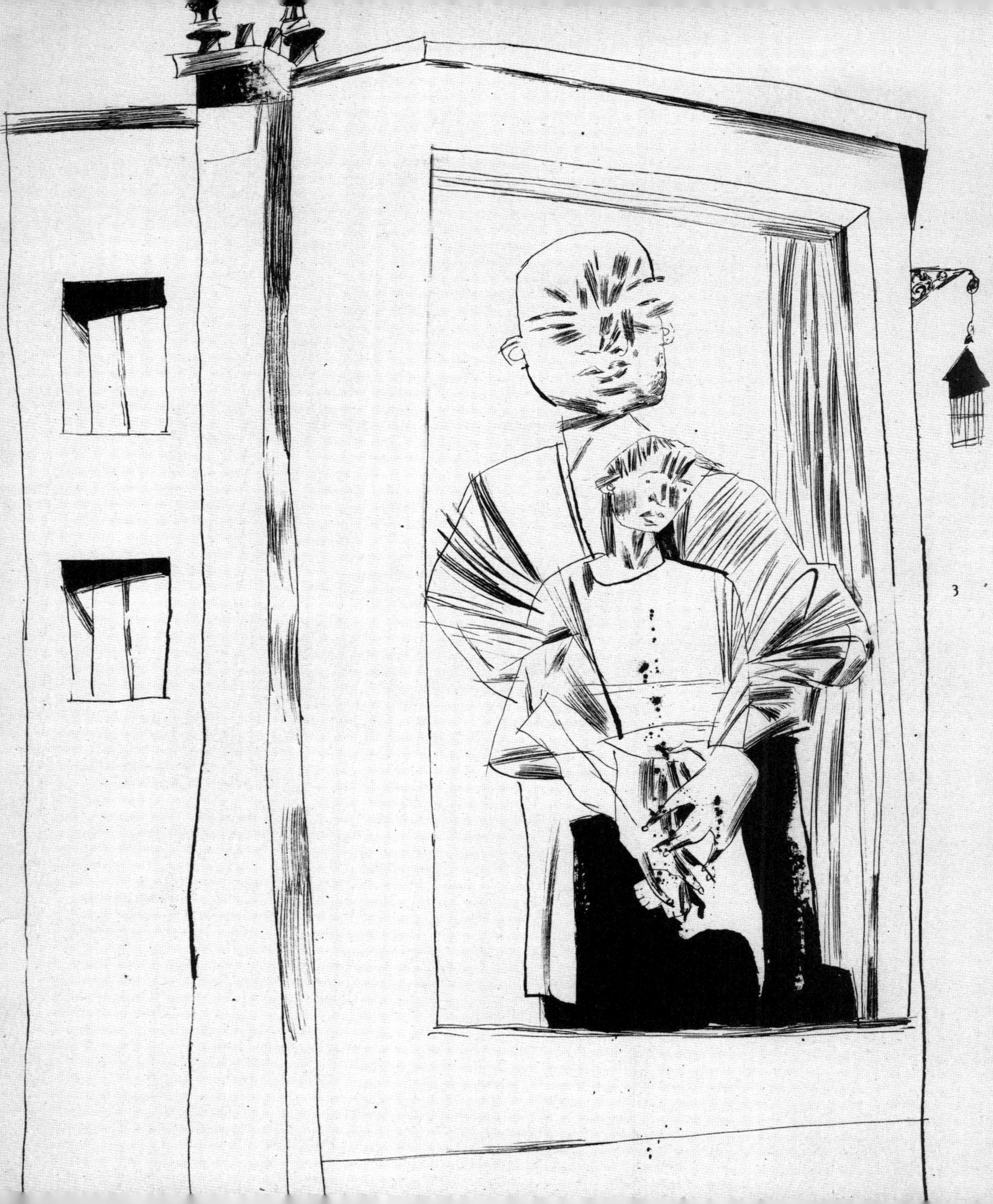

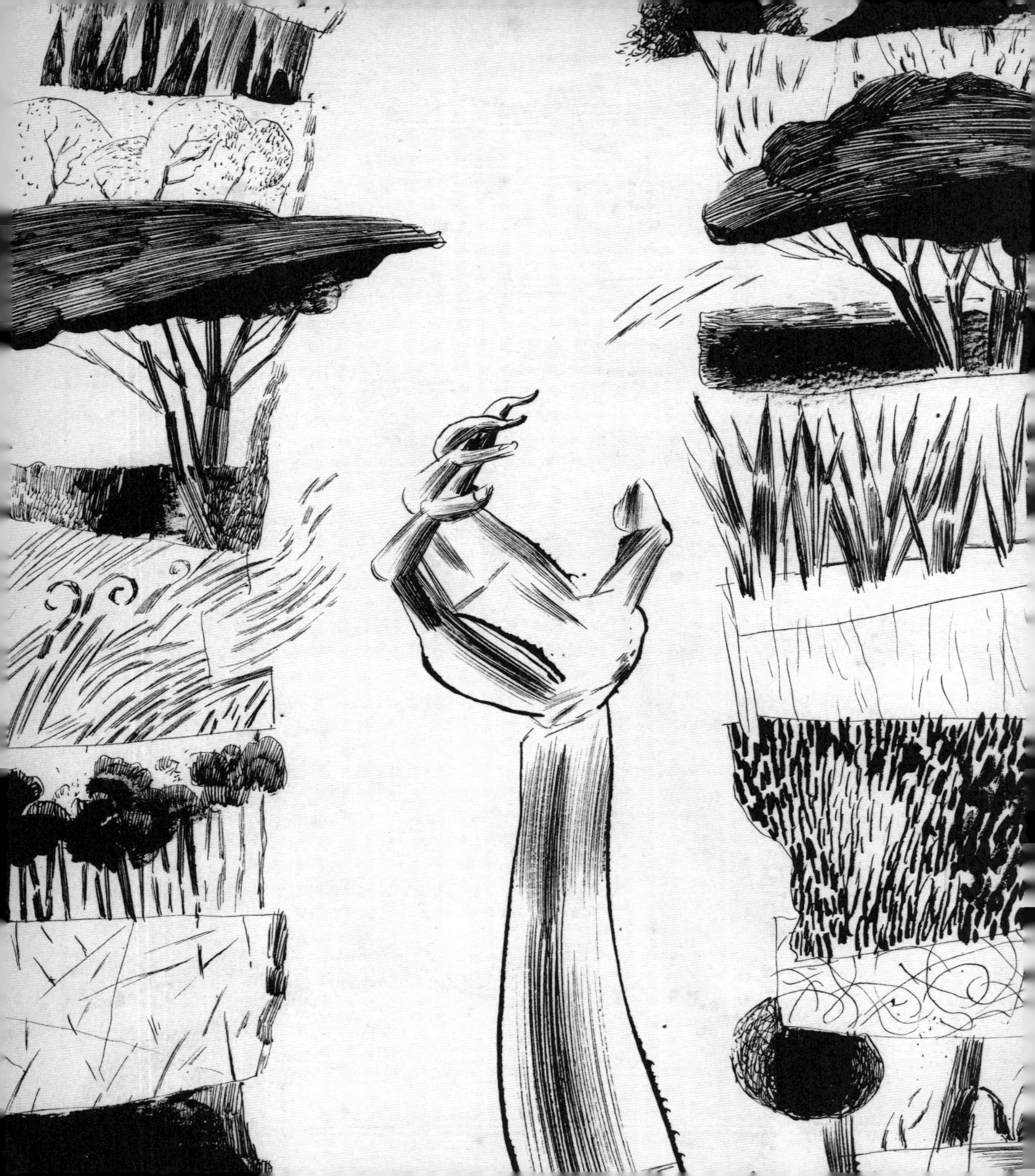

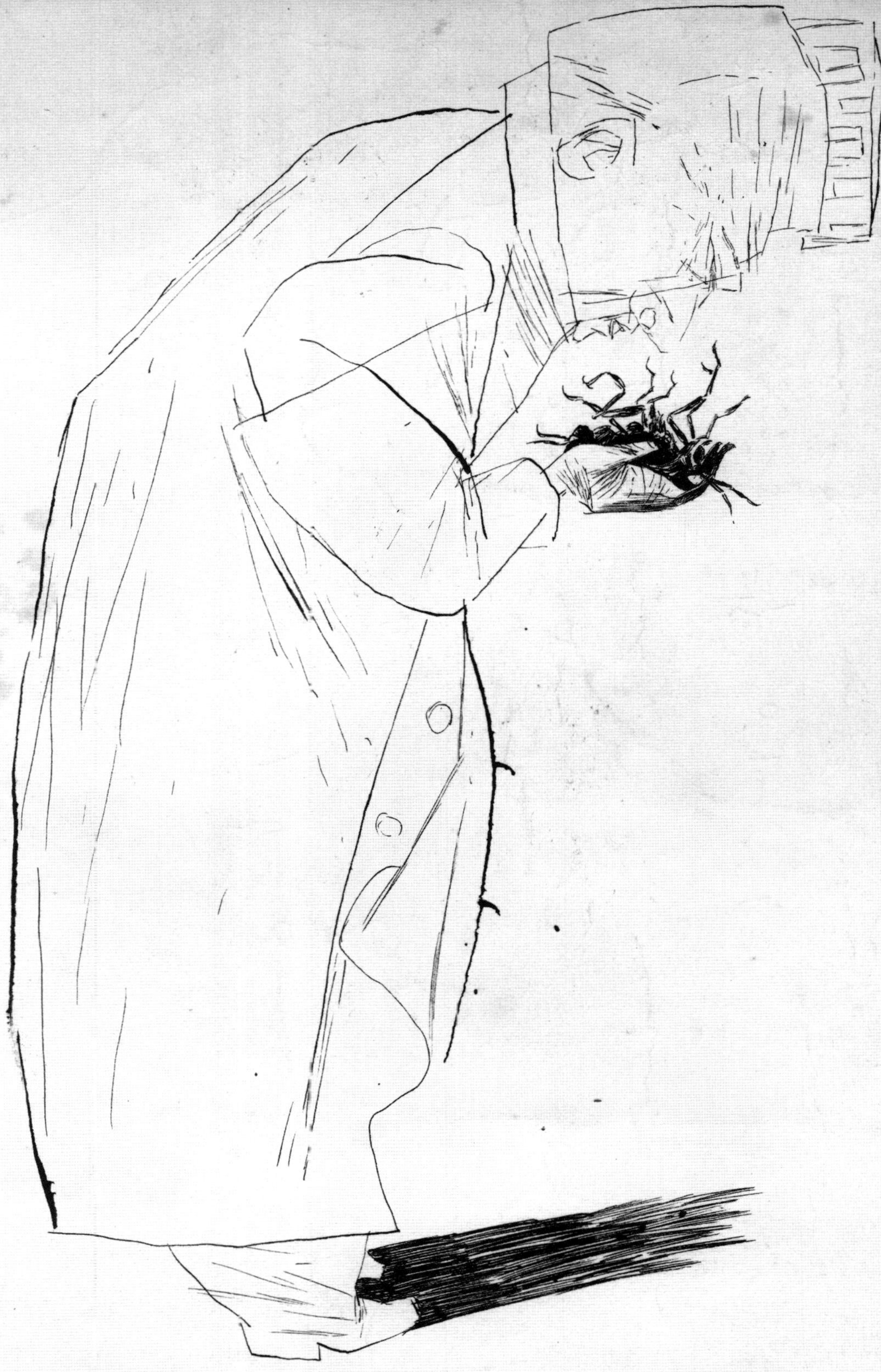

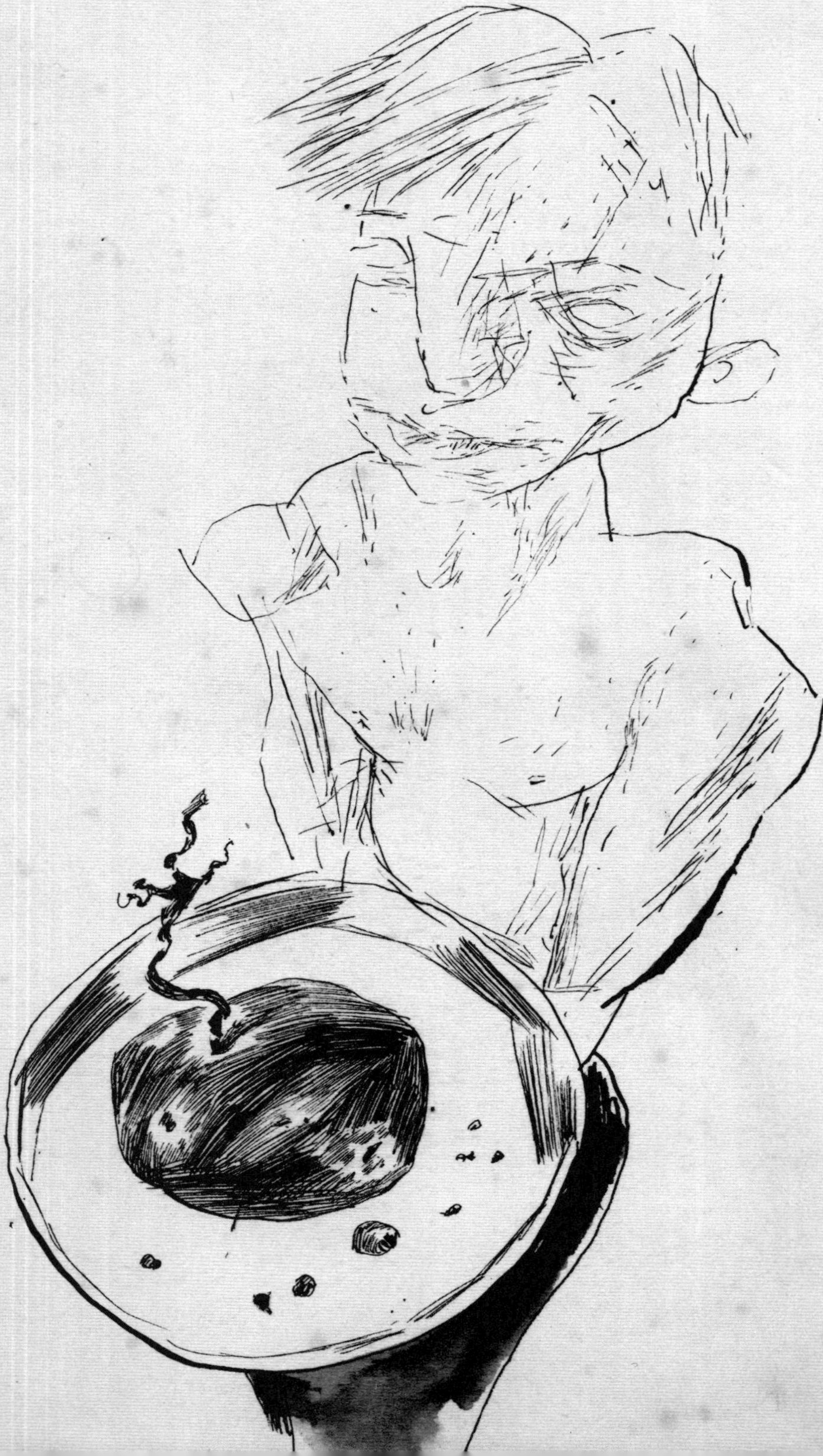

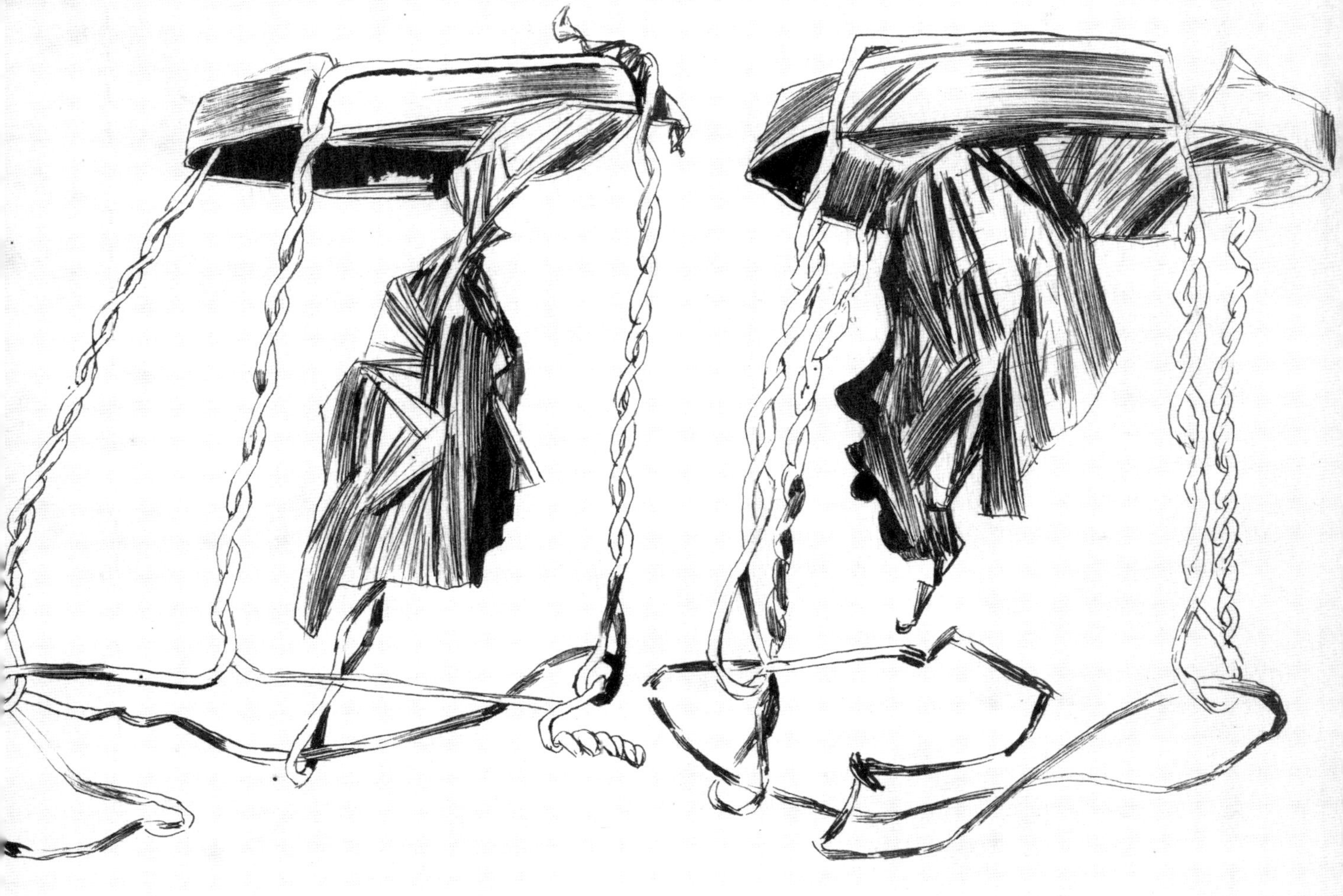

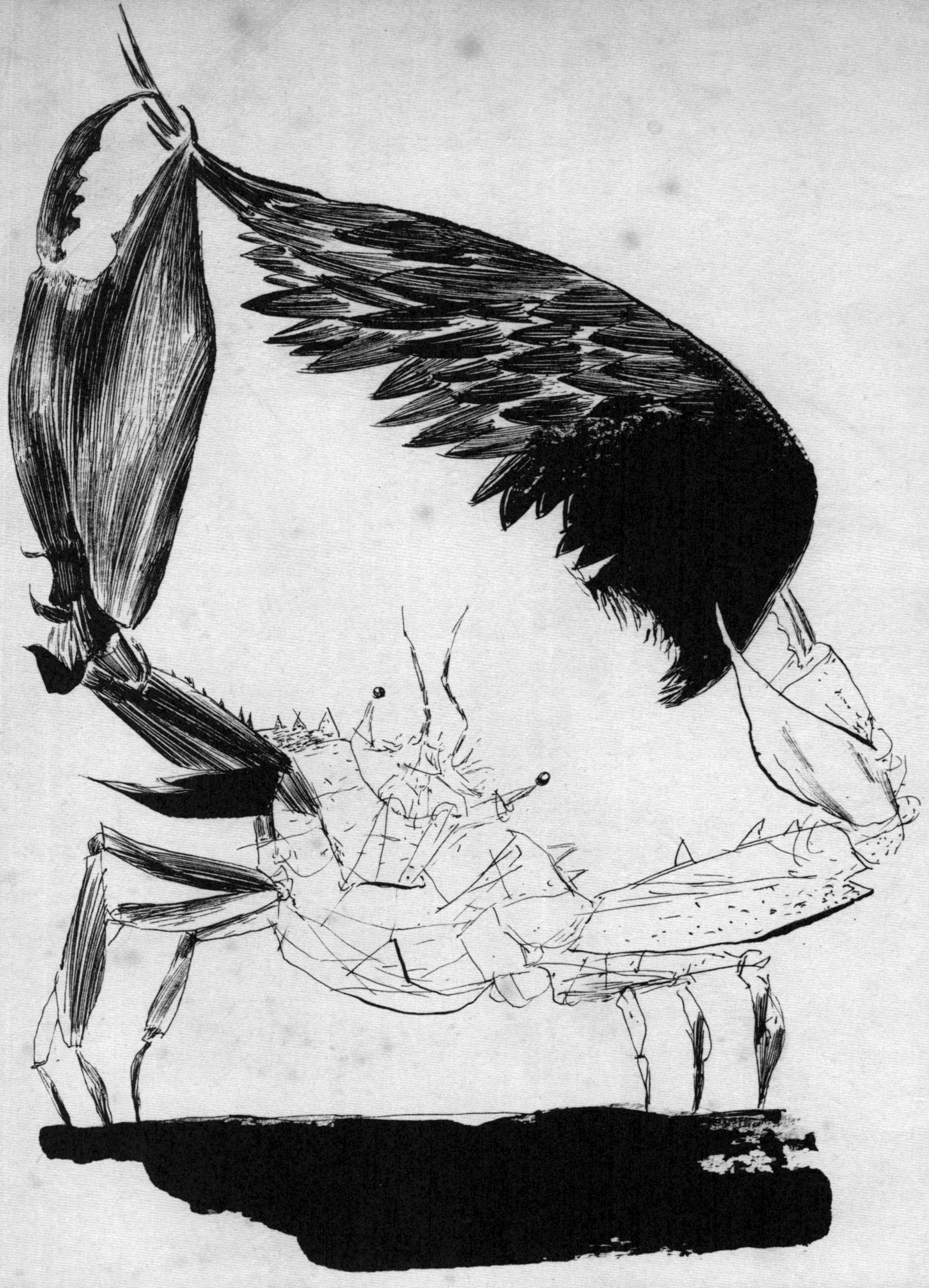

8

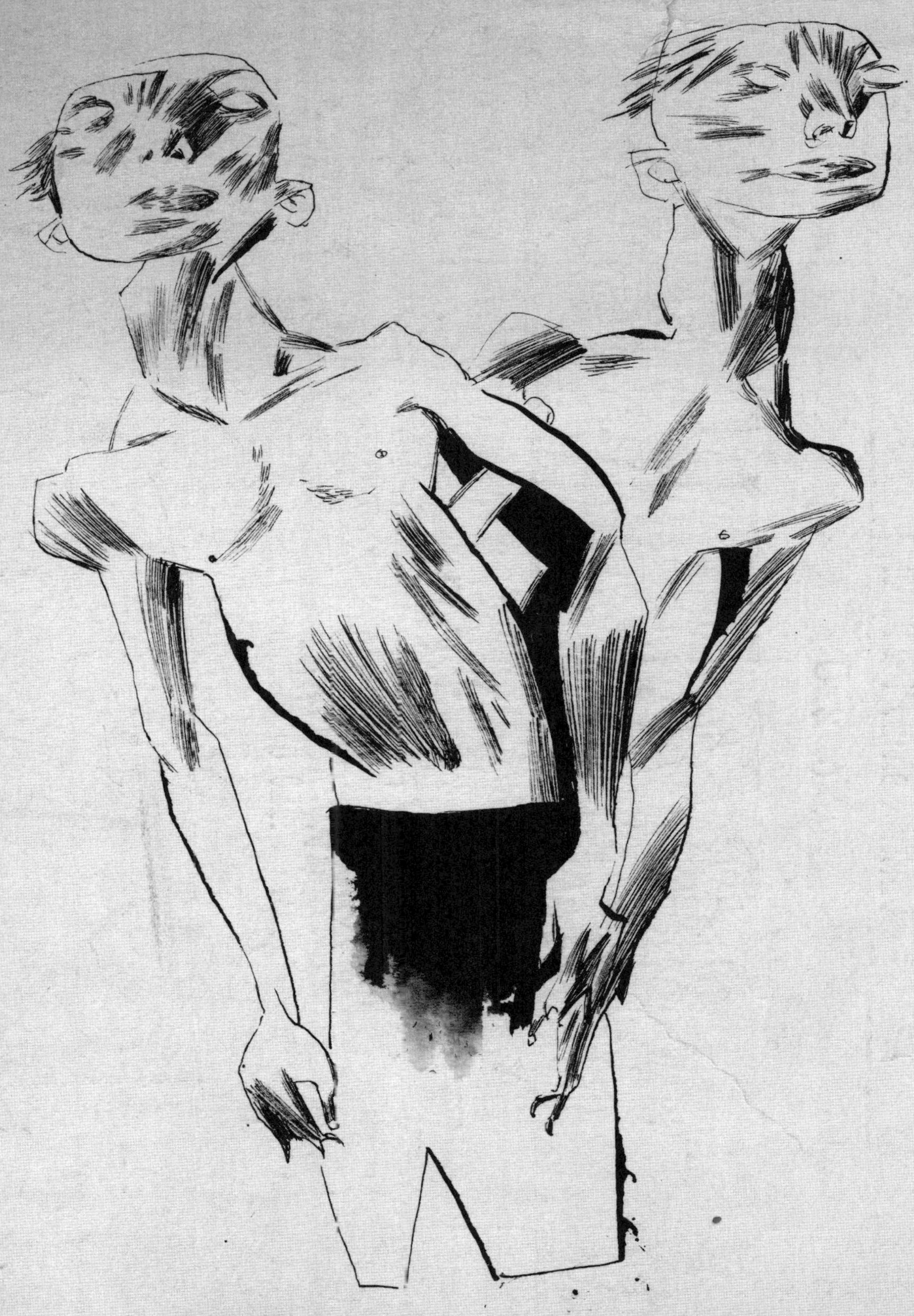

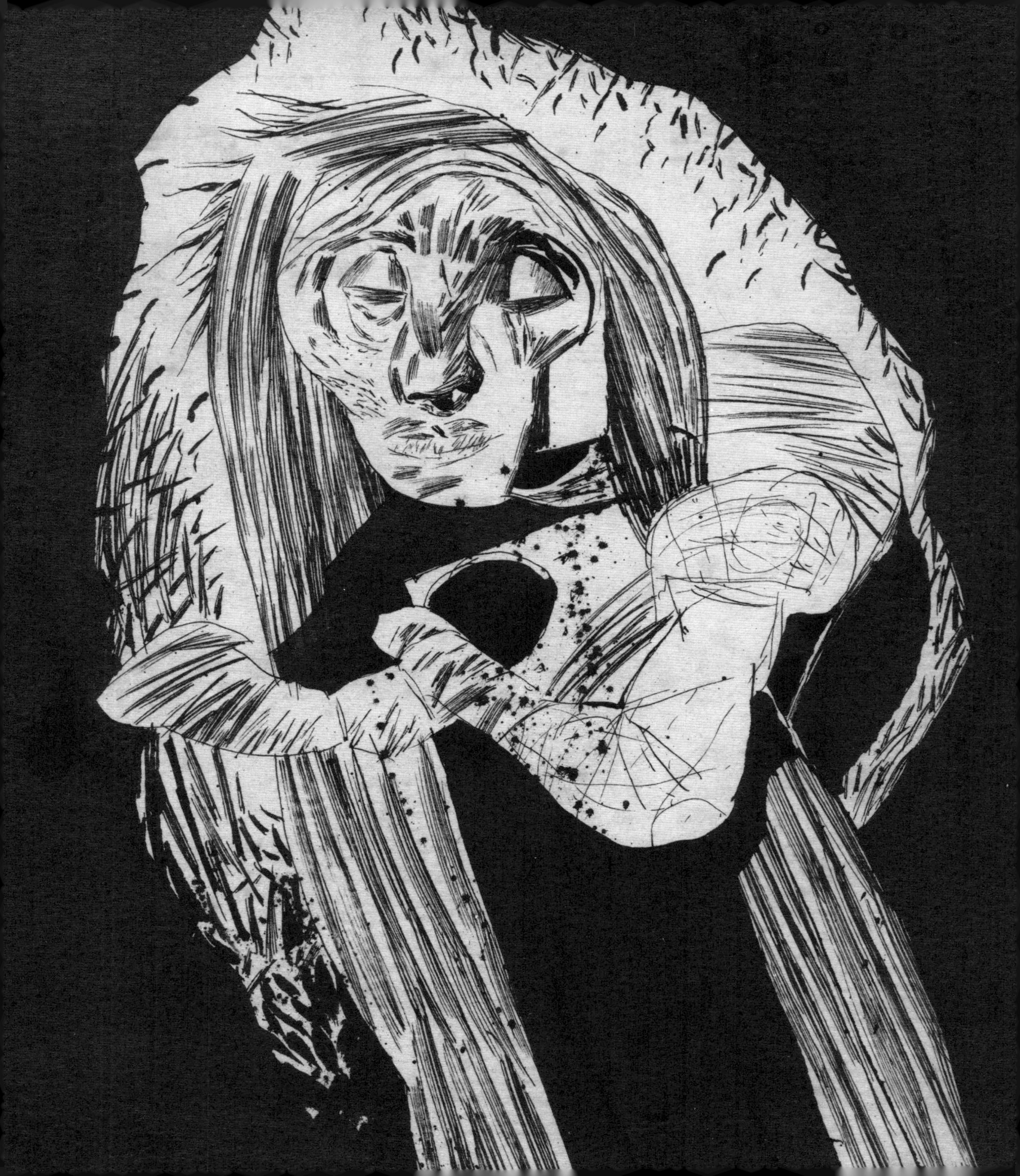

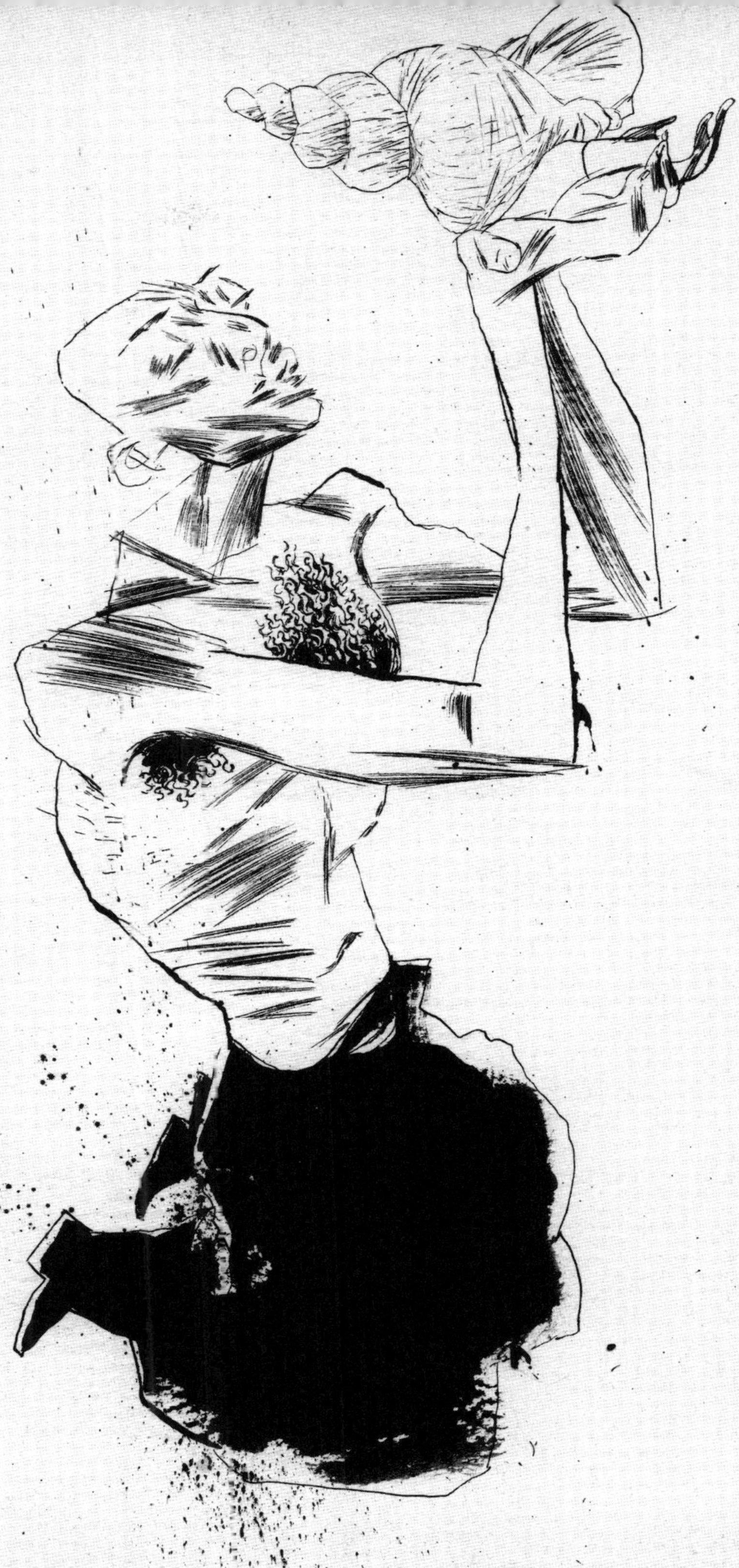

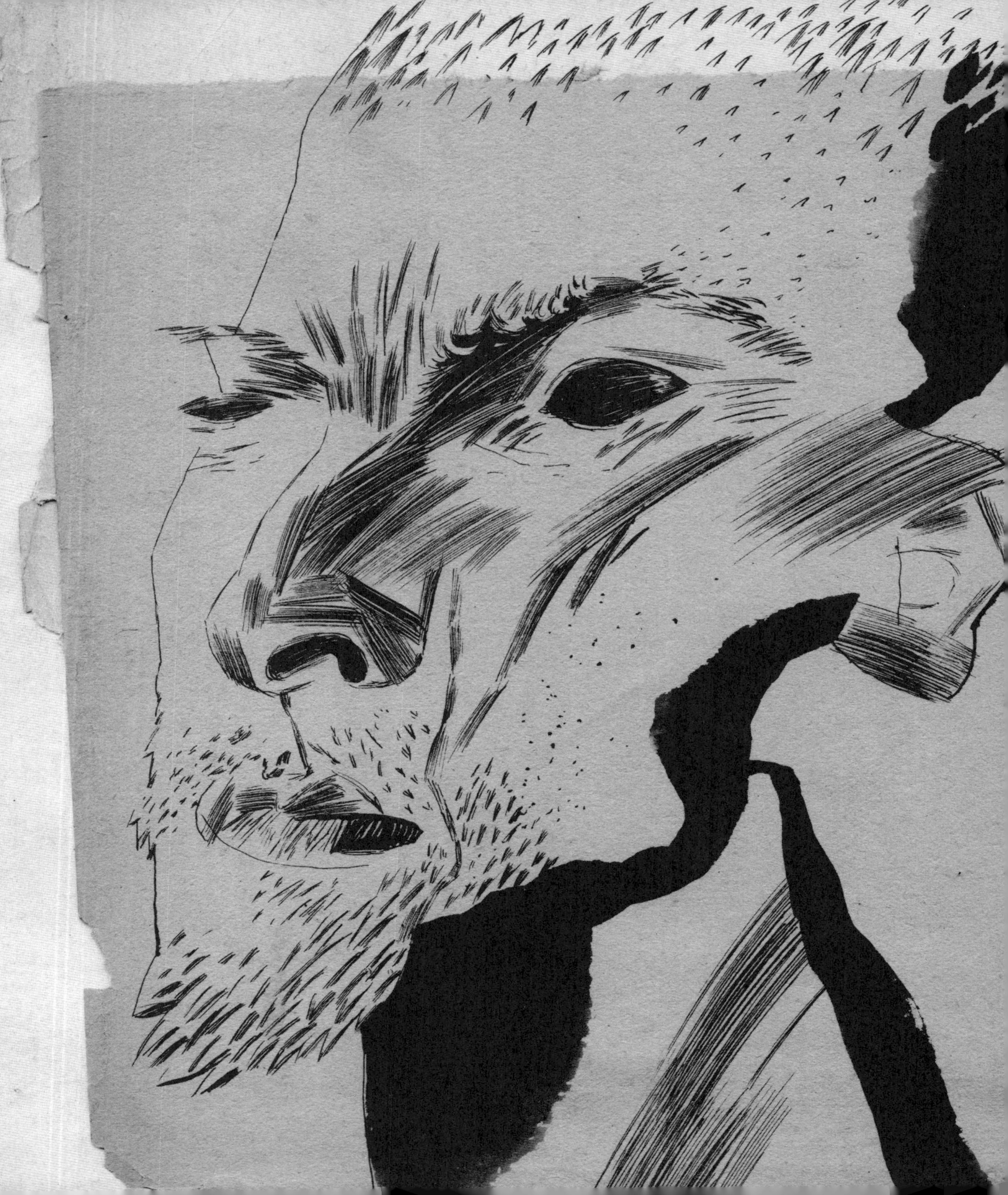

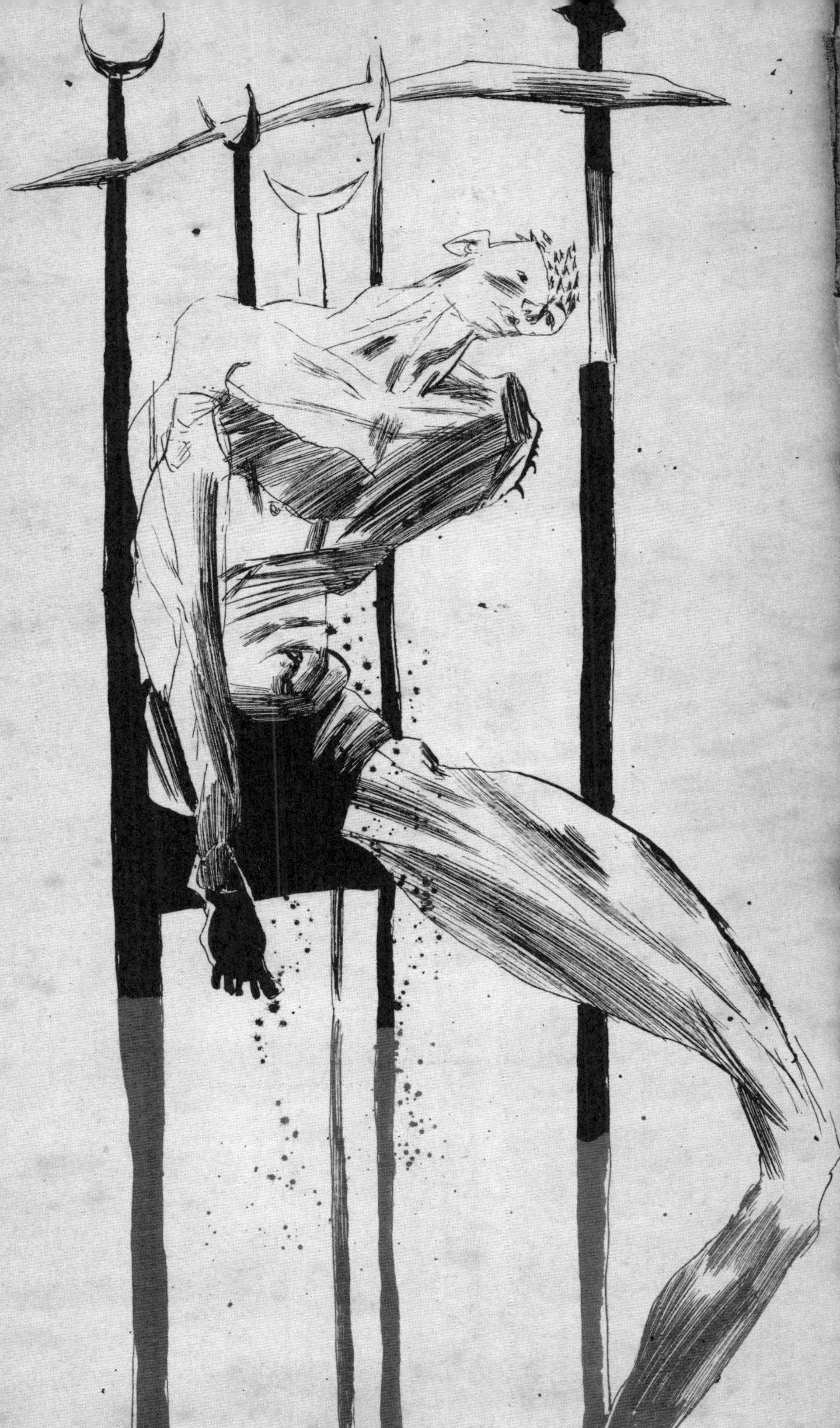

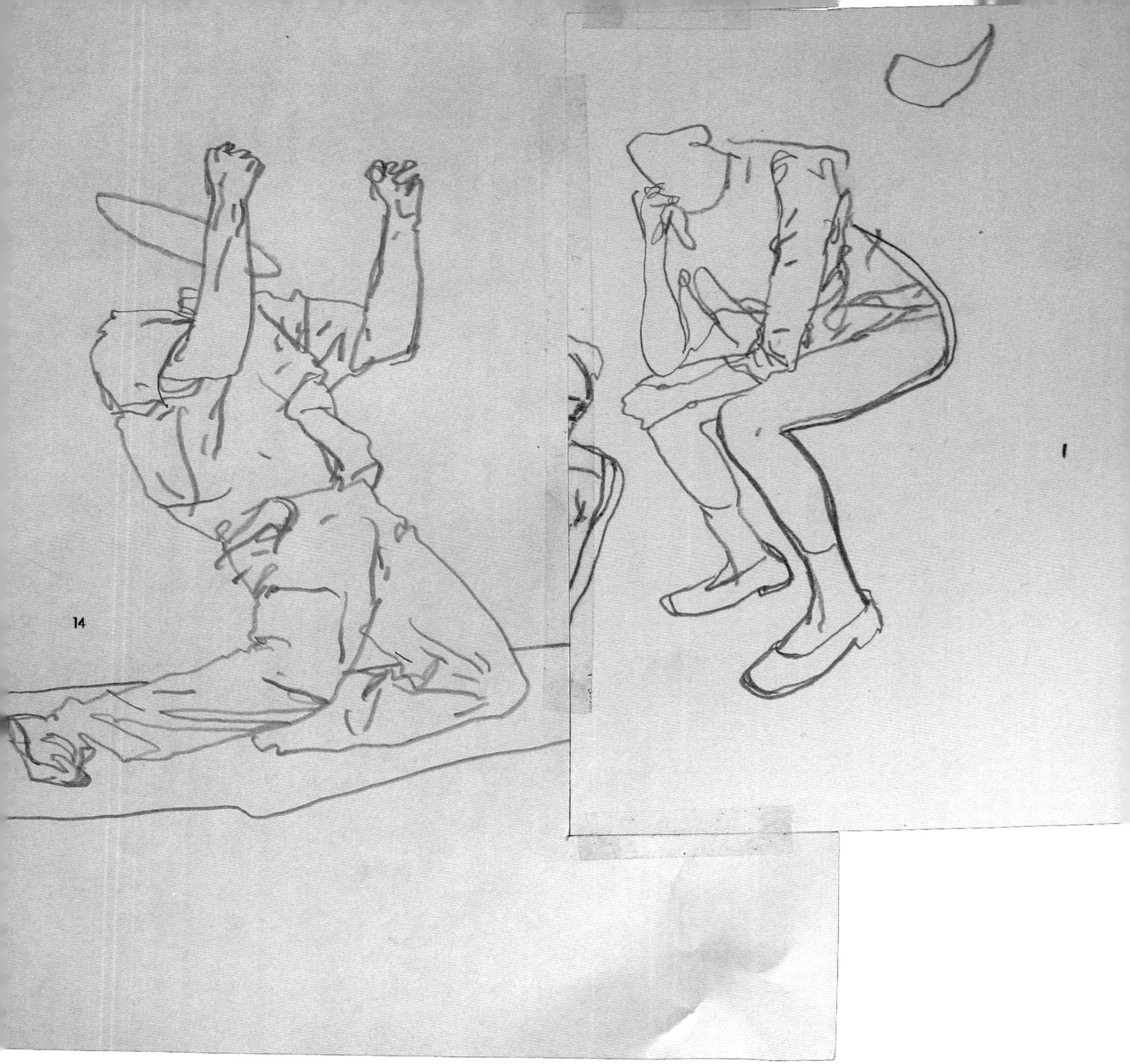

phil hale

13 drawings

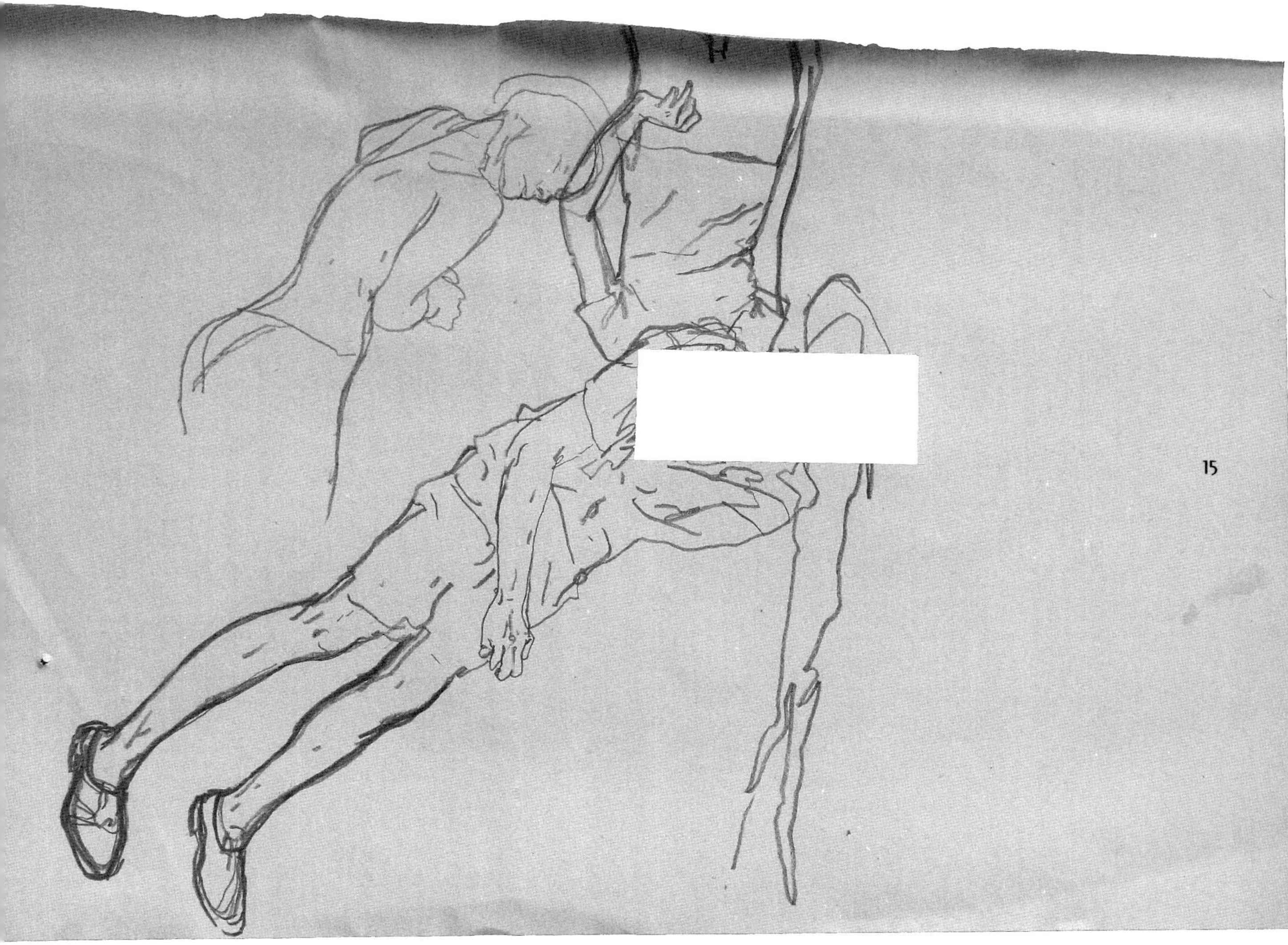

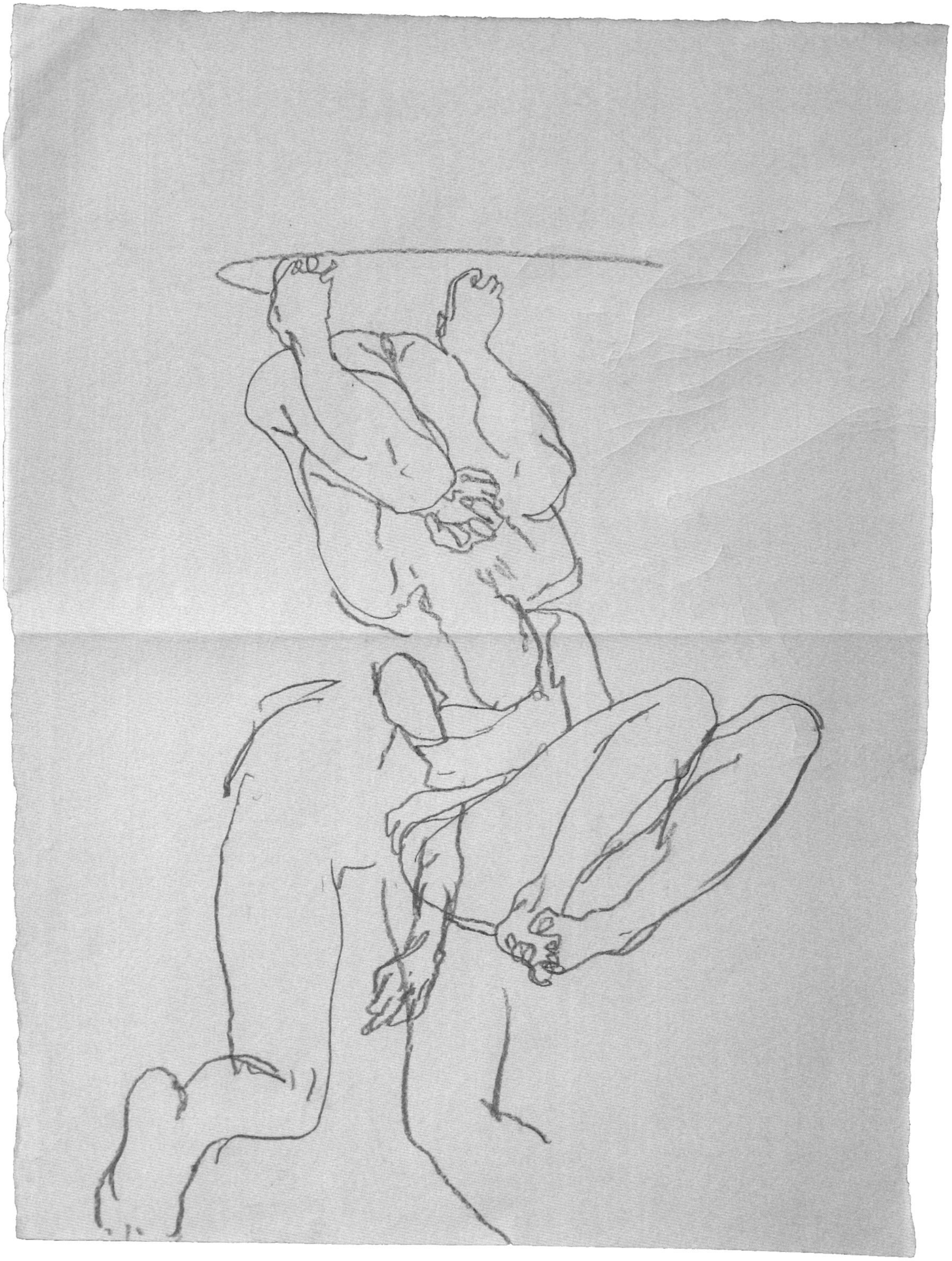

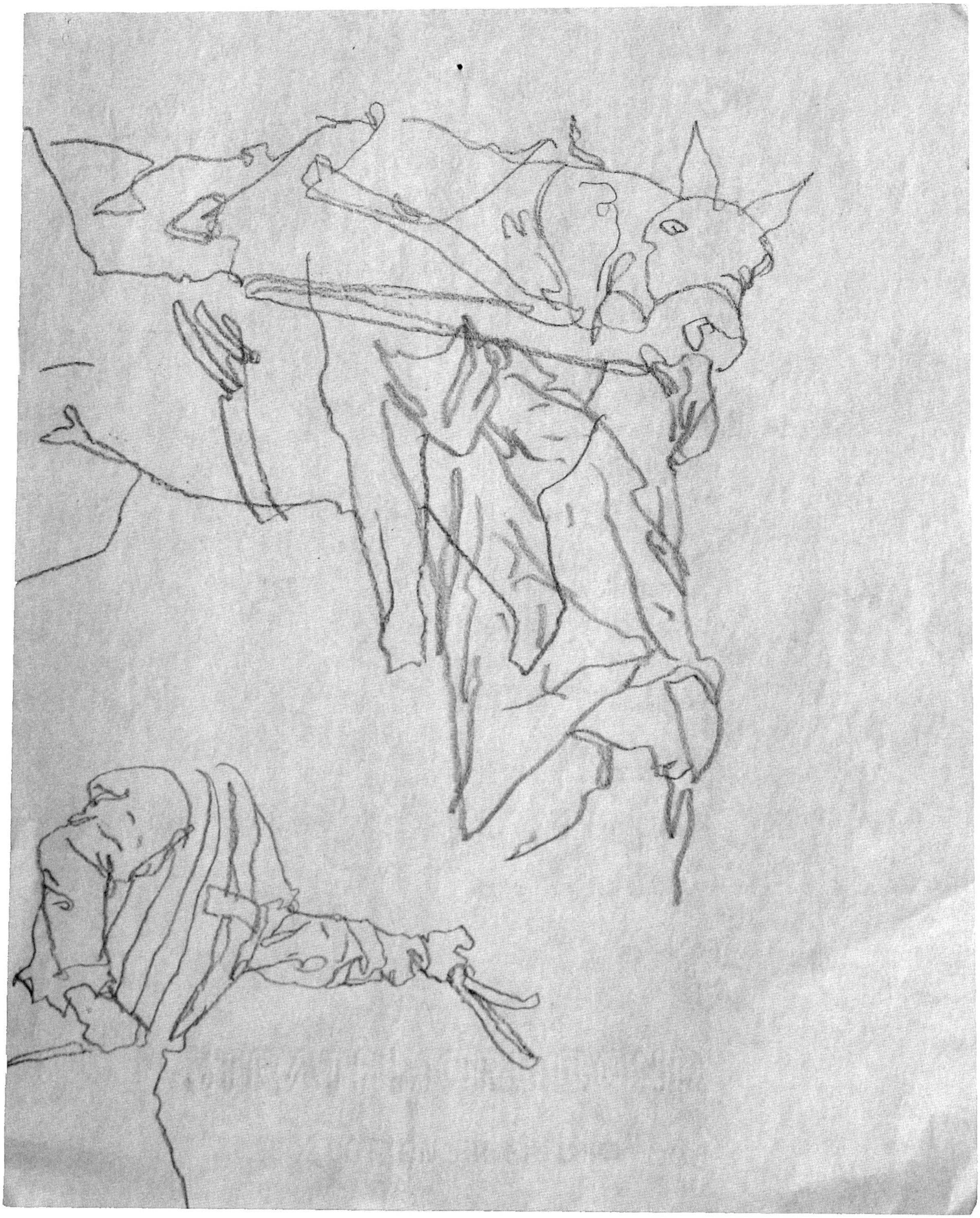

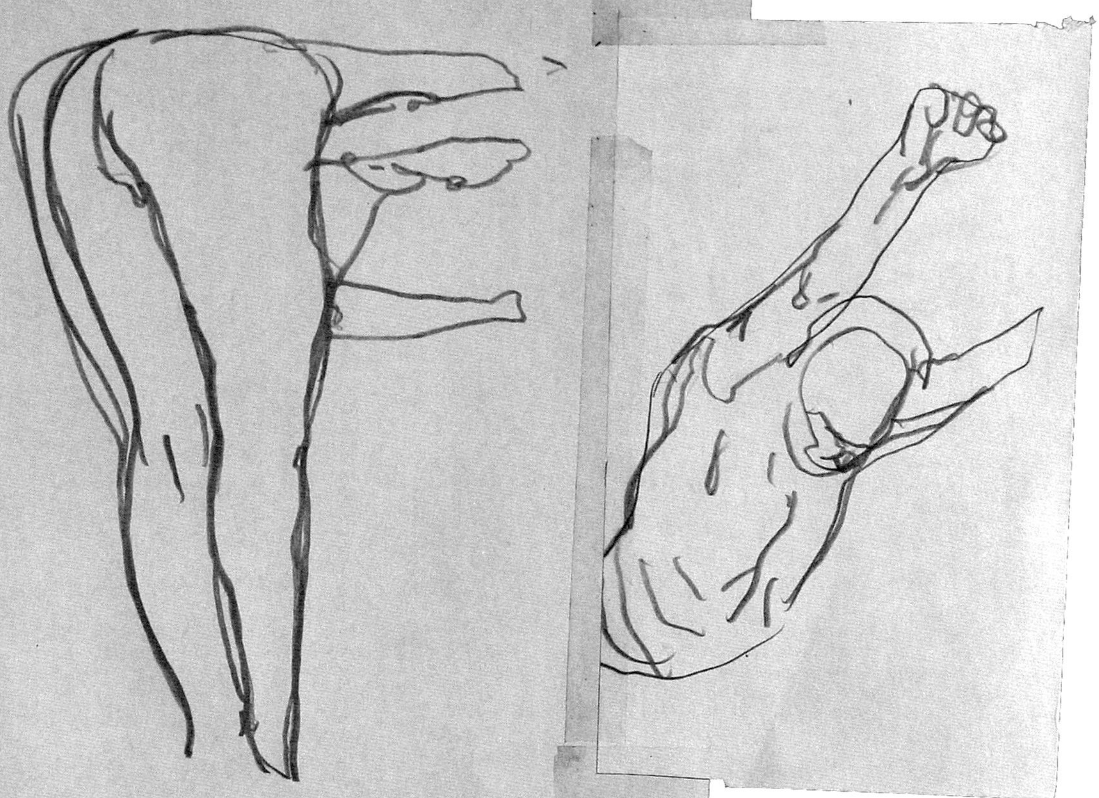

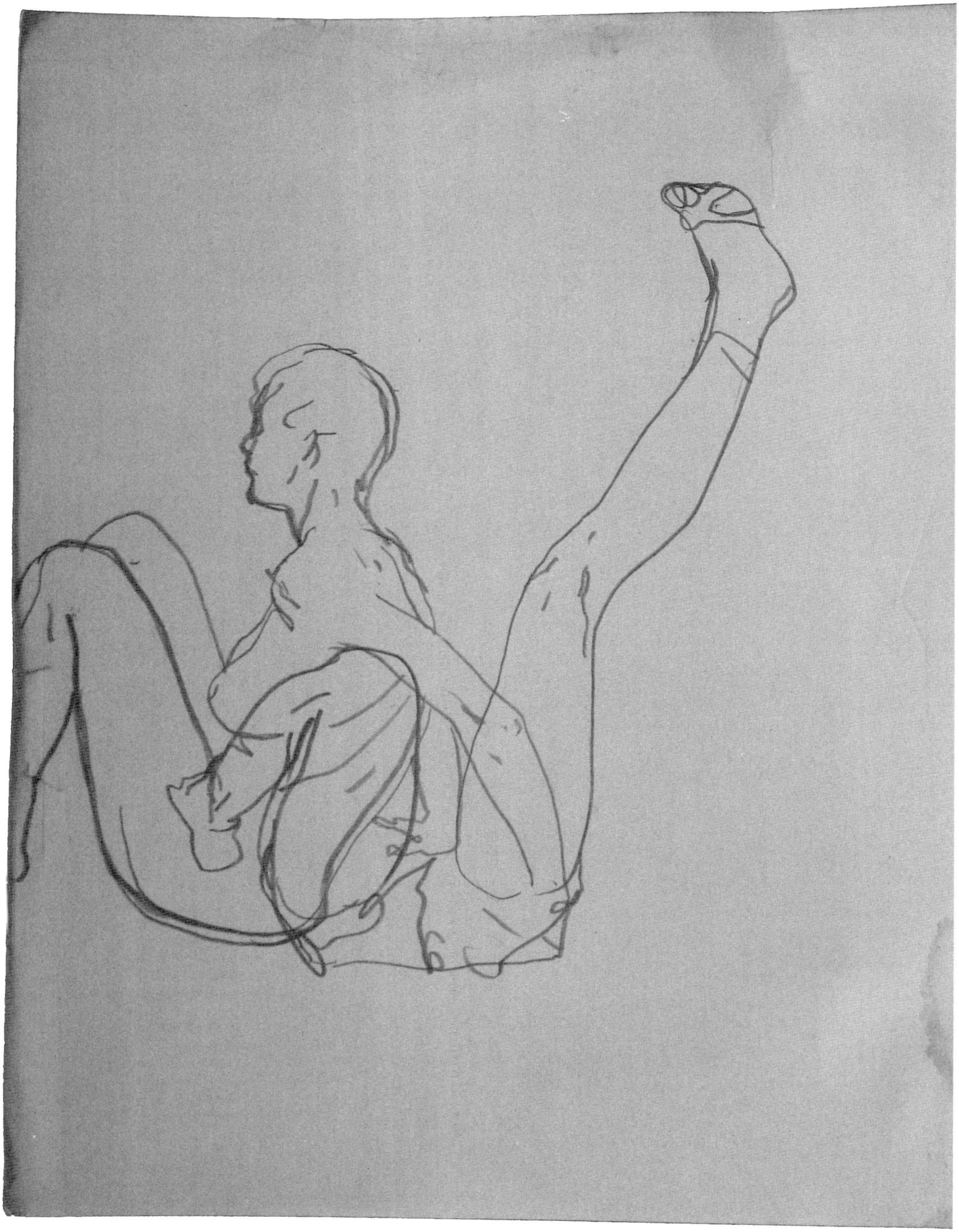

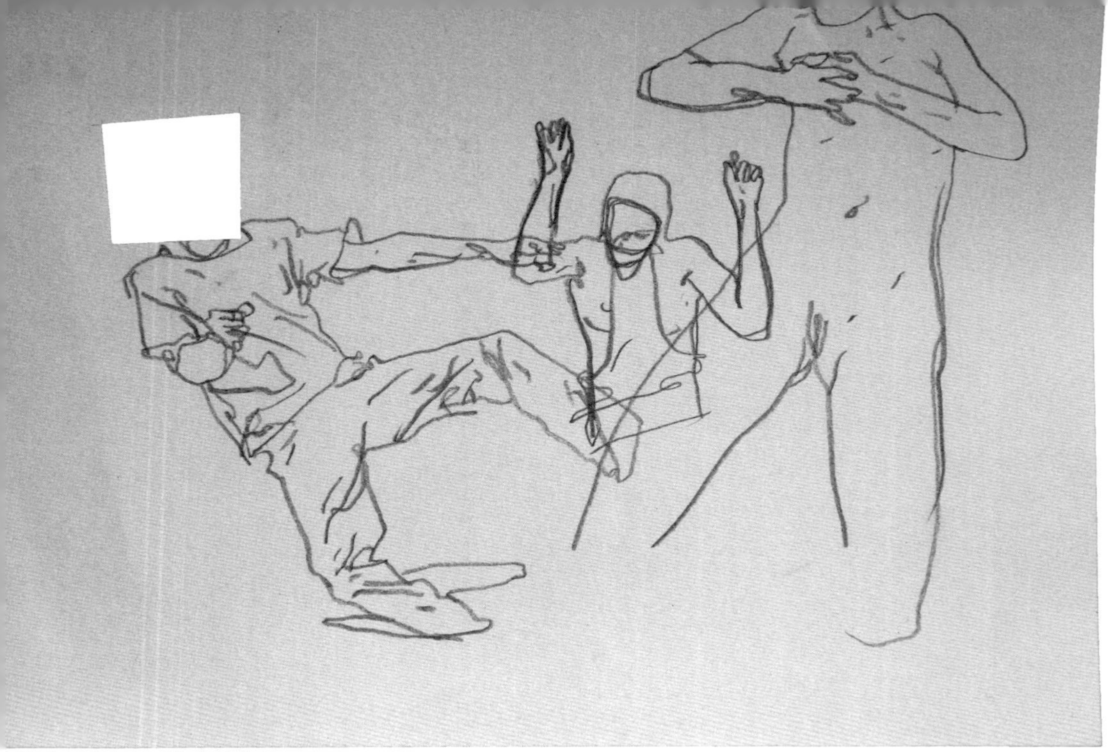

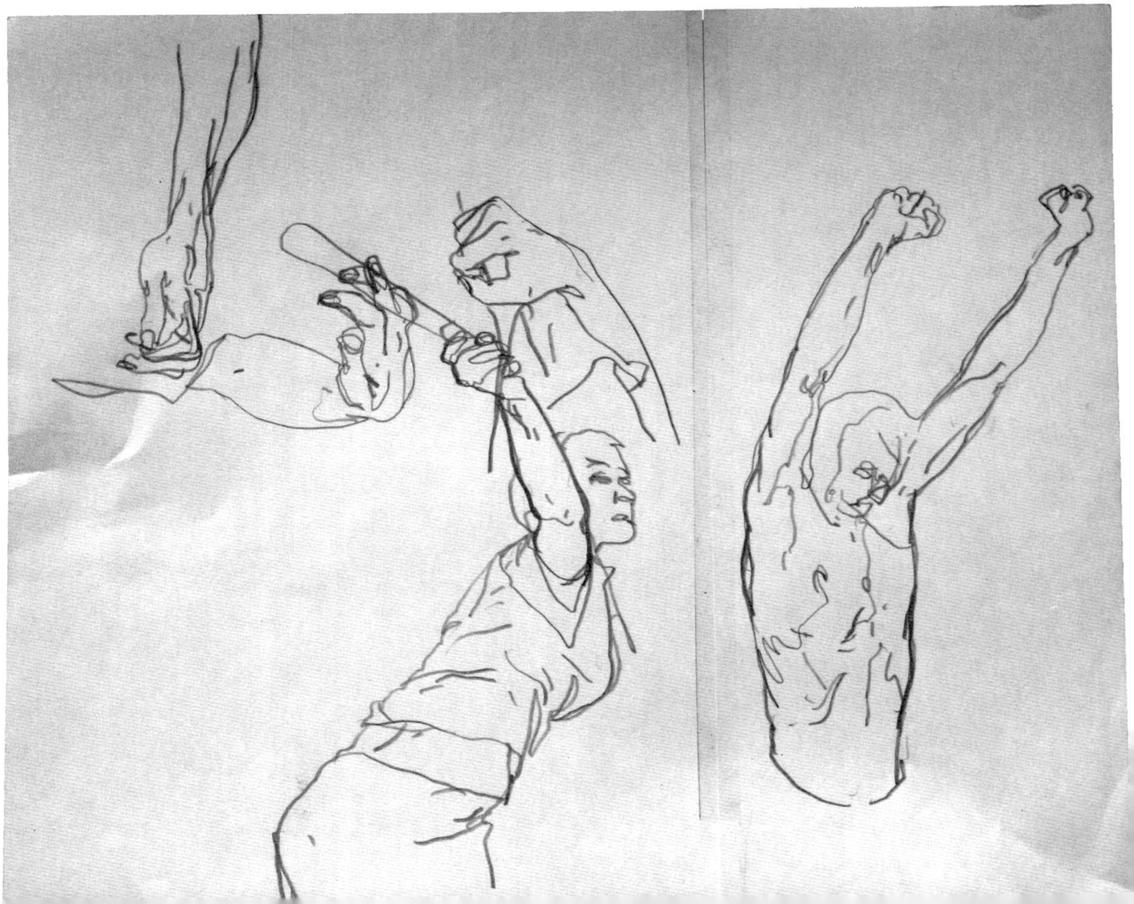

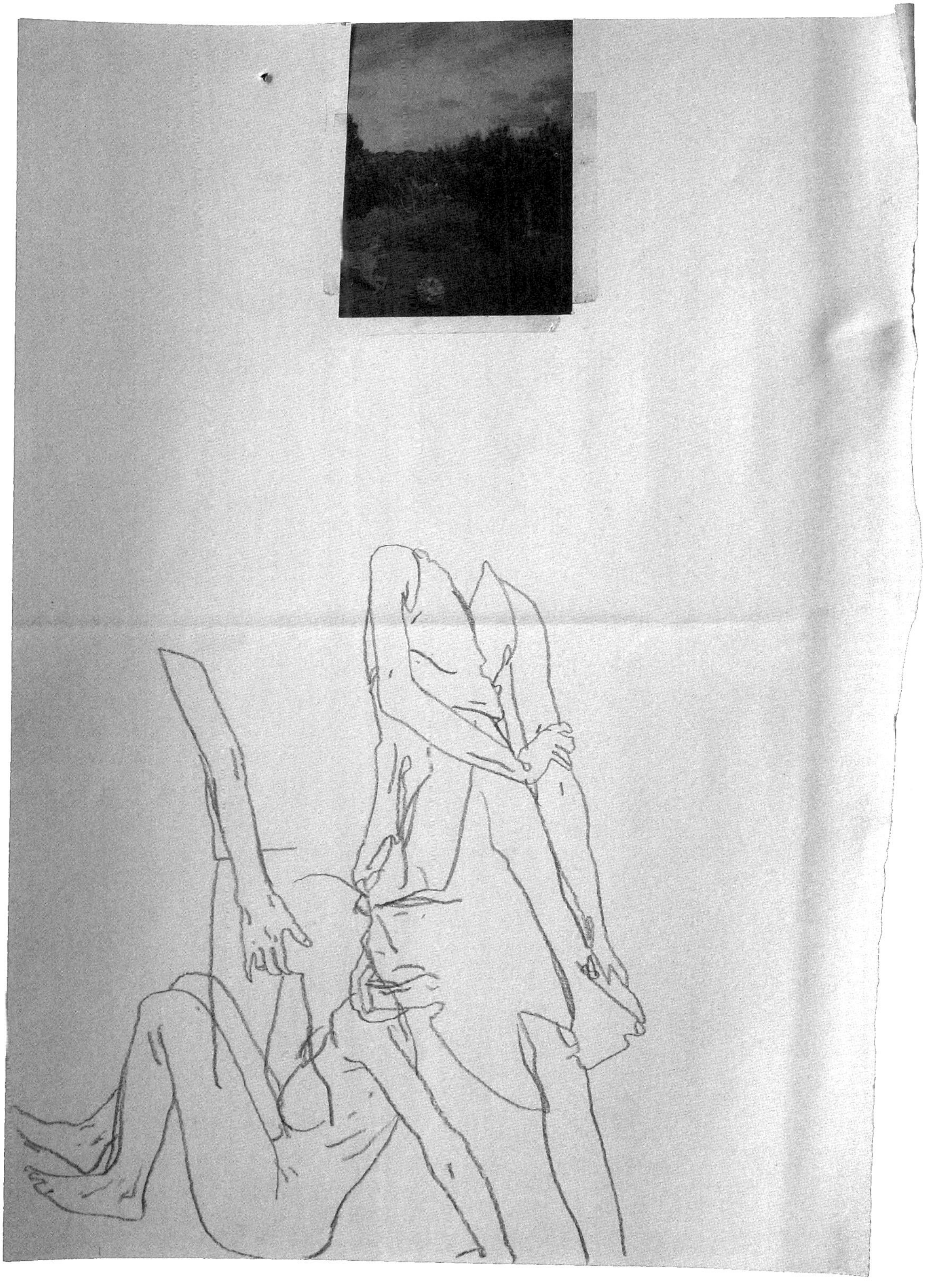

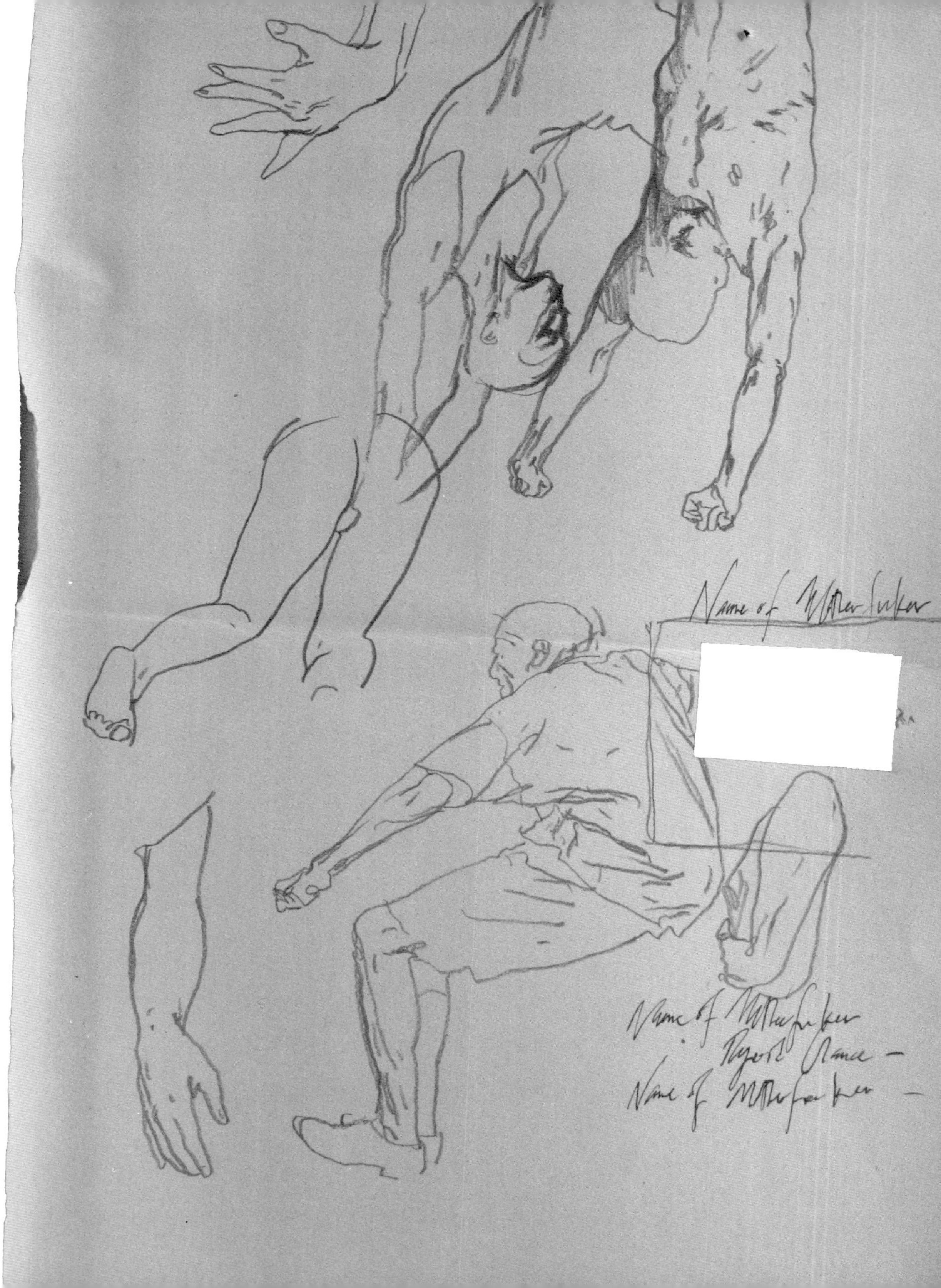

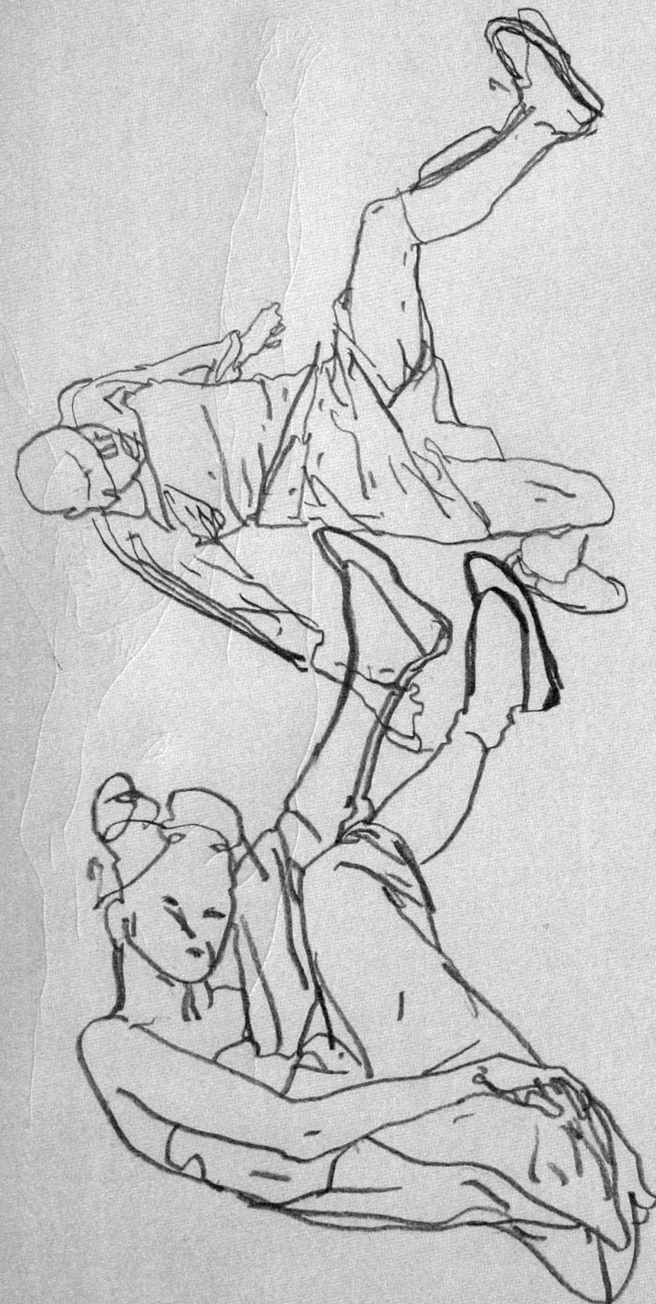

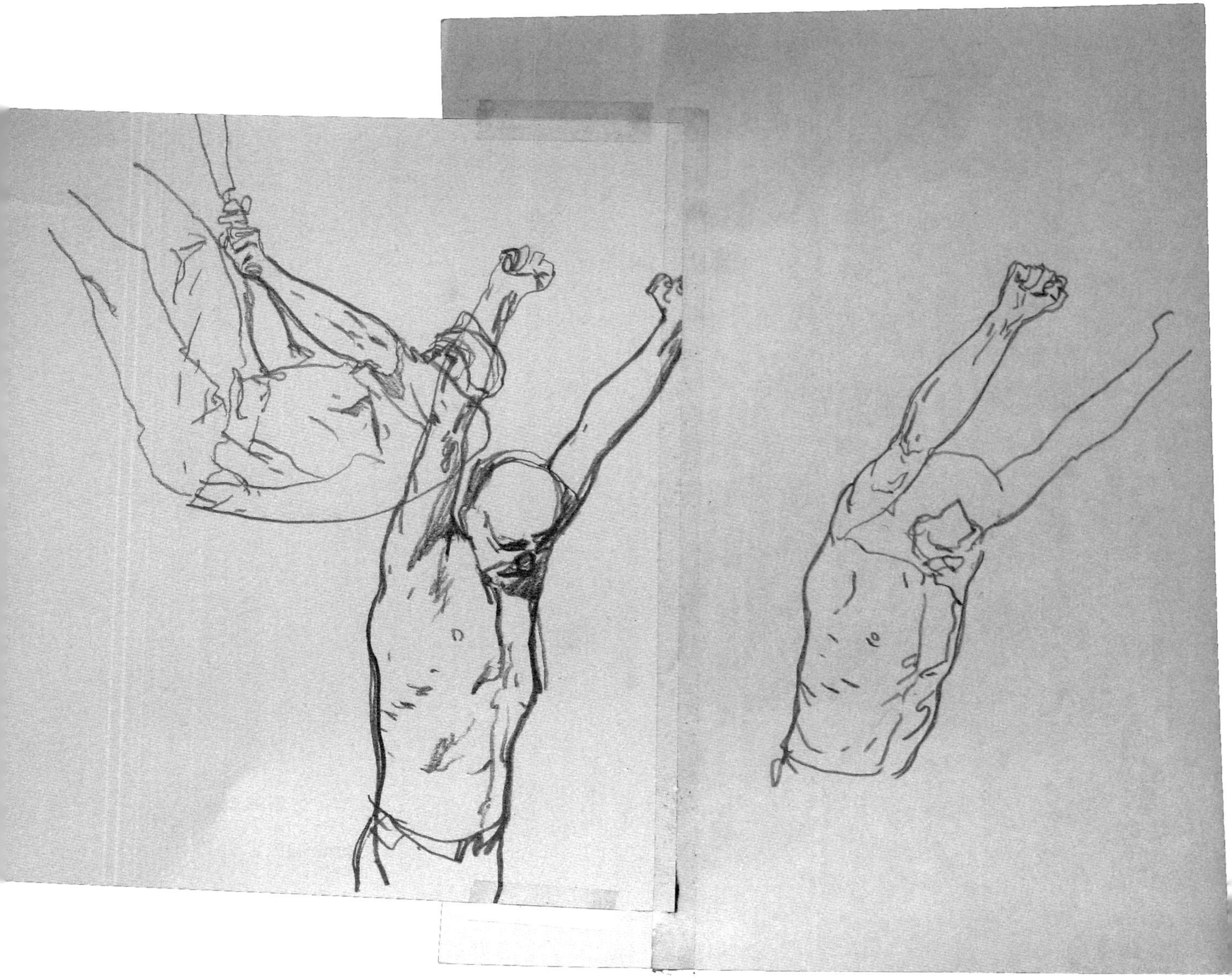

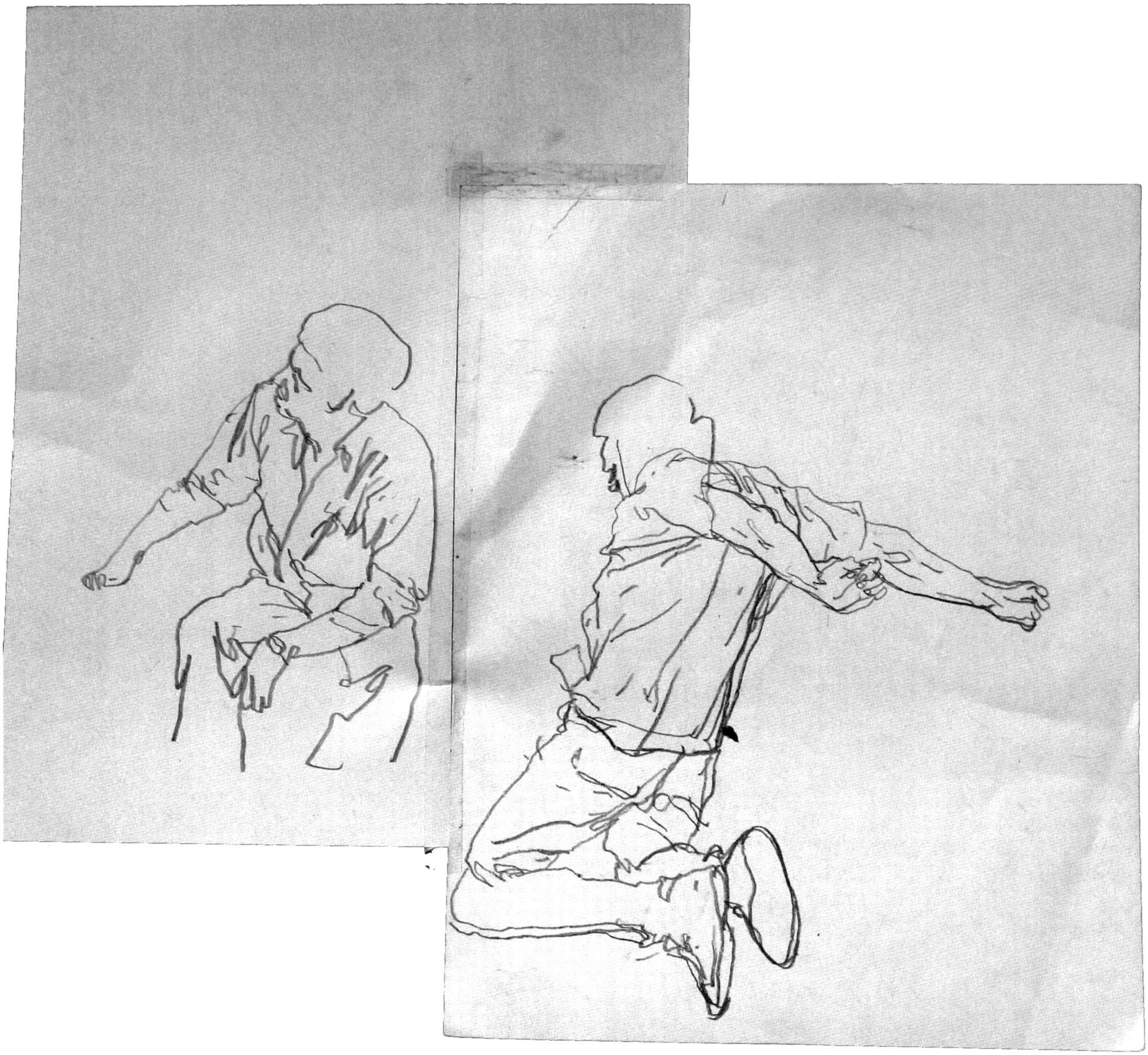

jon j muth

sumi-e

11 drawings

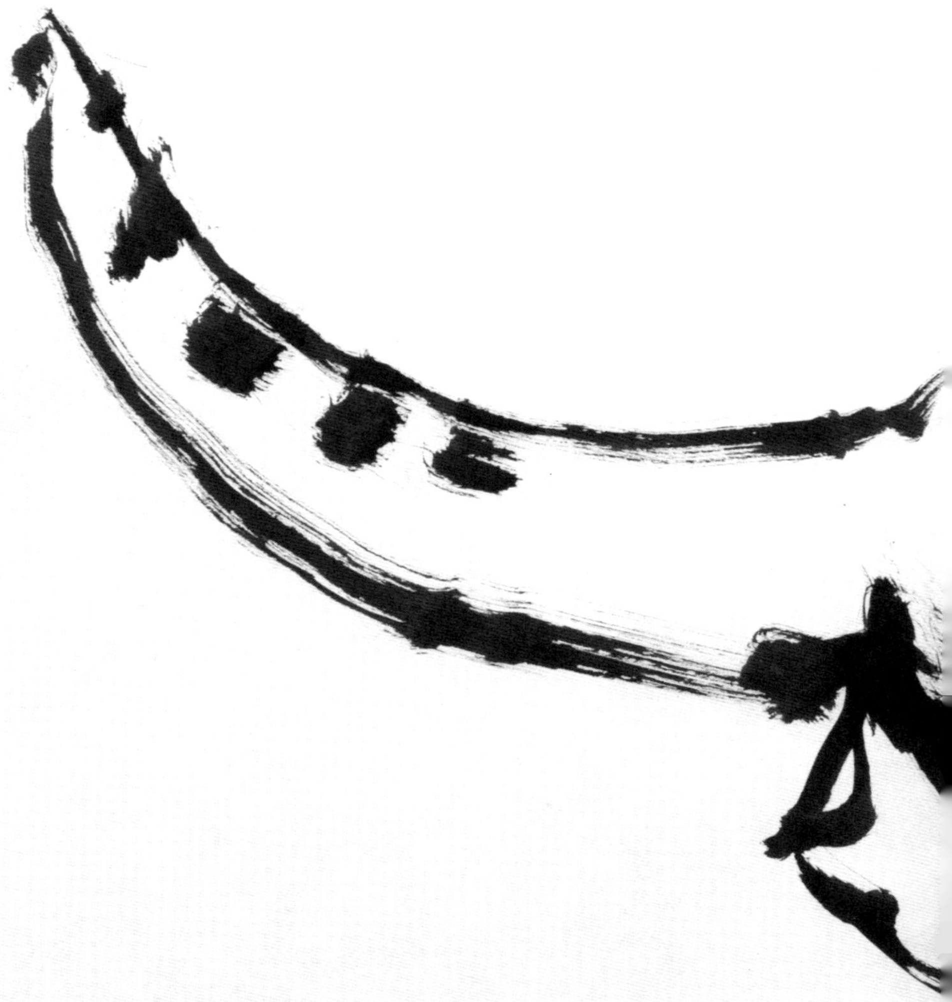

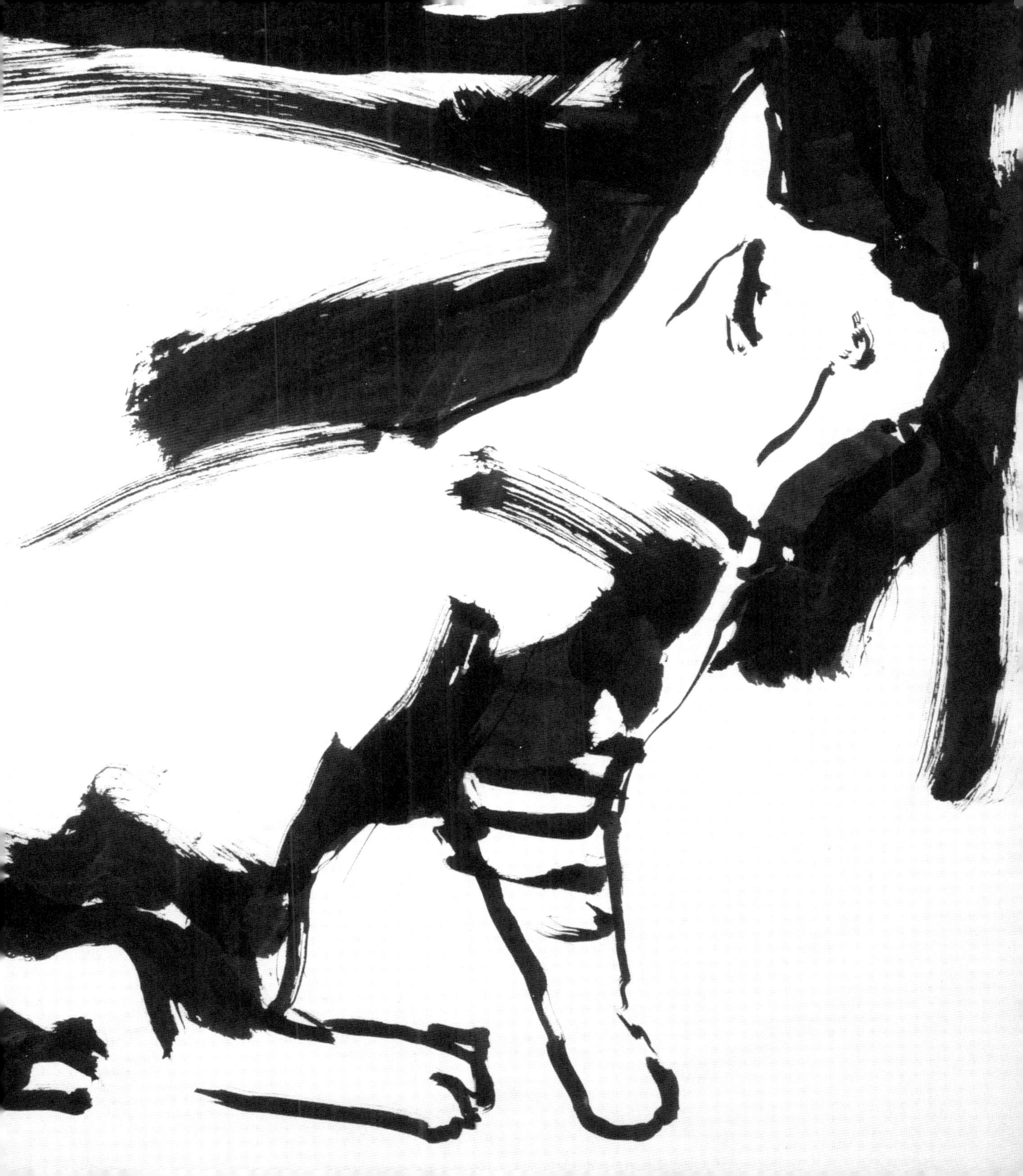

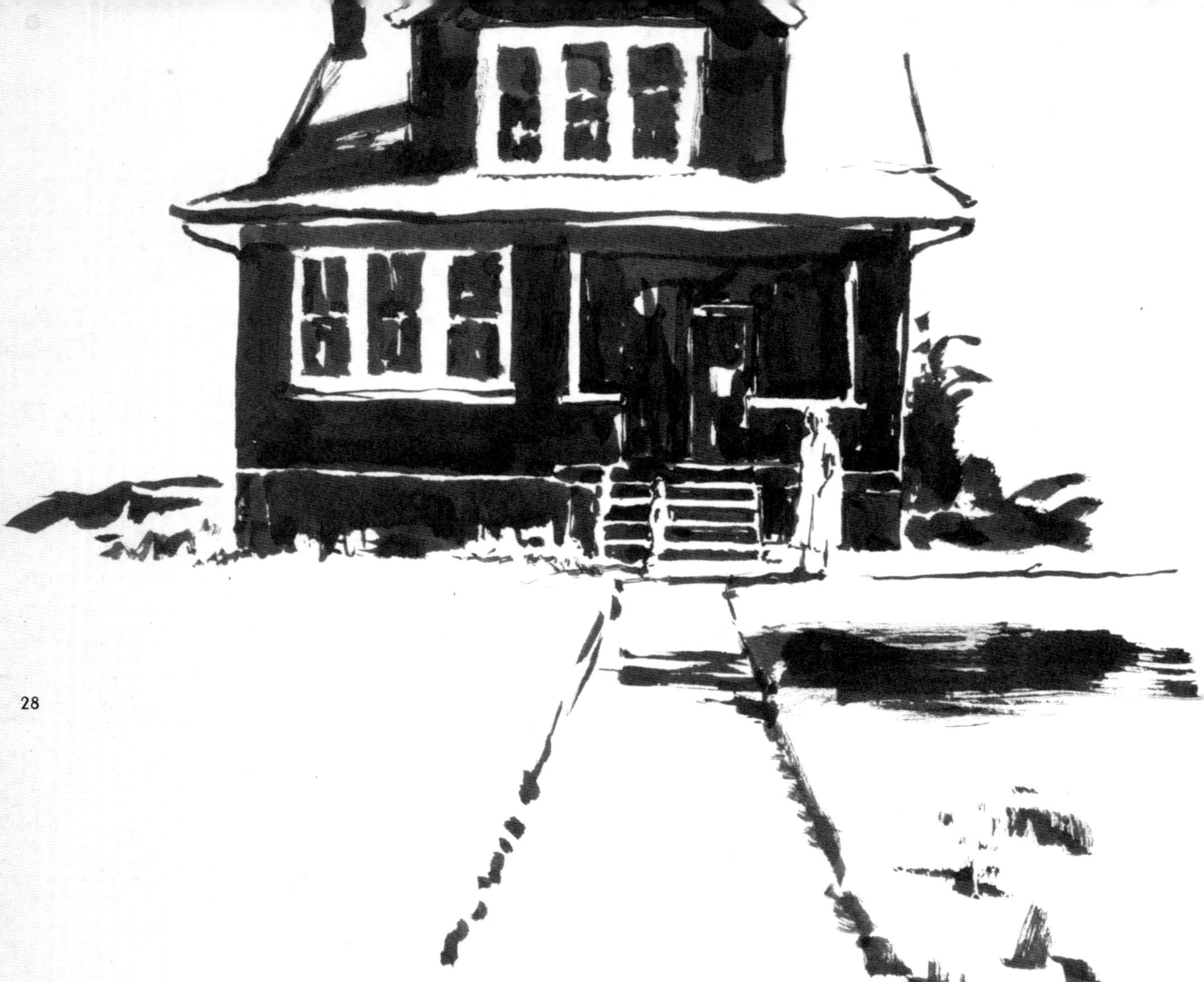

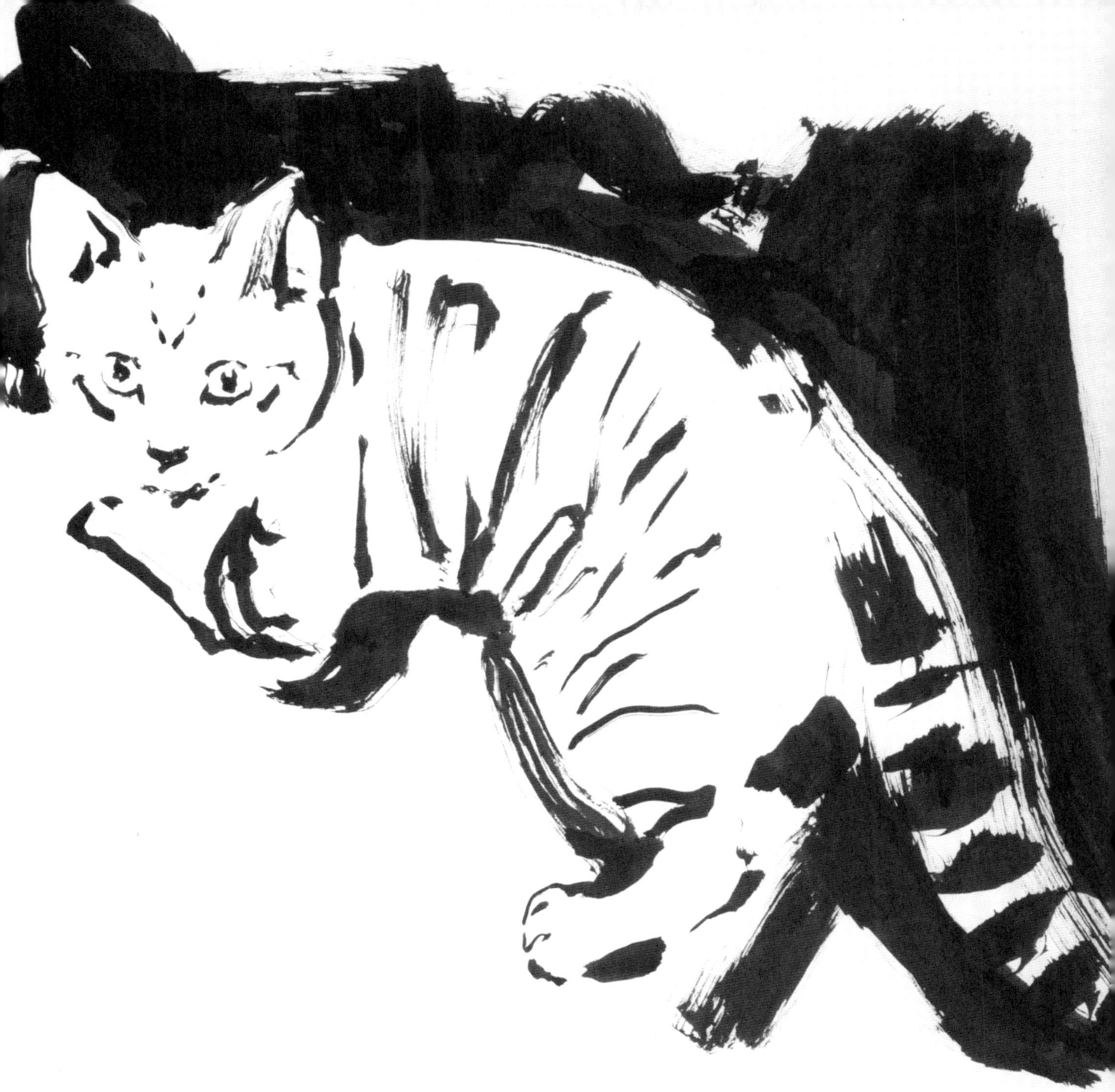

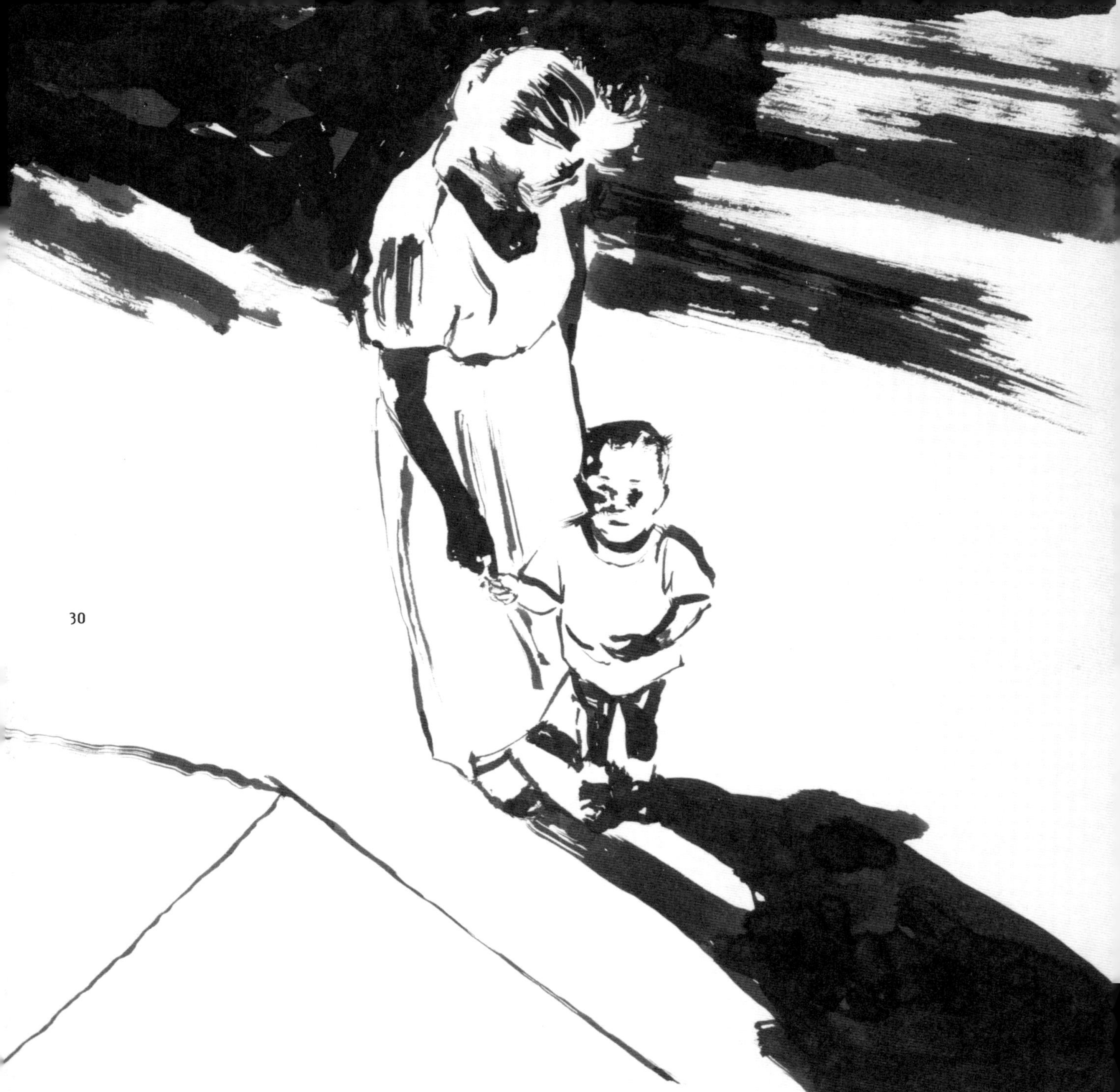

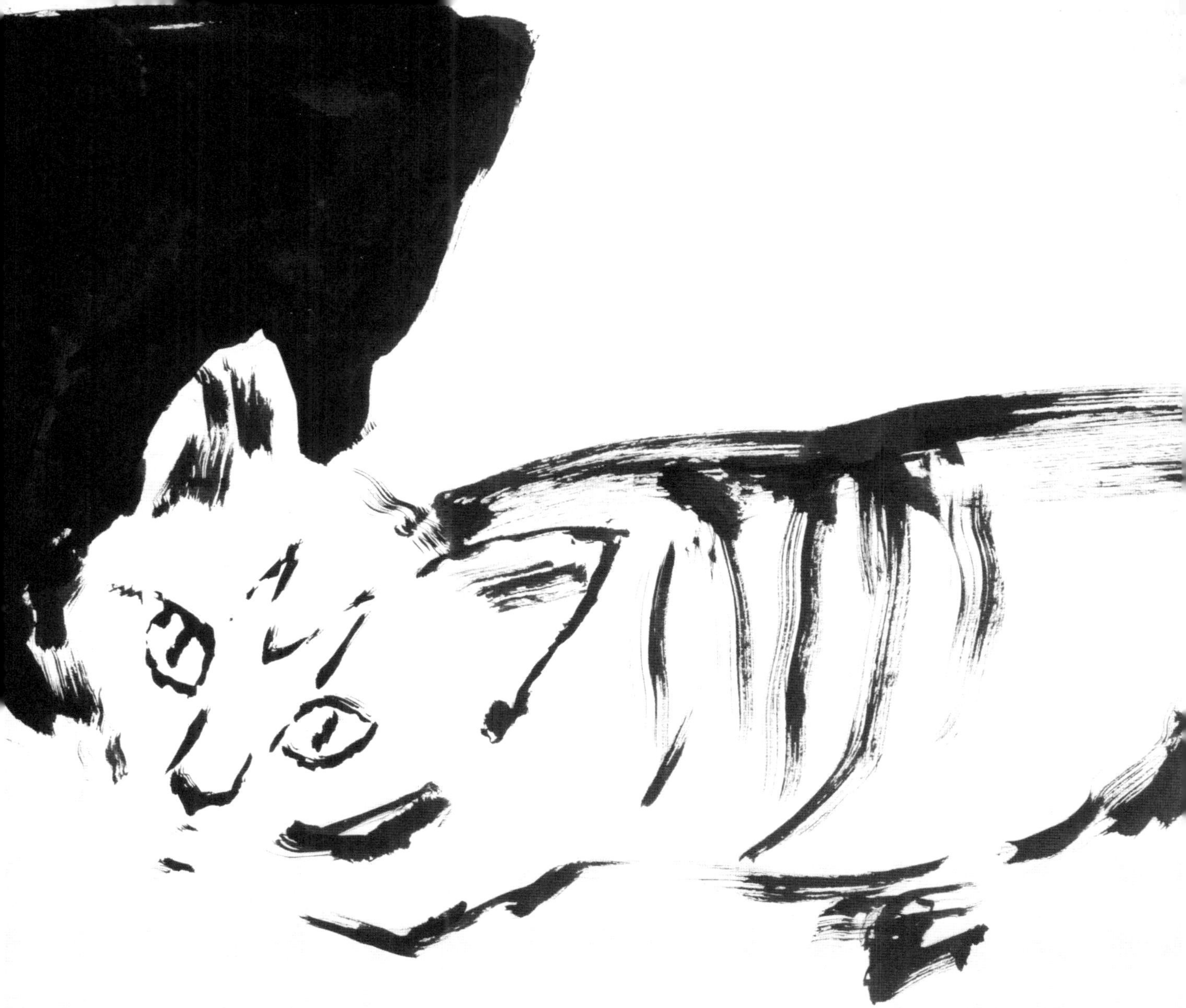

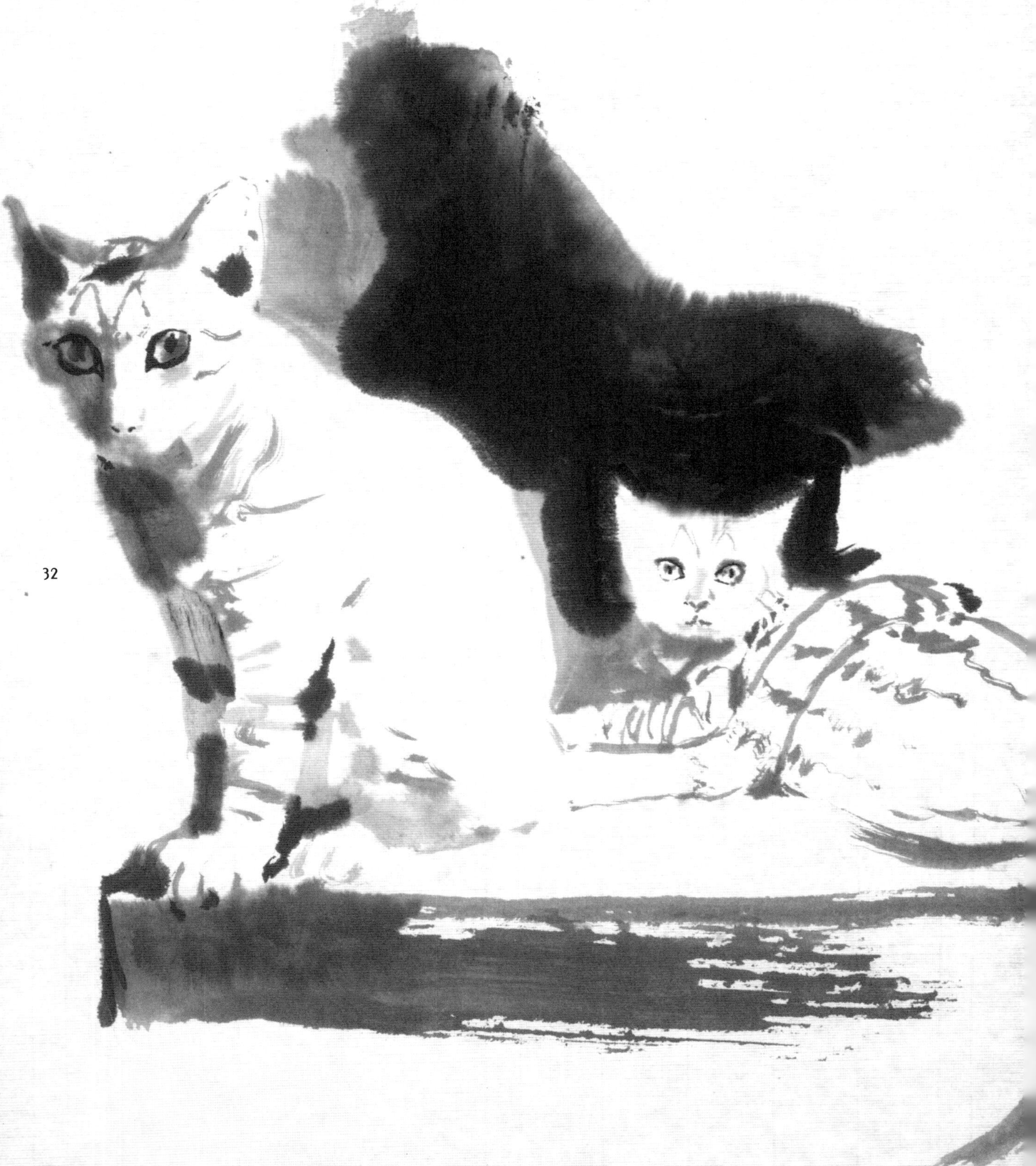

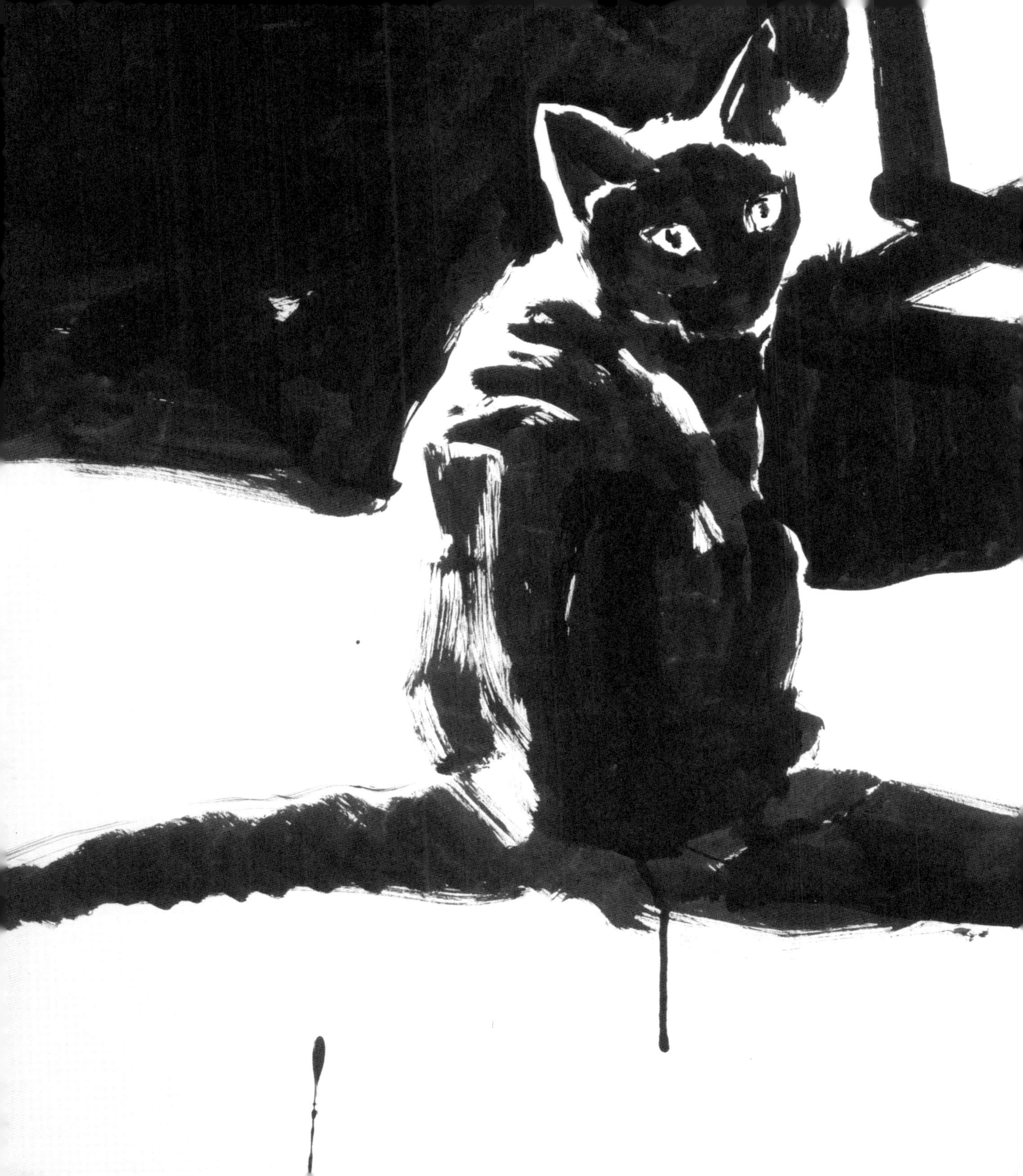

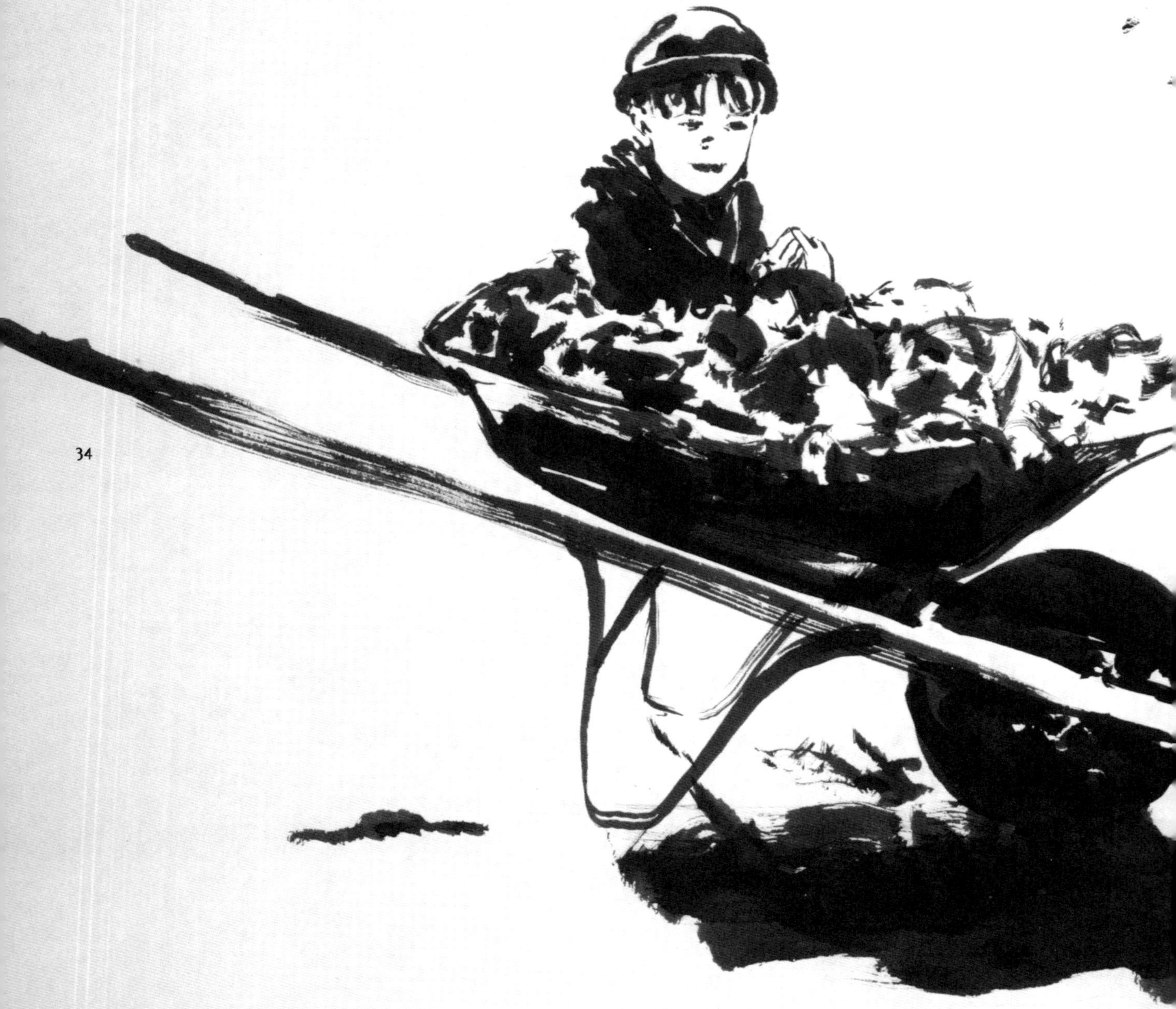

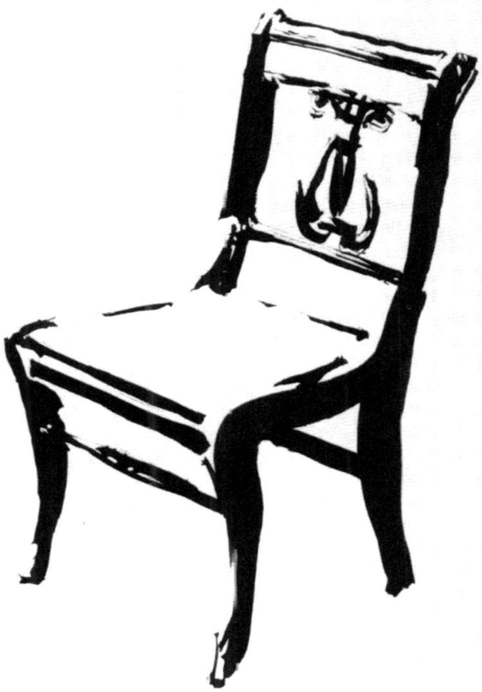

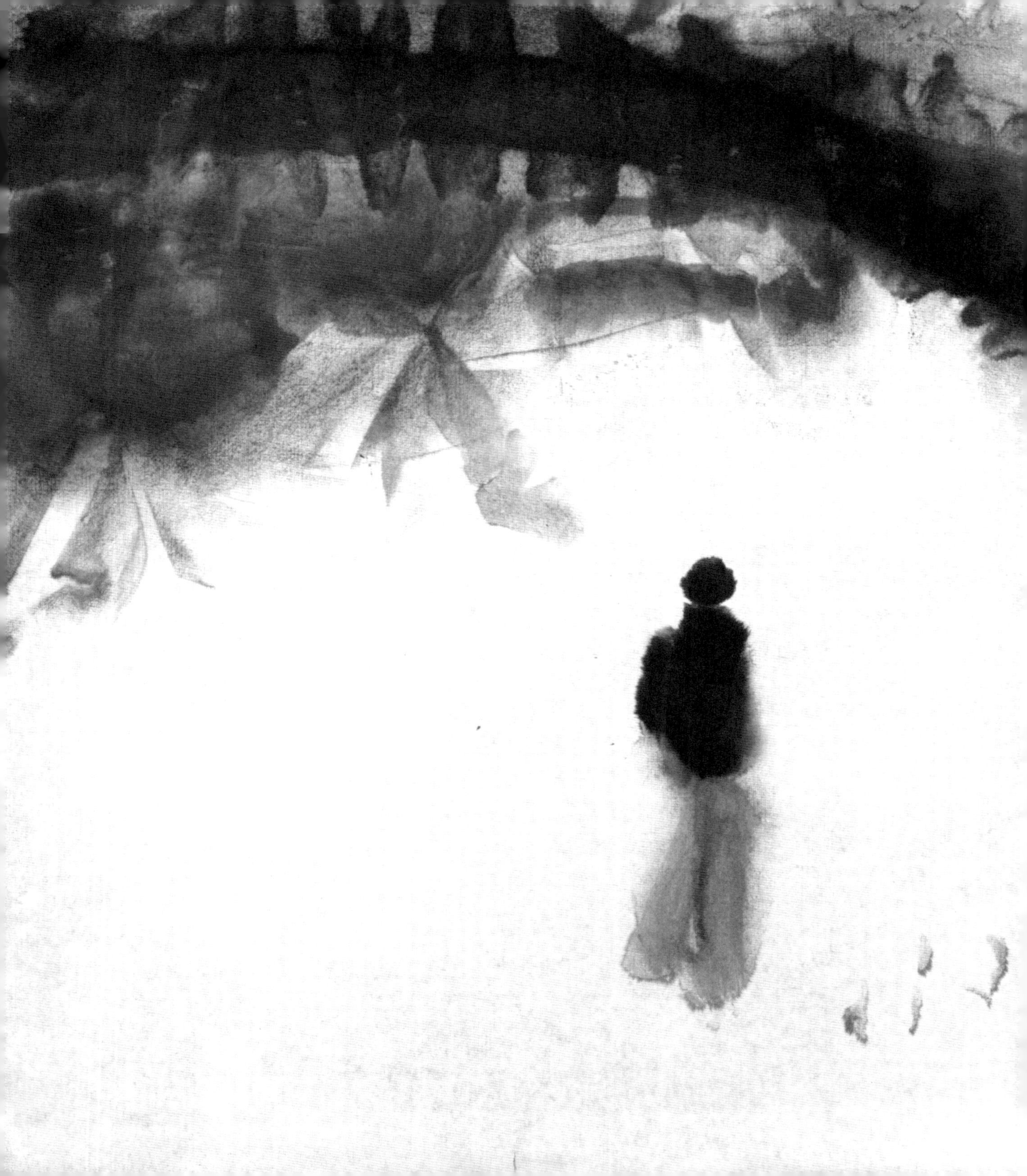

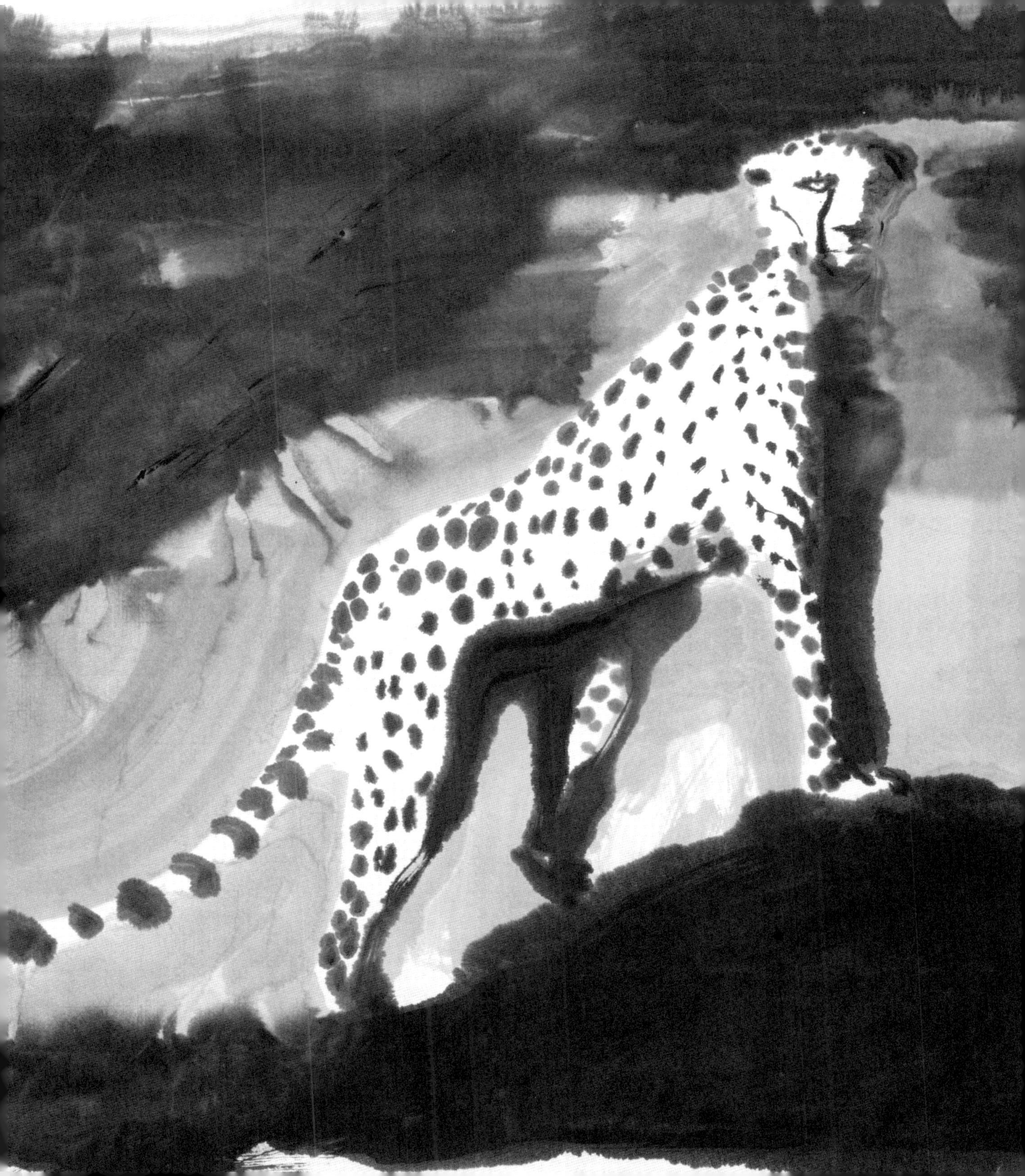

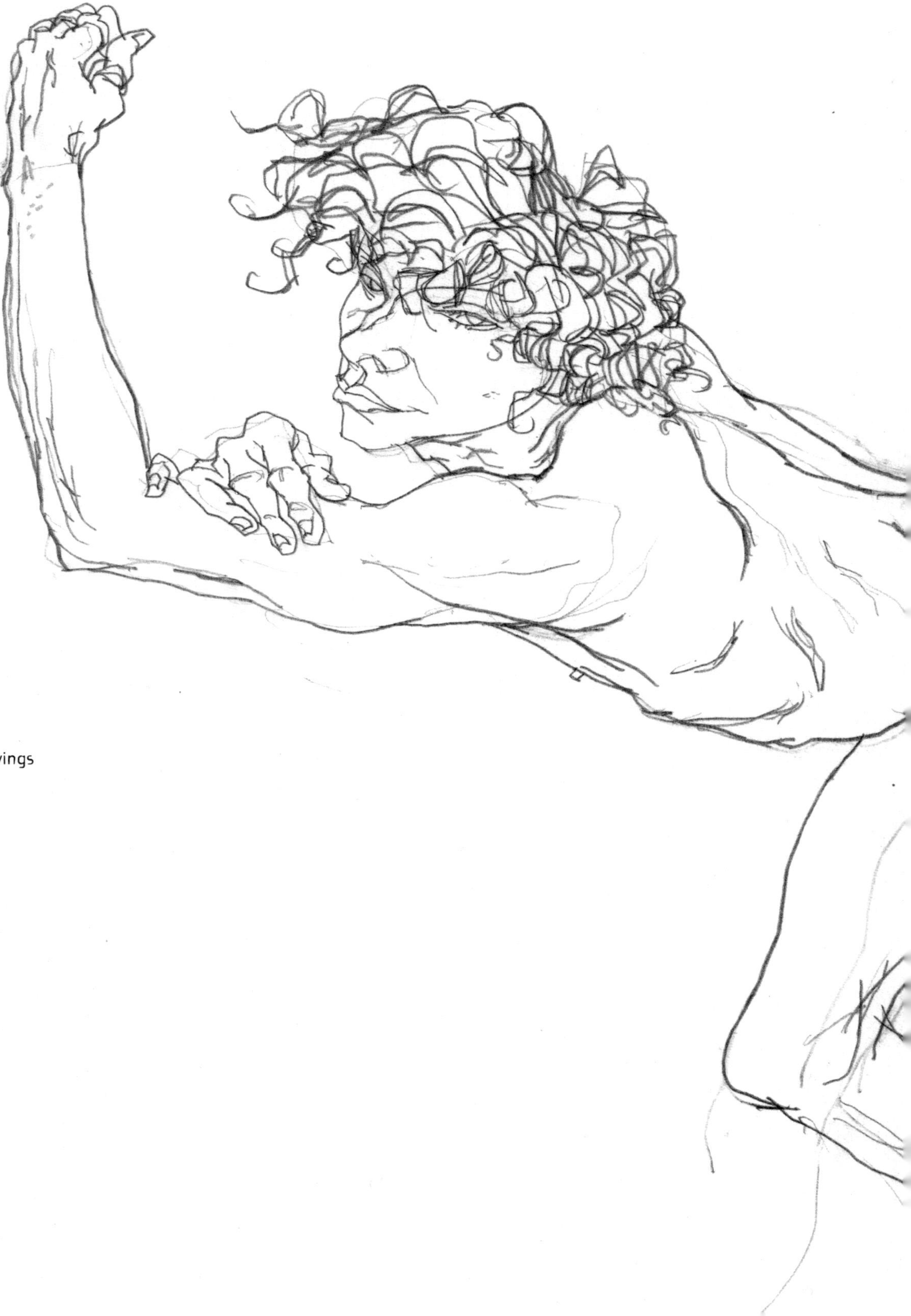

kent williams 14 drawings

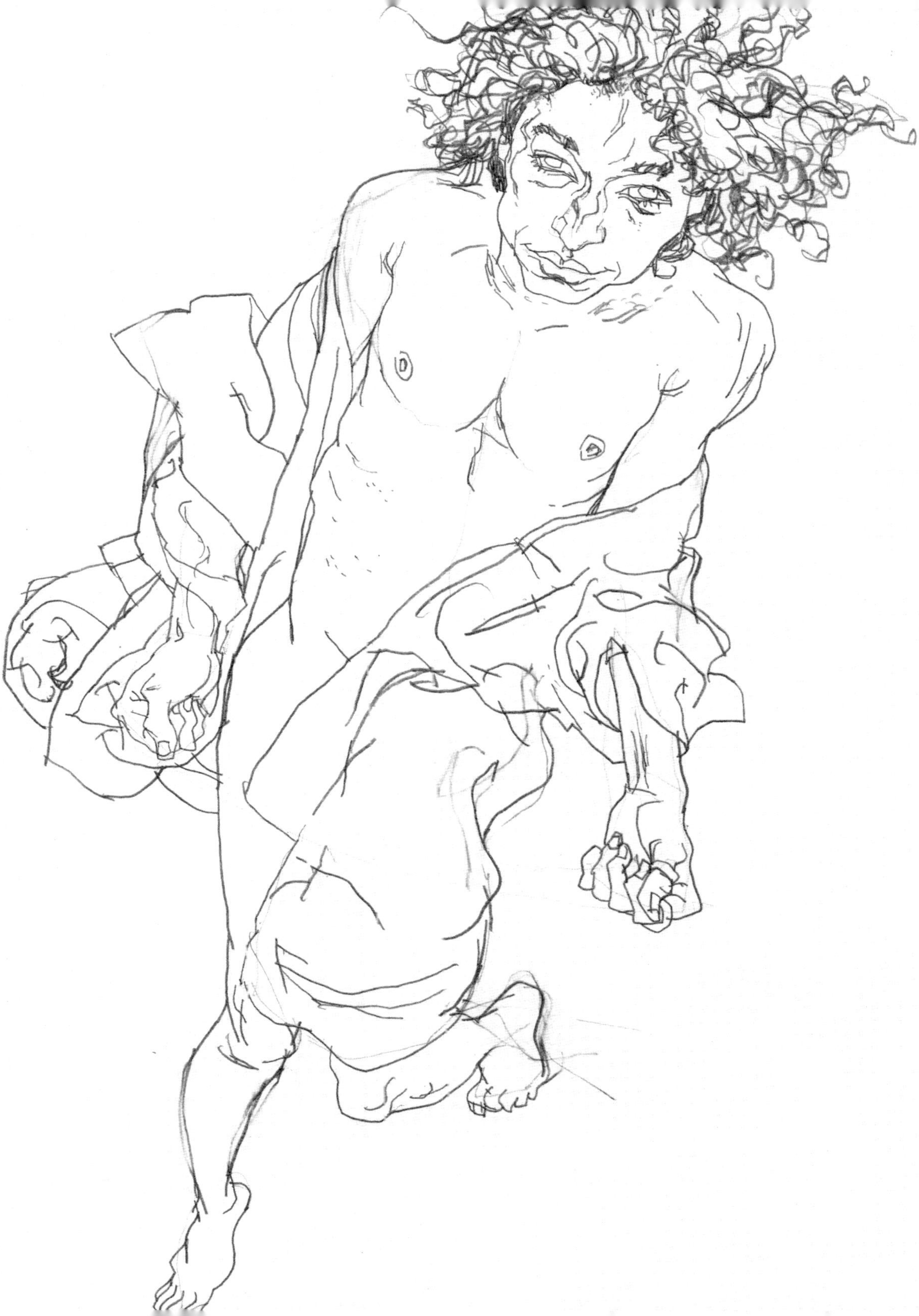

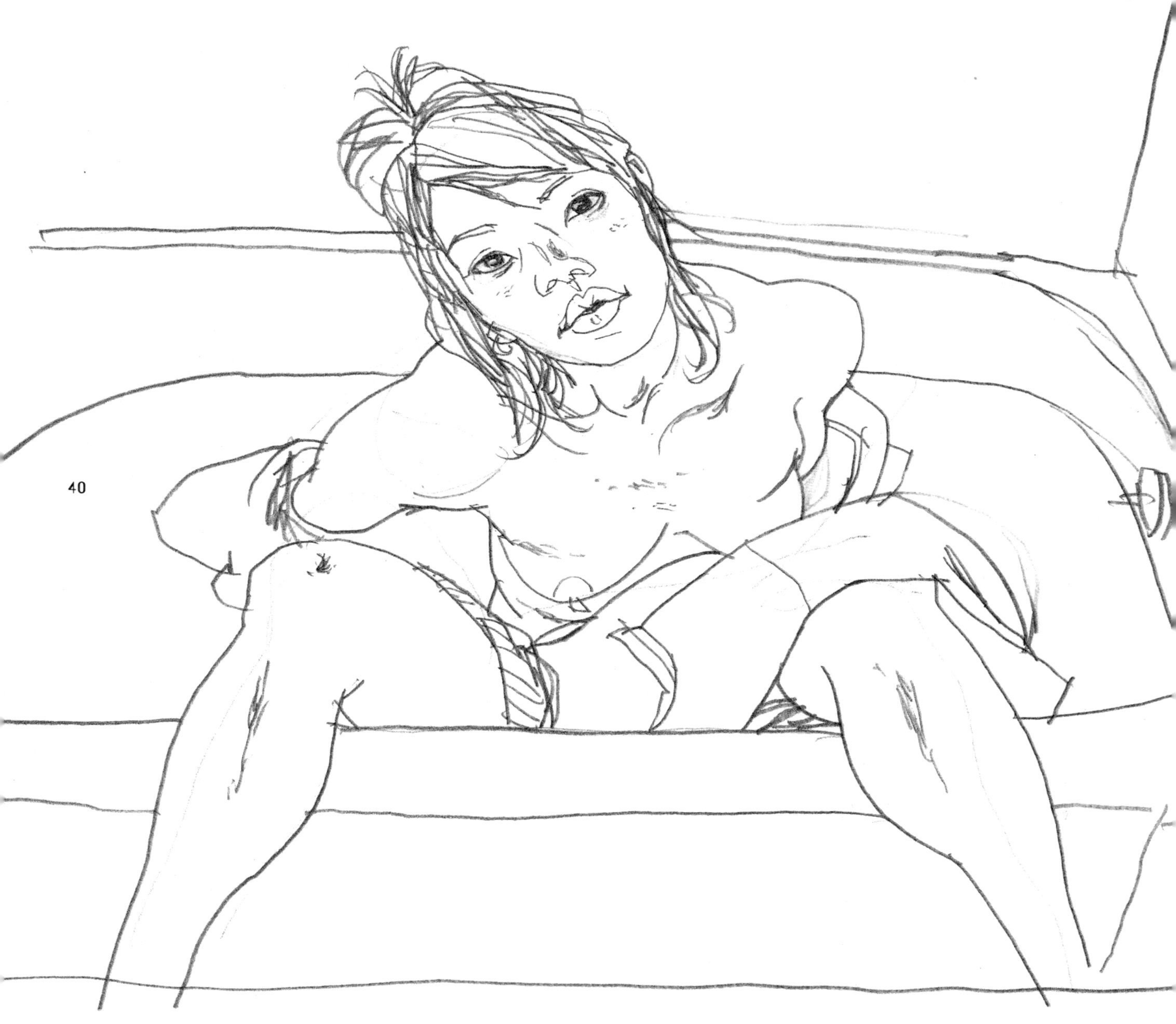

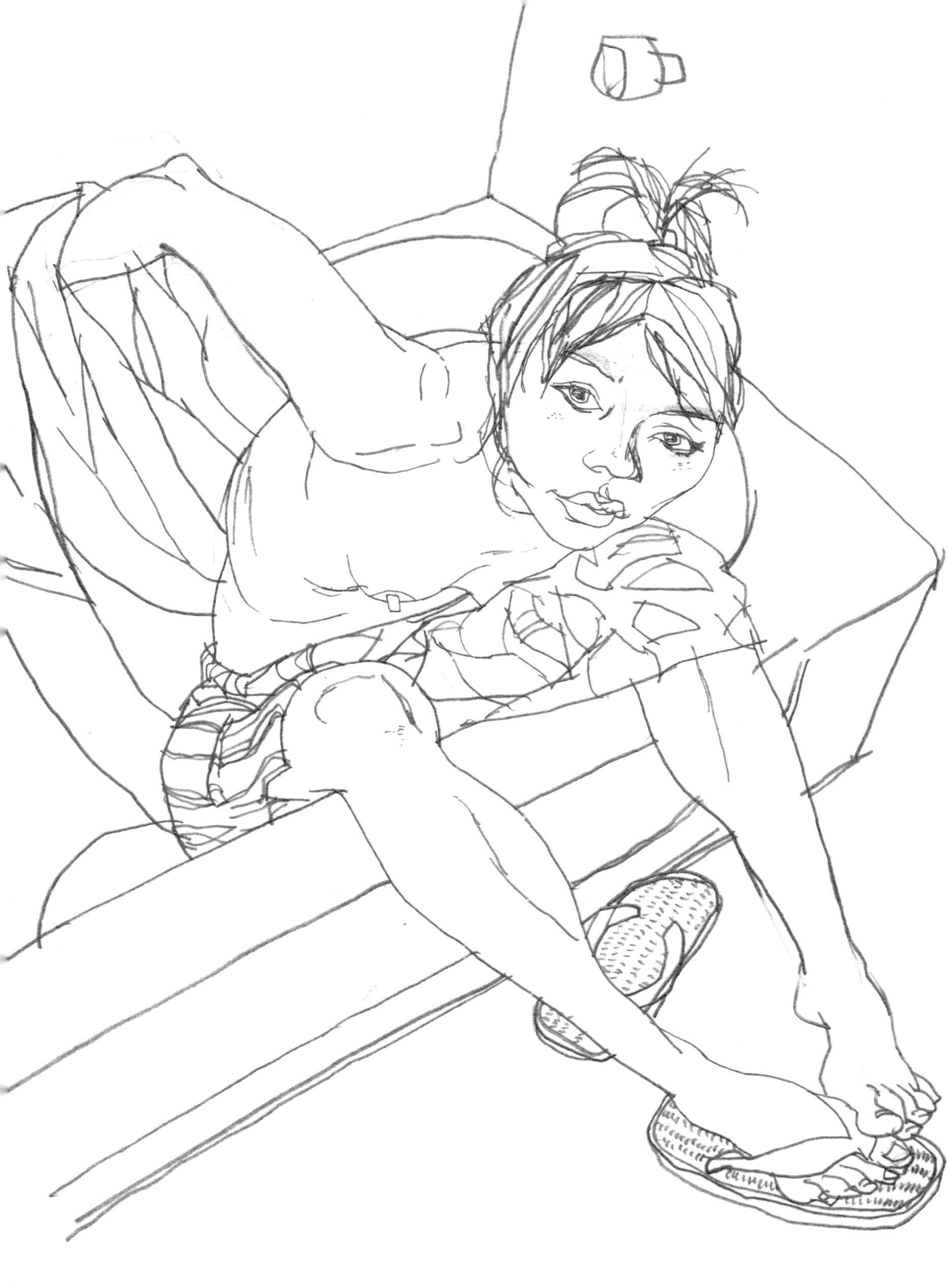

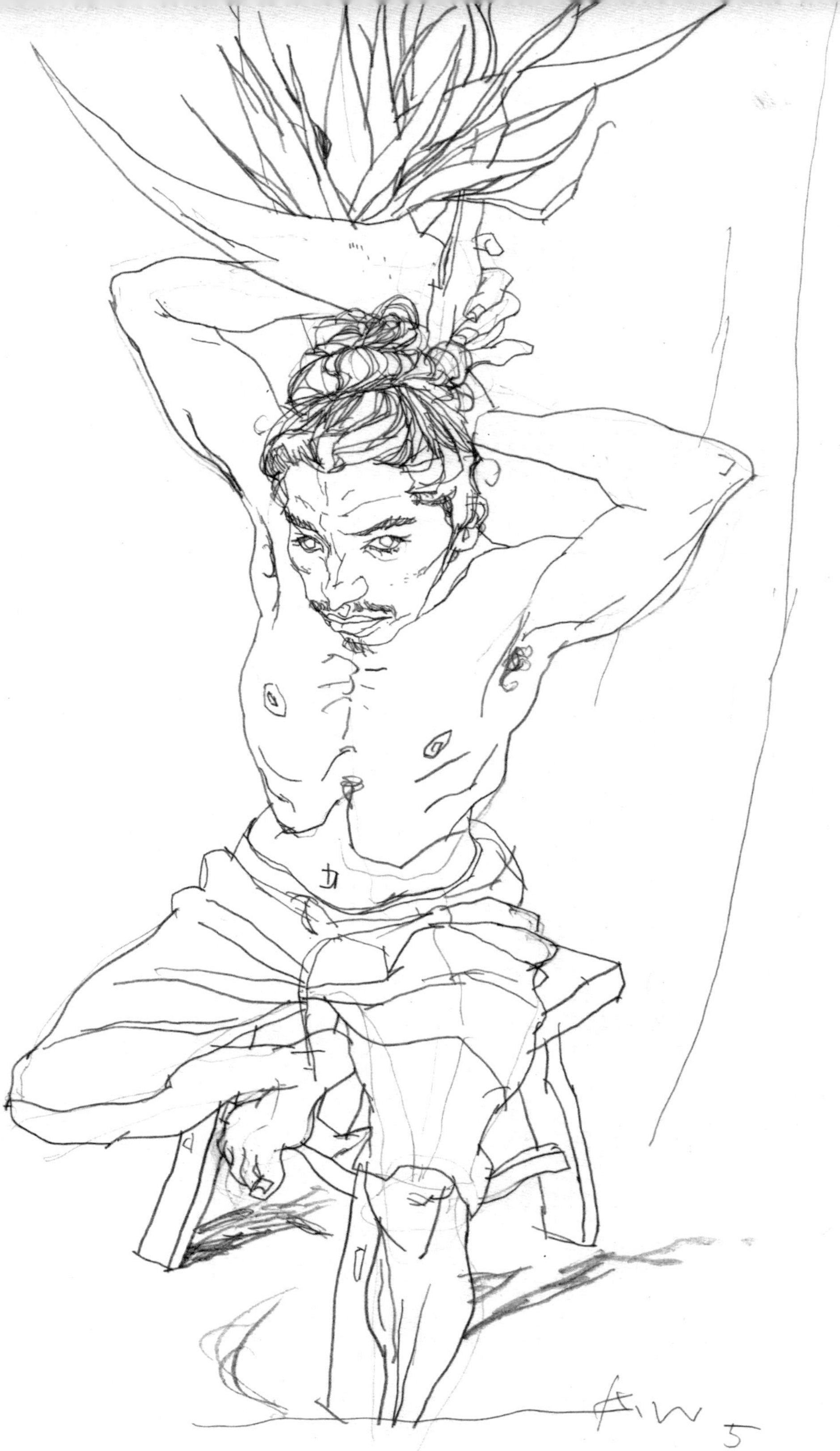

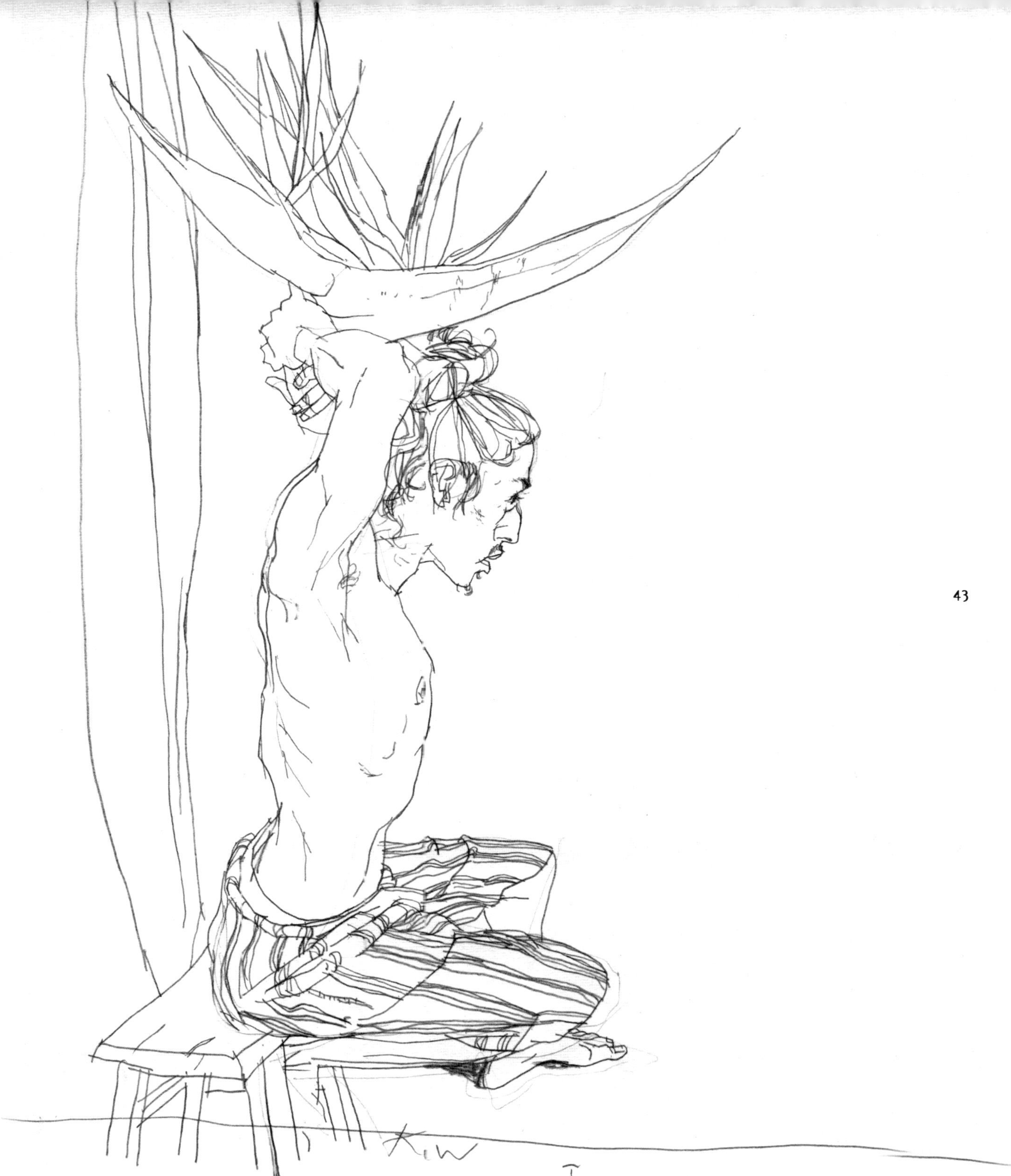

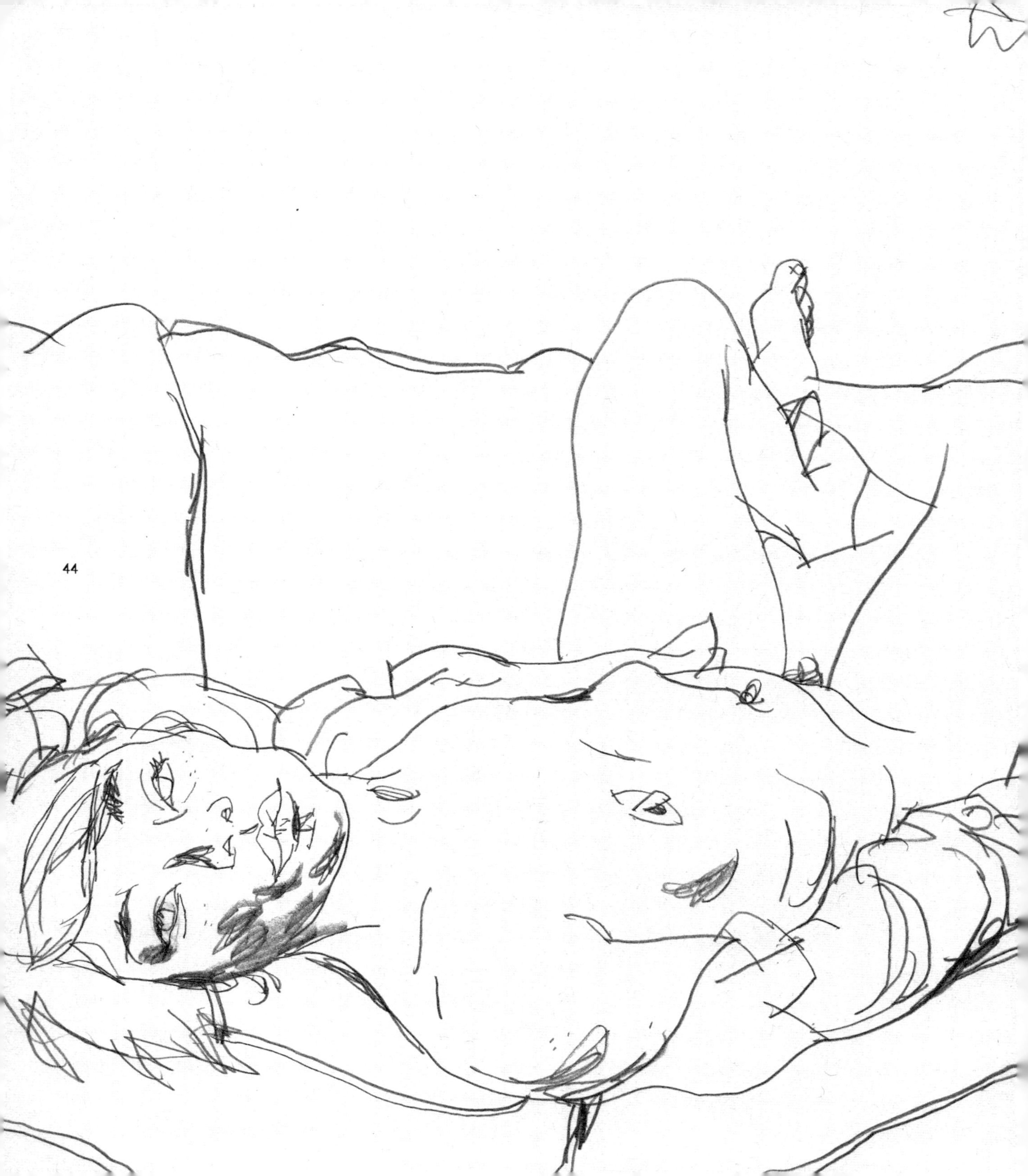

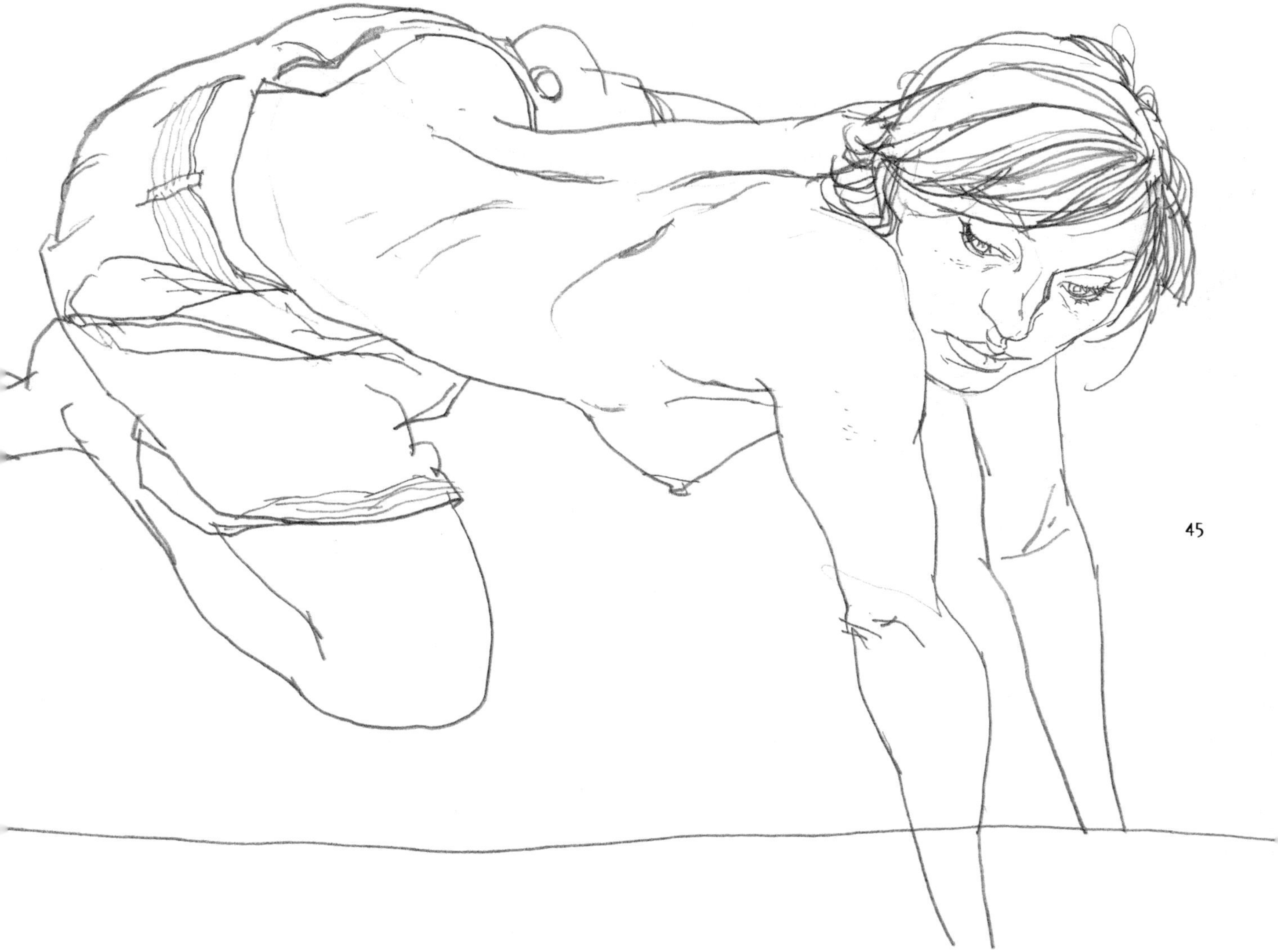

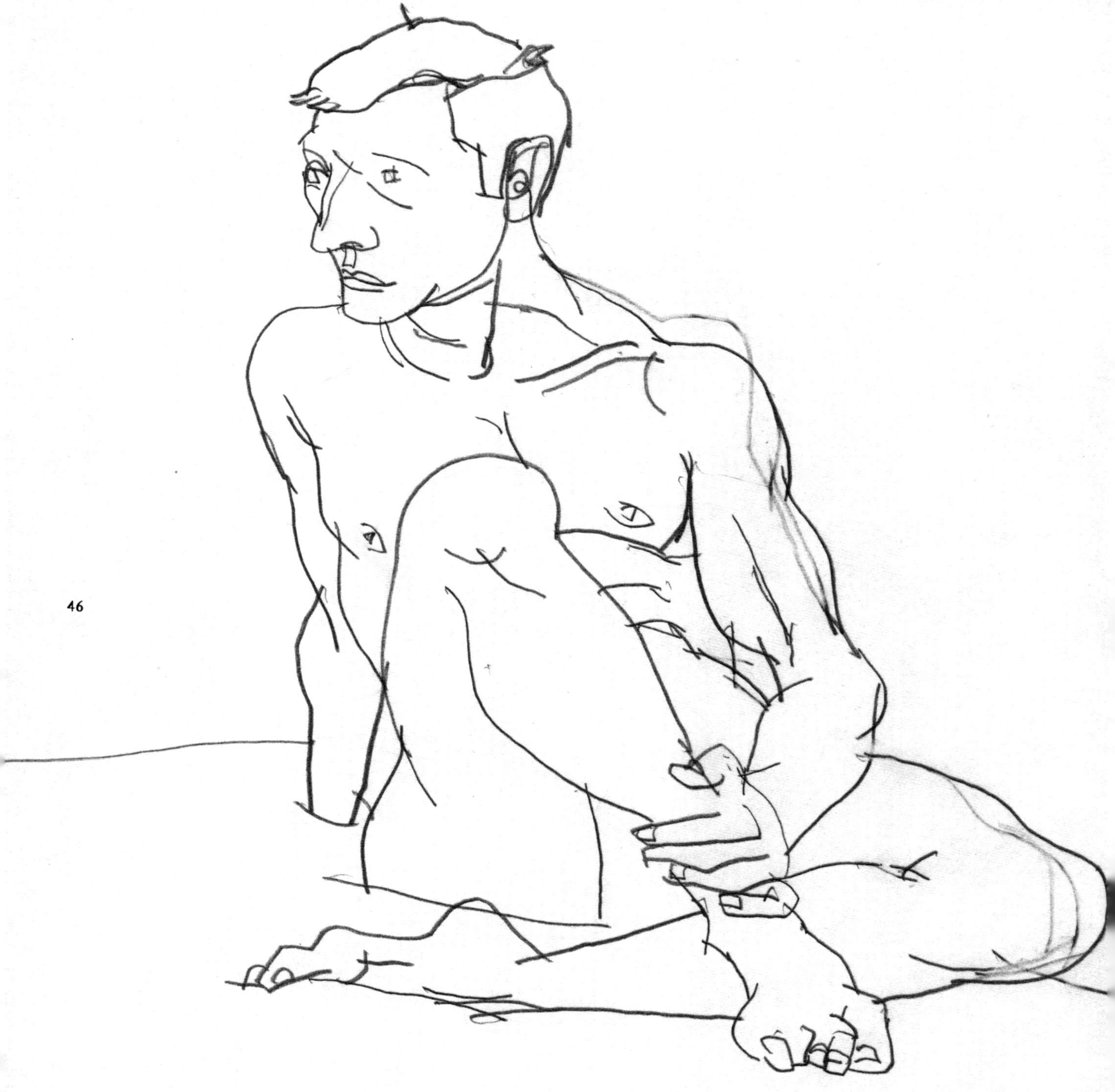

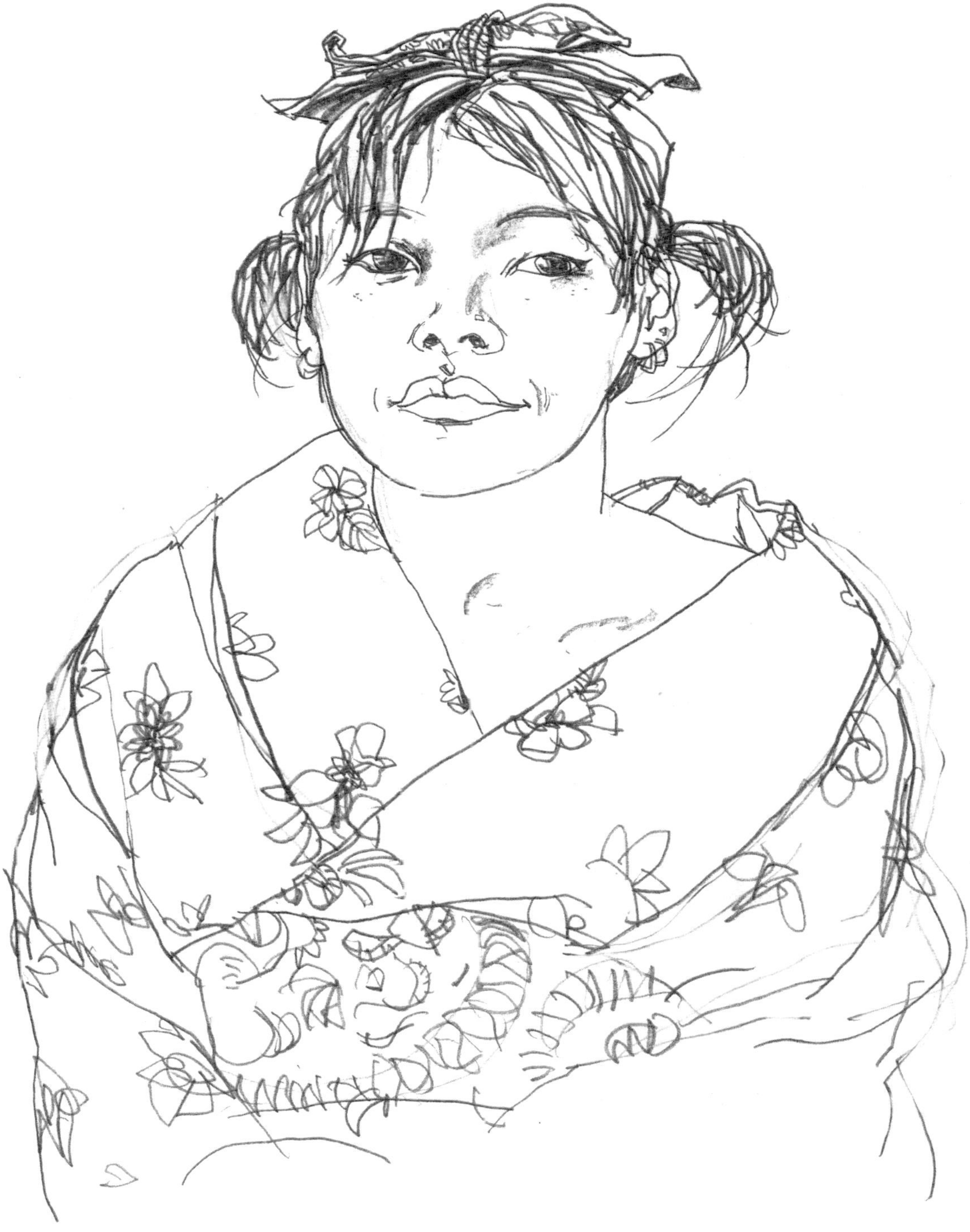

47

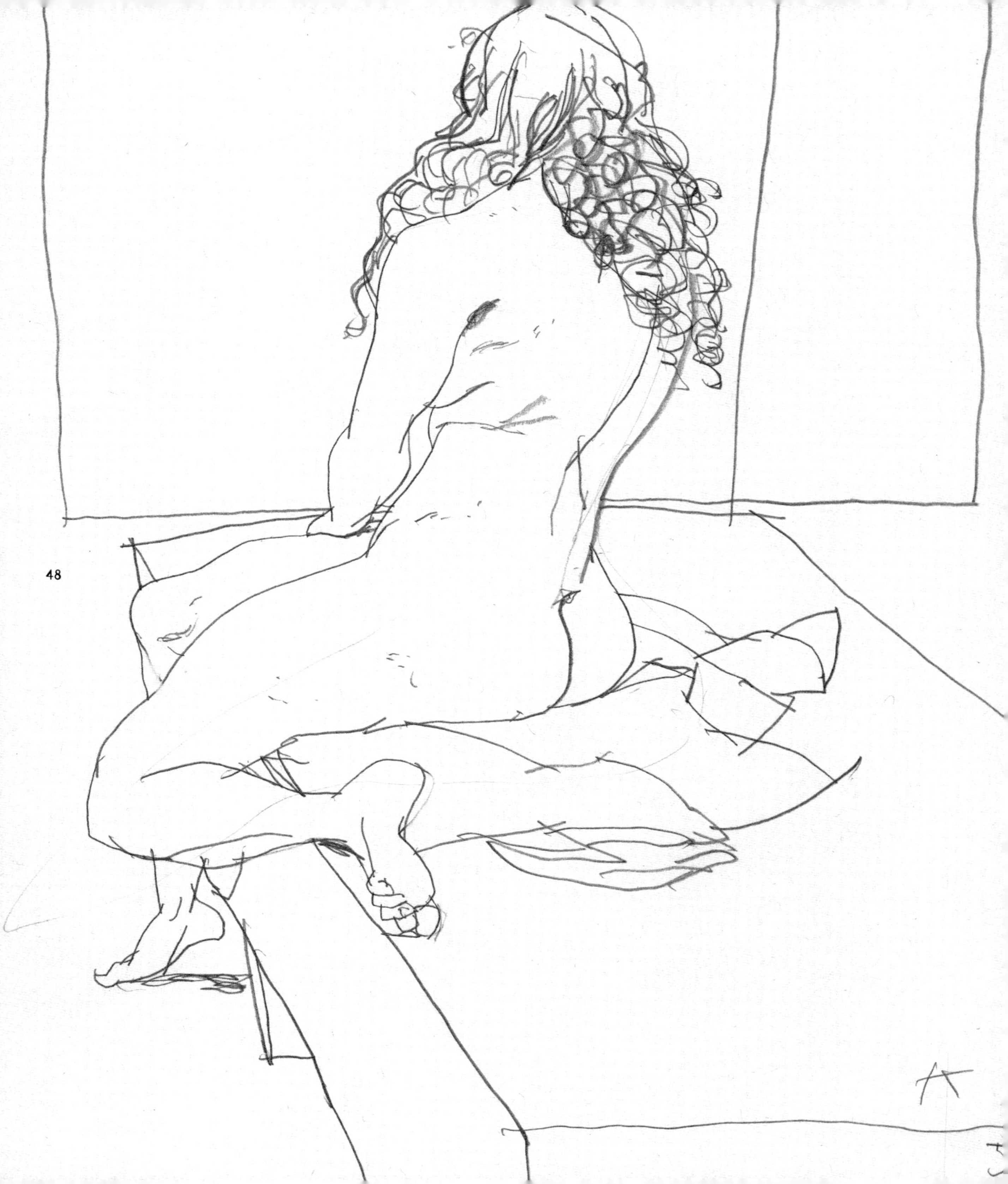

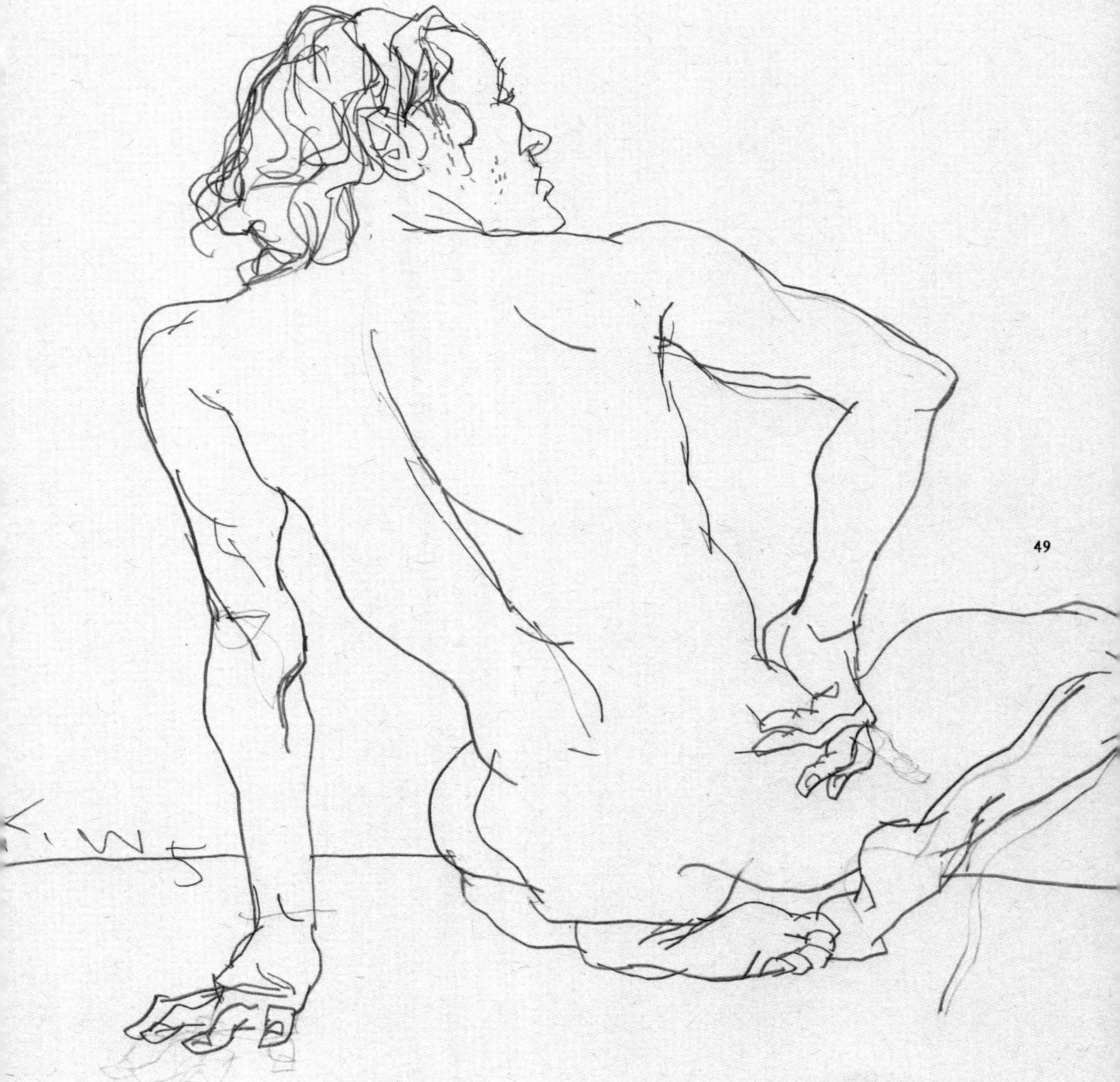

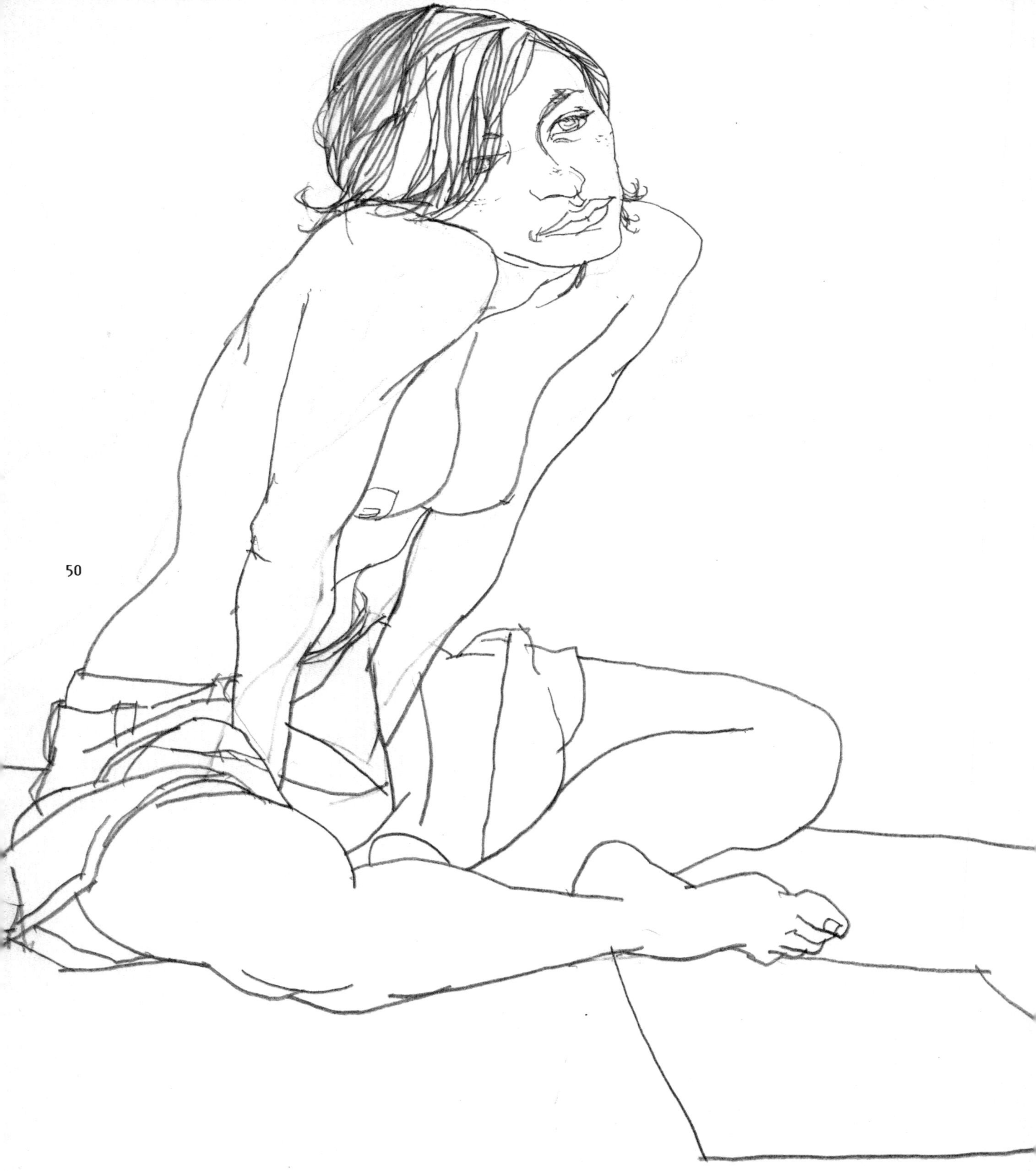

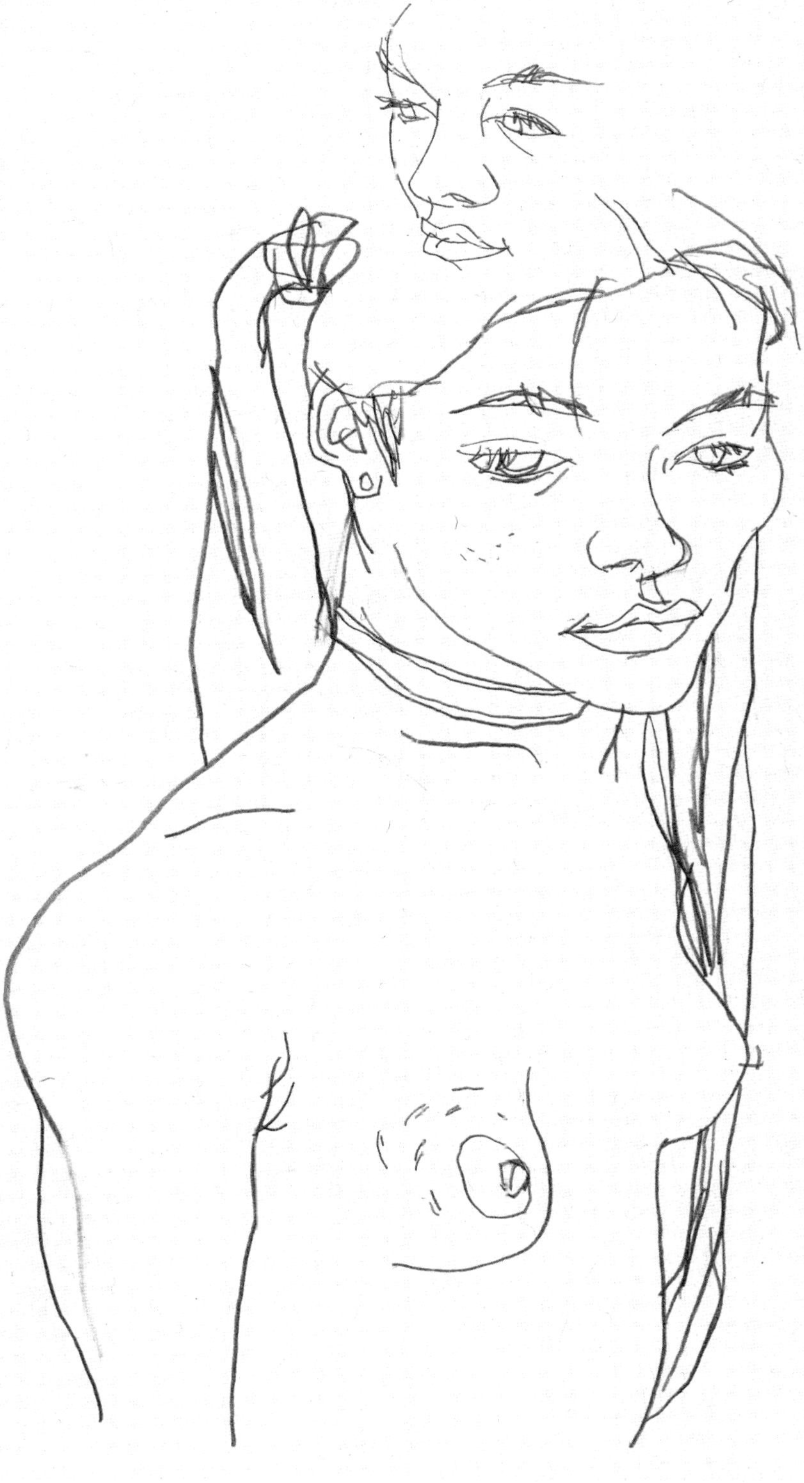

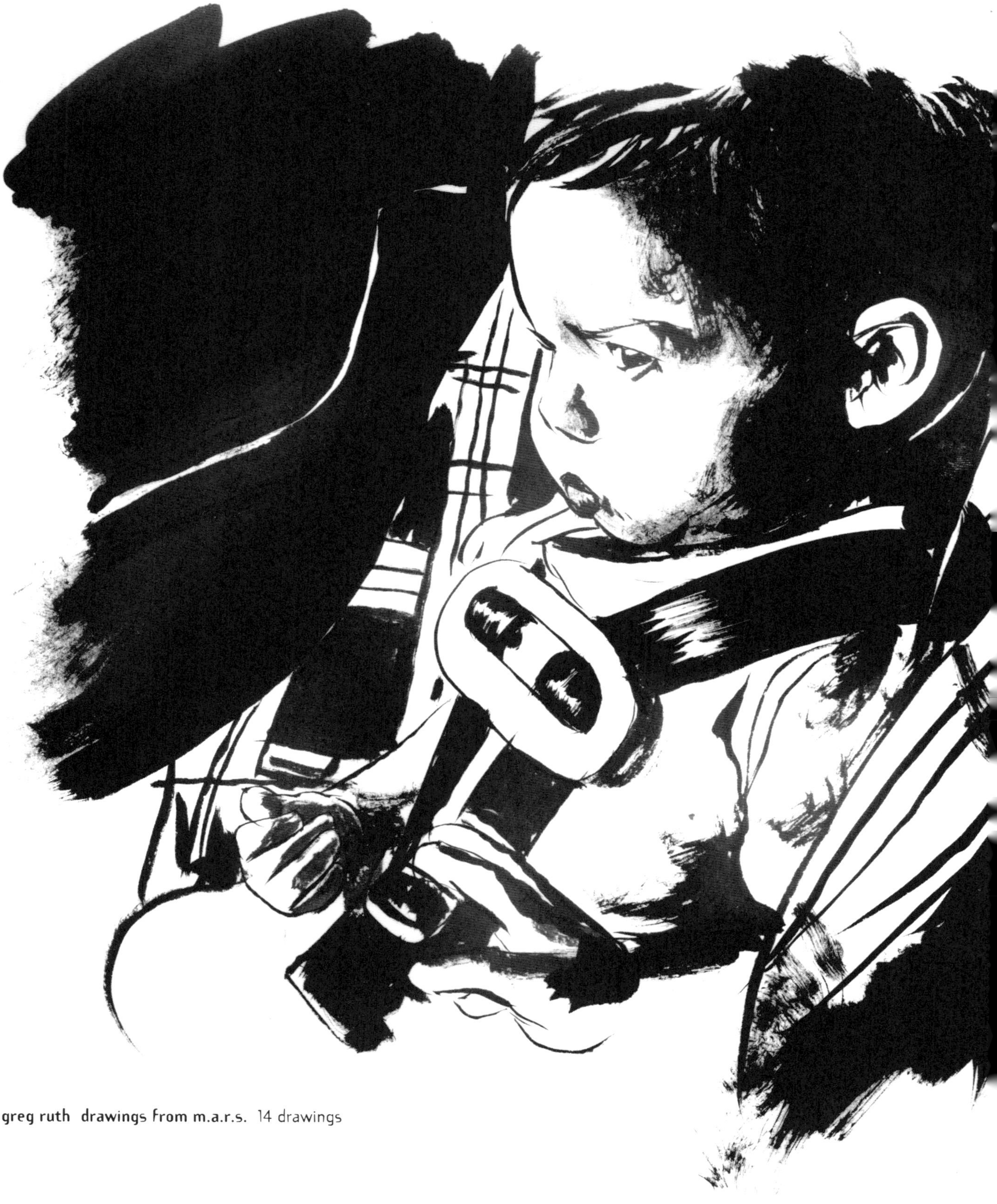

greg ruth drawings from m.a.r.s. 14 drawings

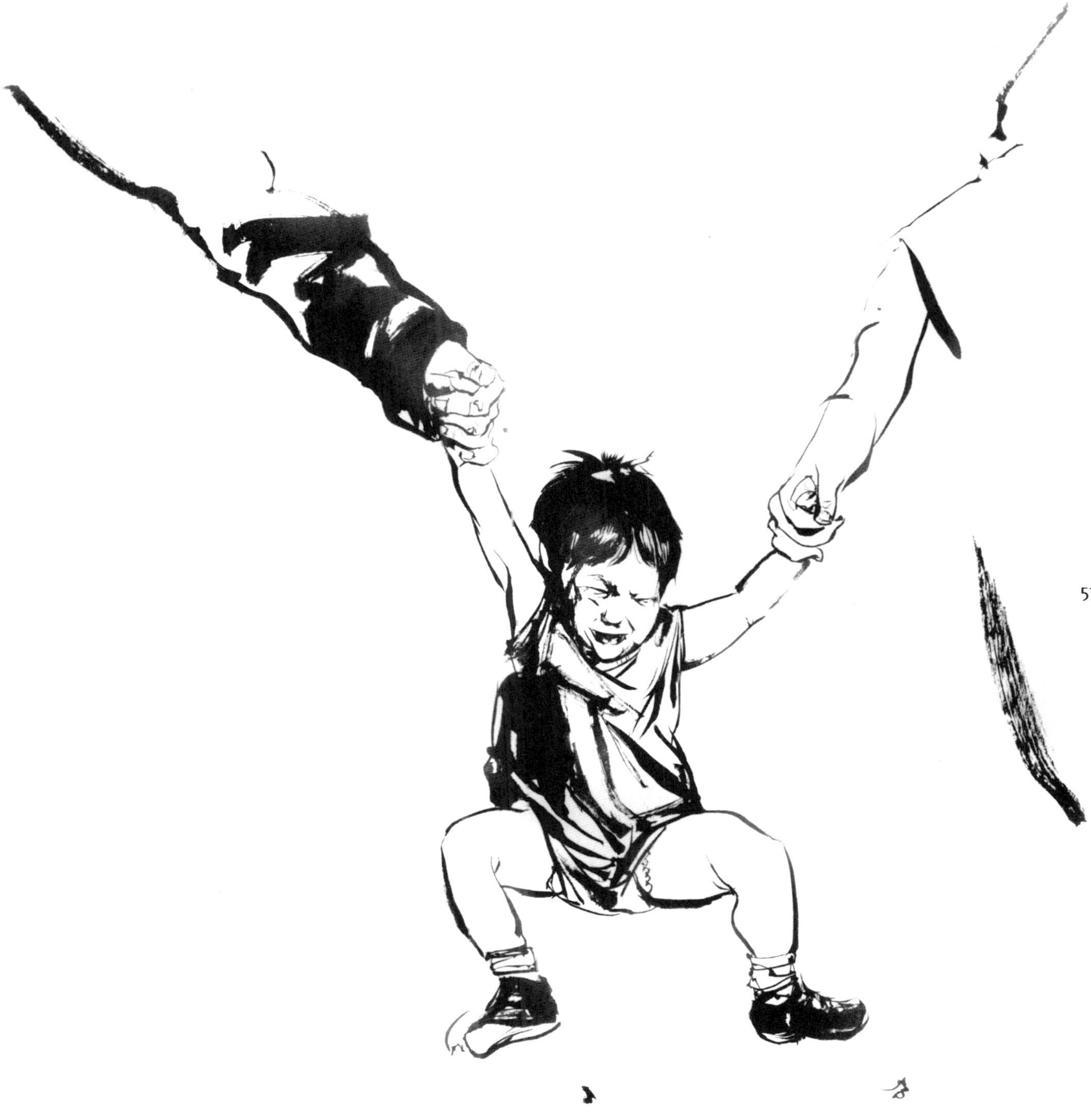

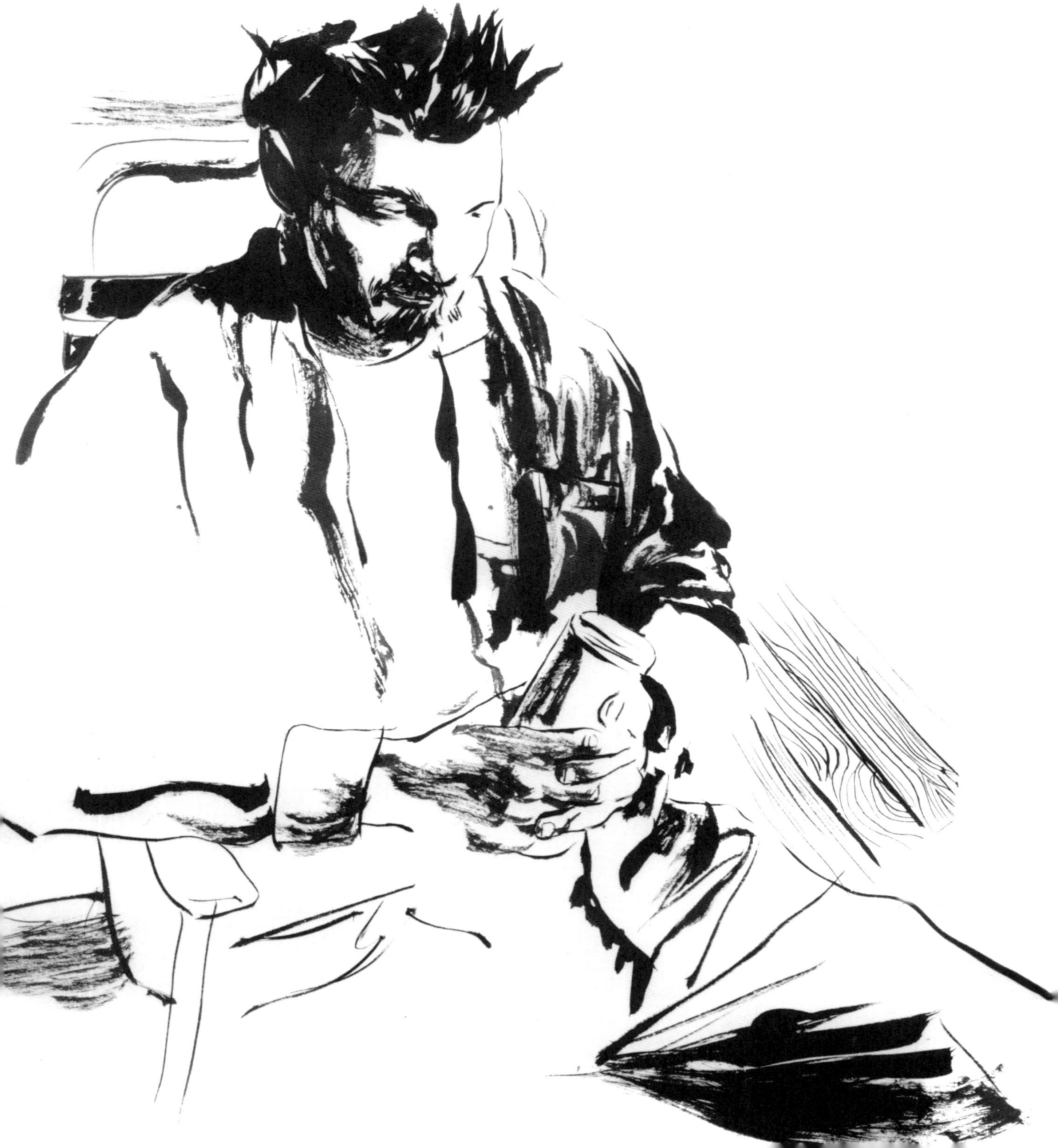

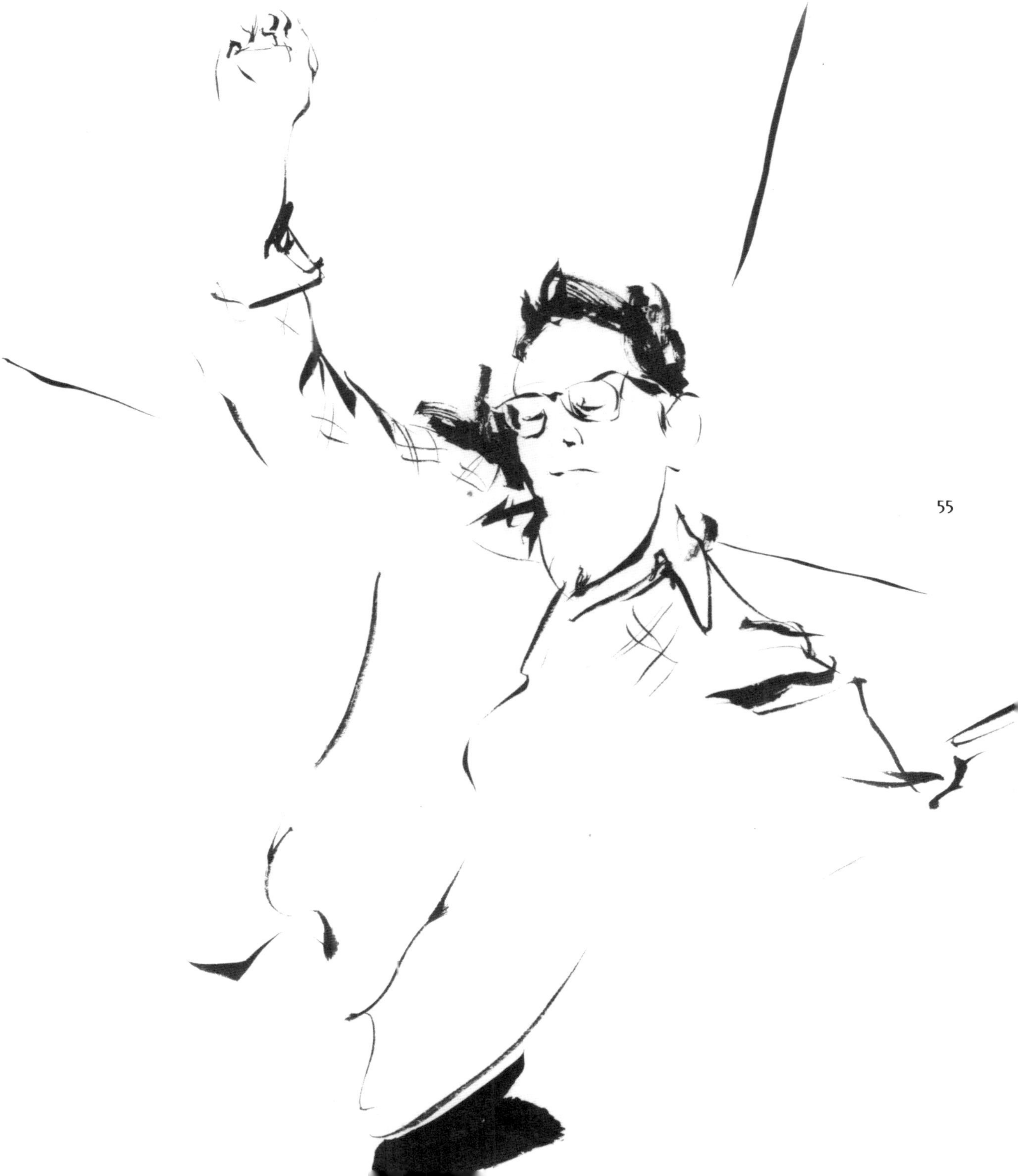

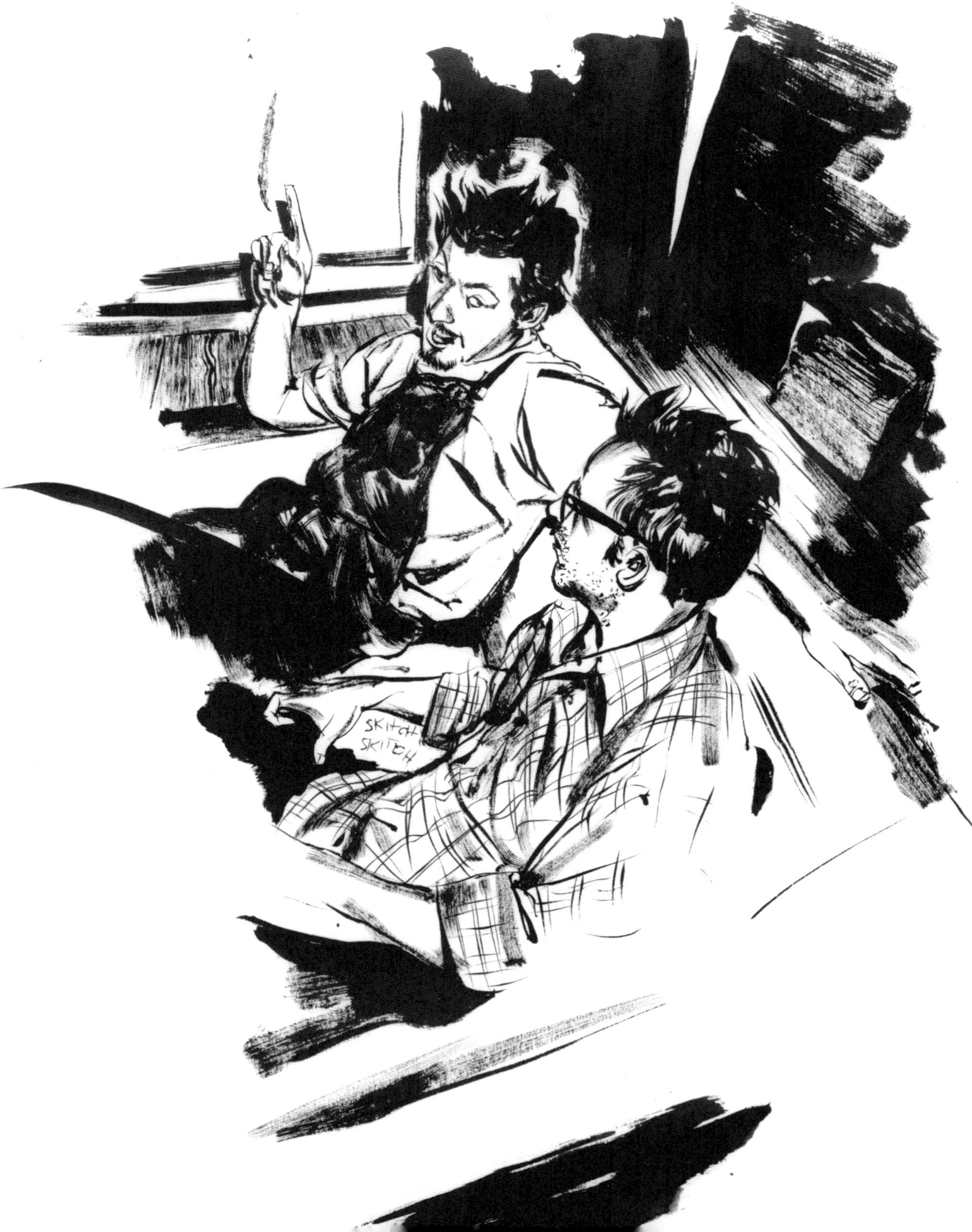
SKITCH
SKITCH

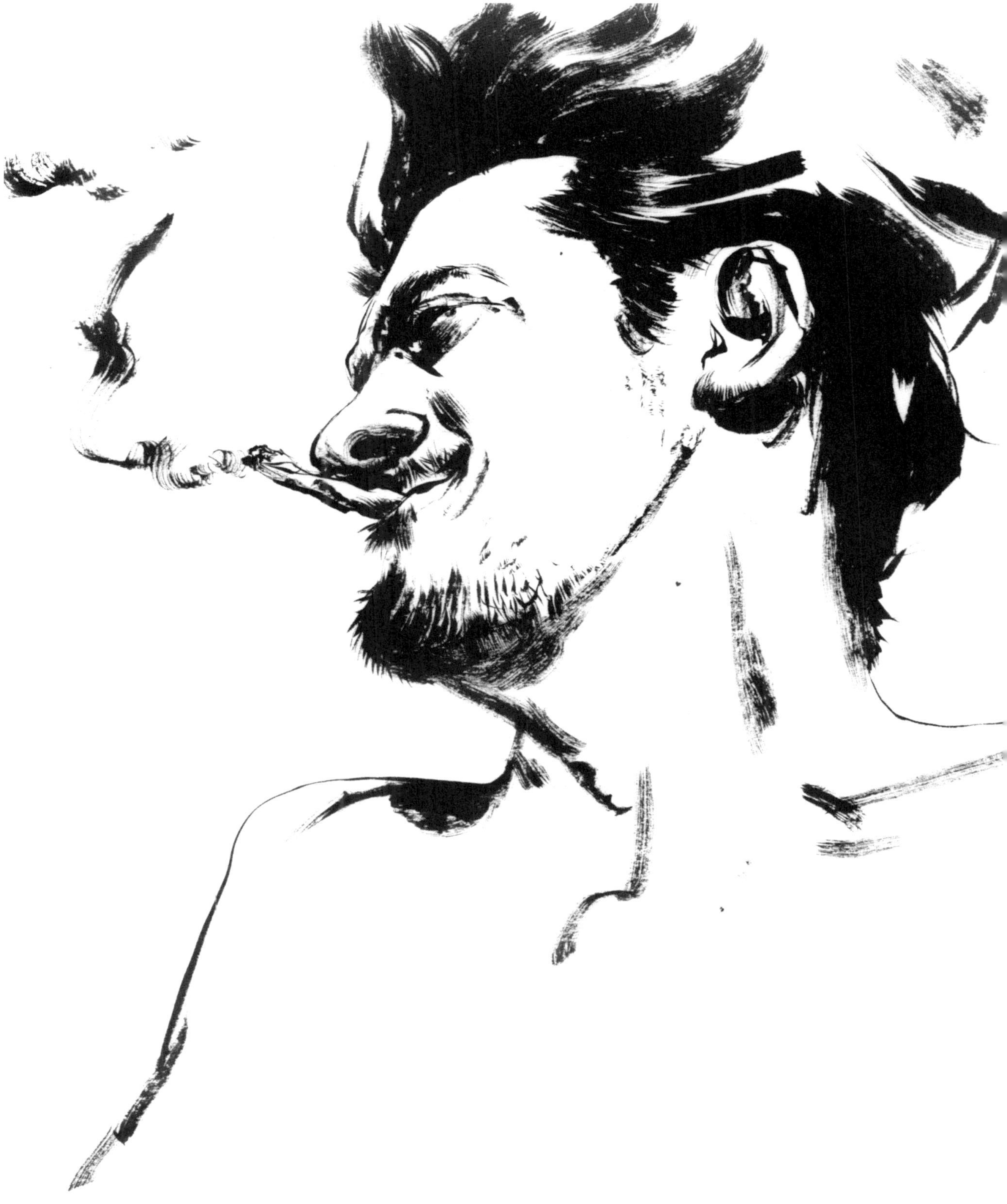

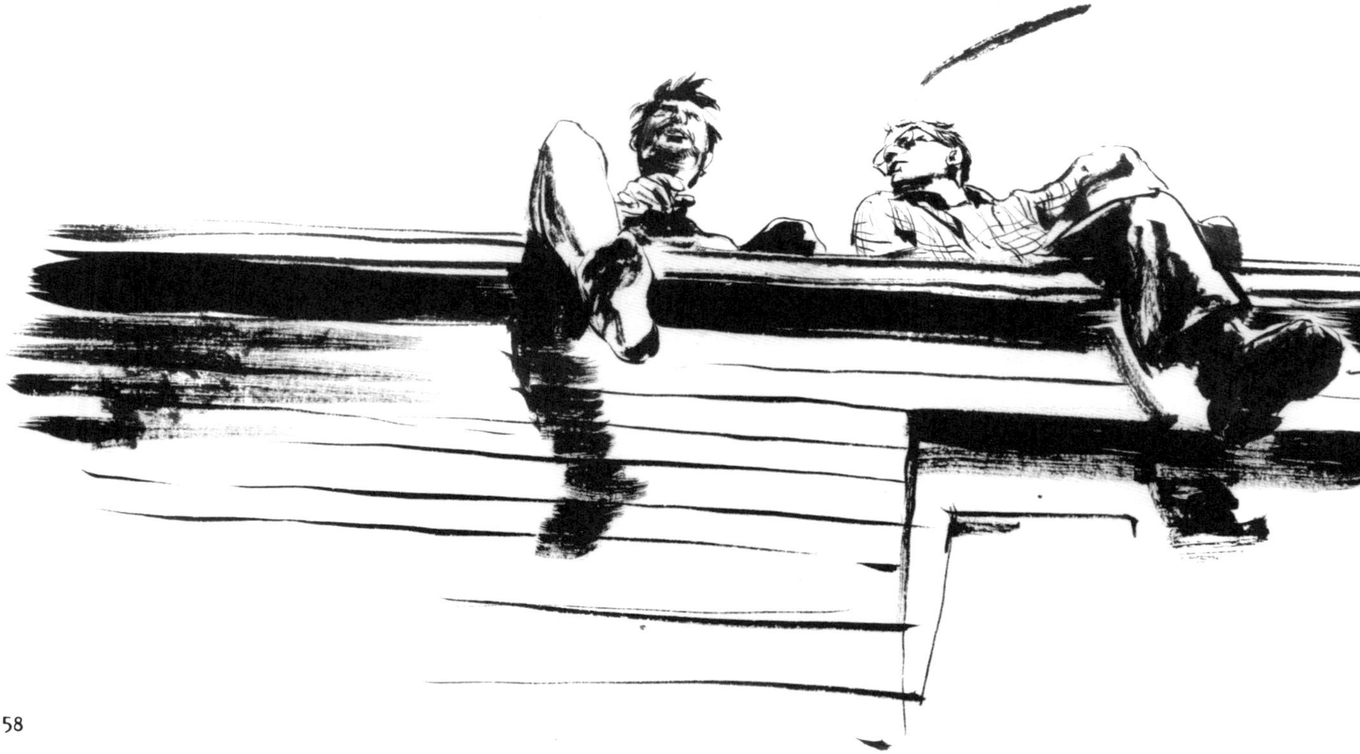

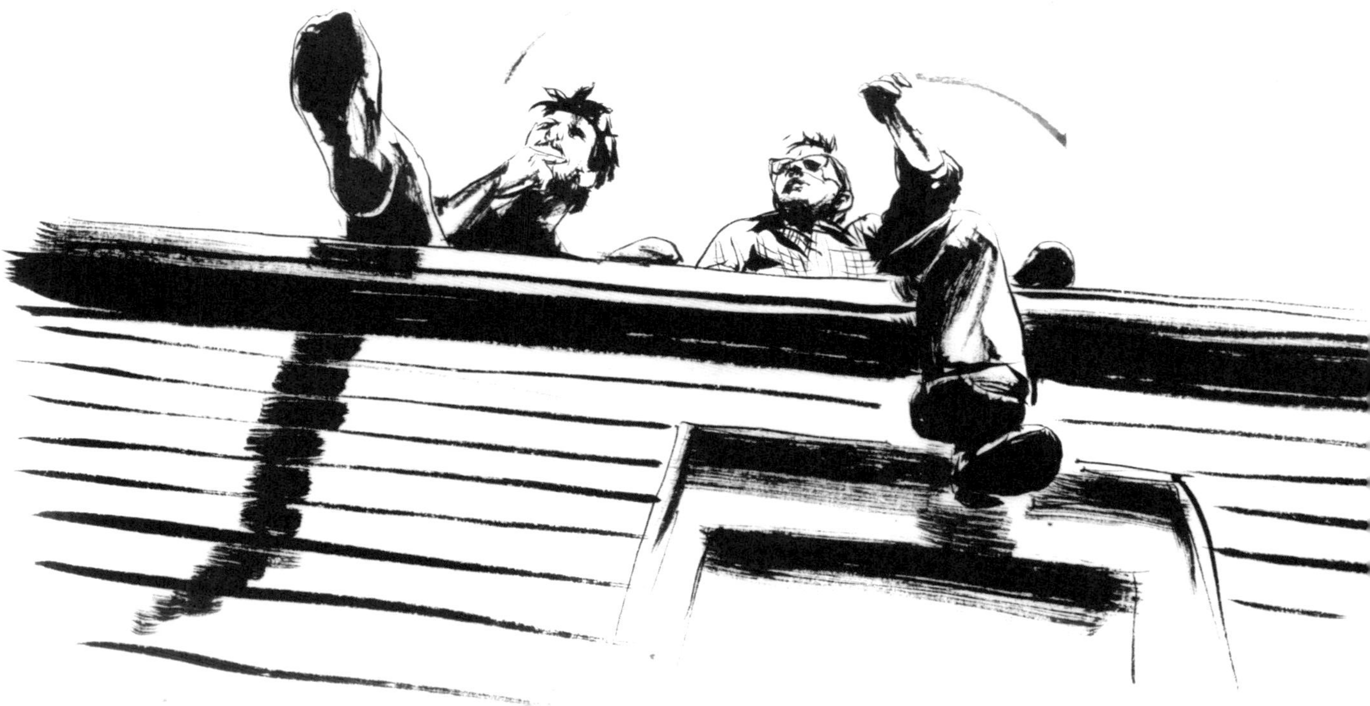

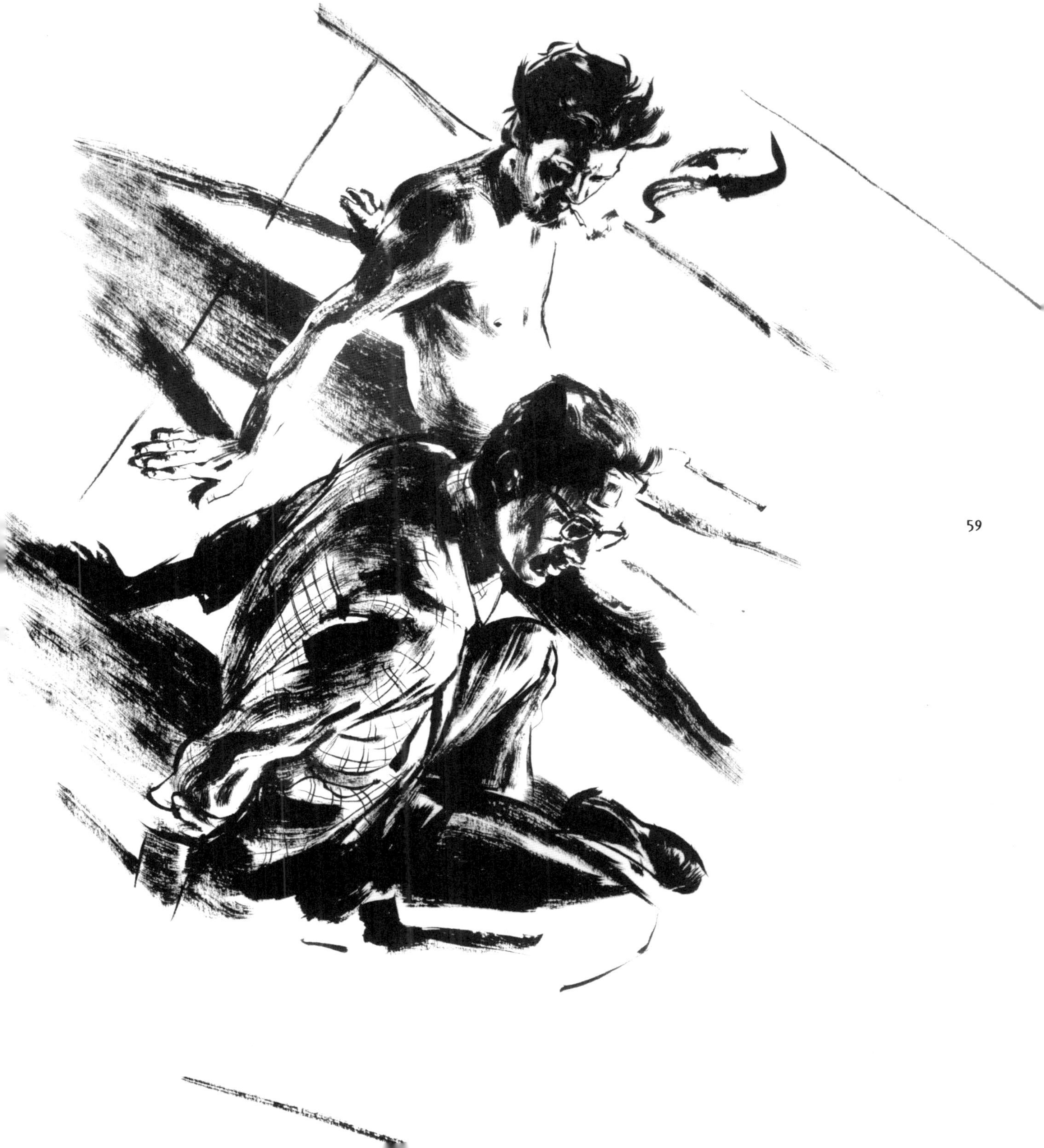

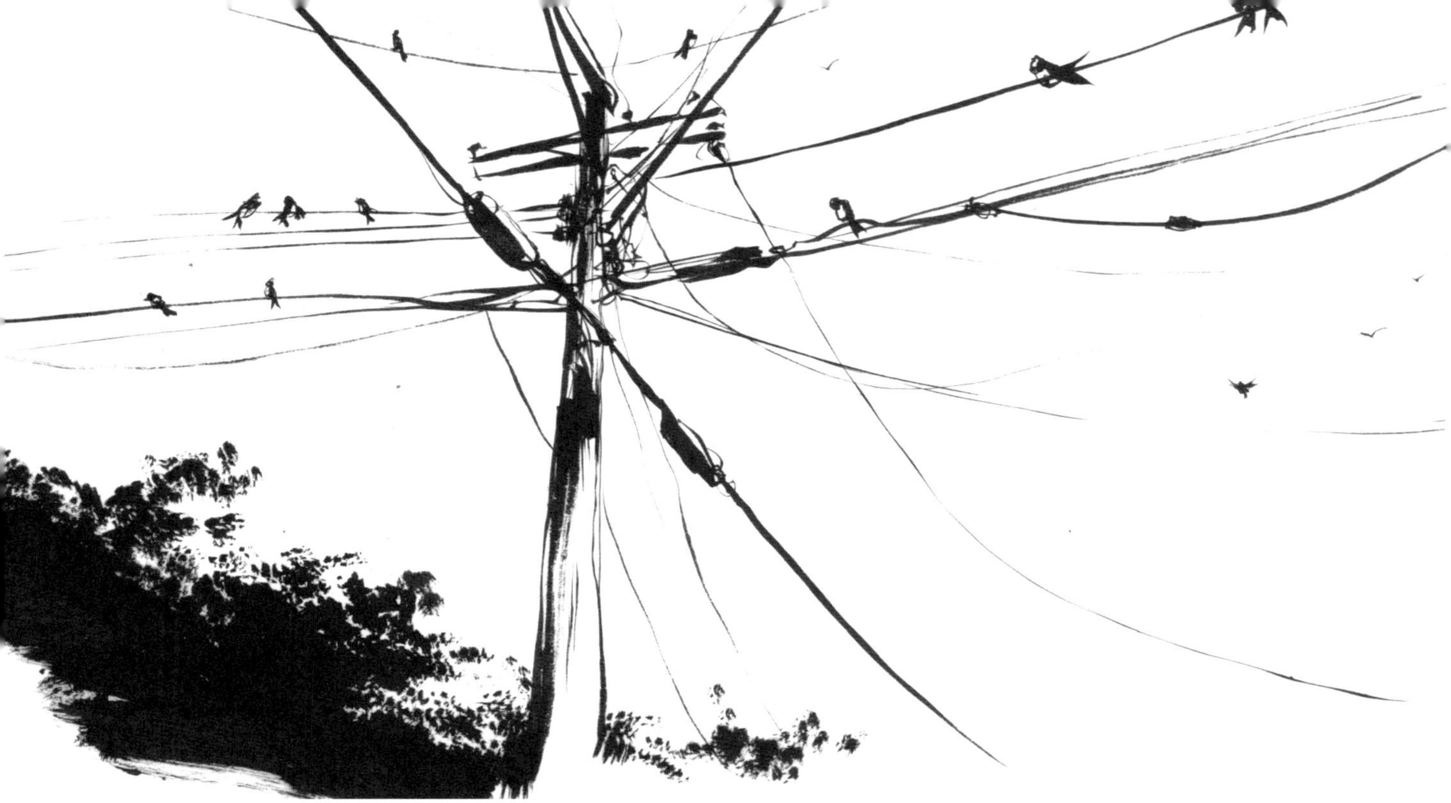

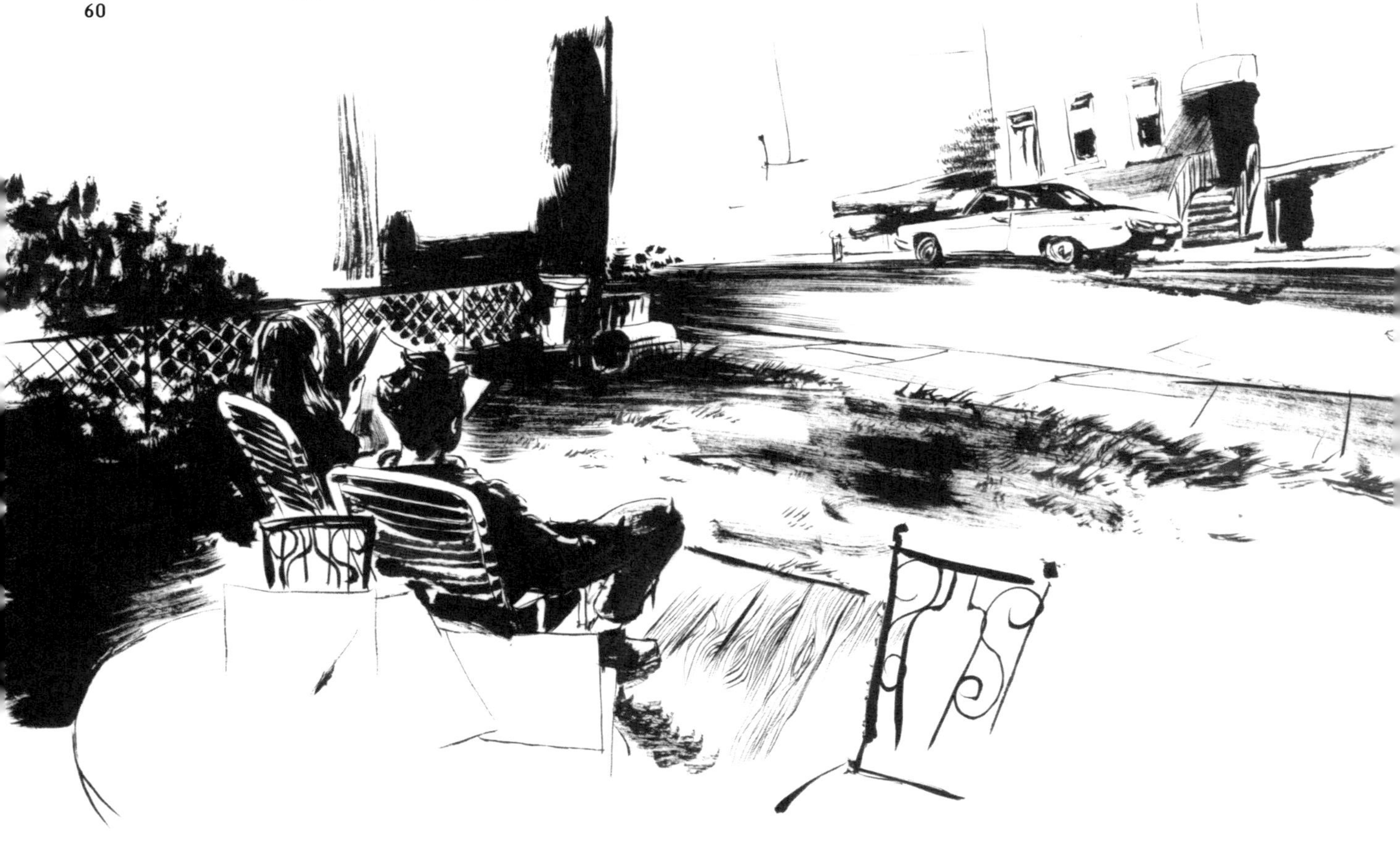

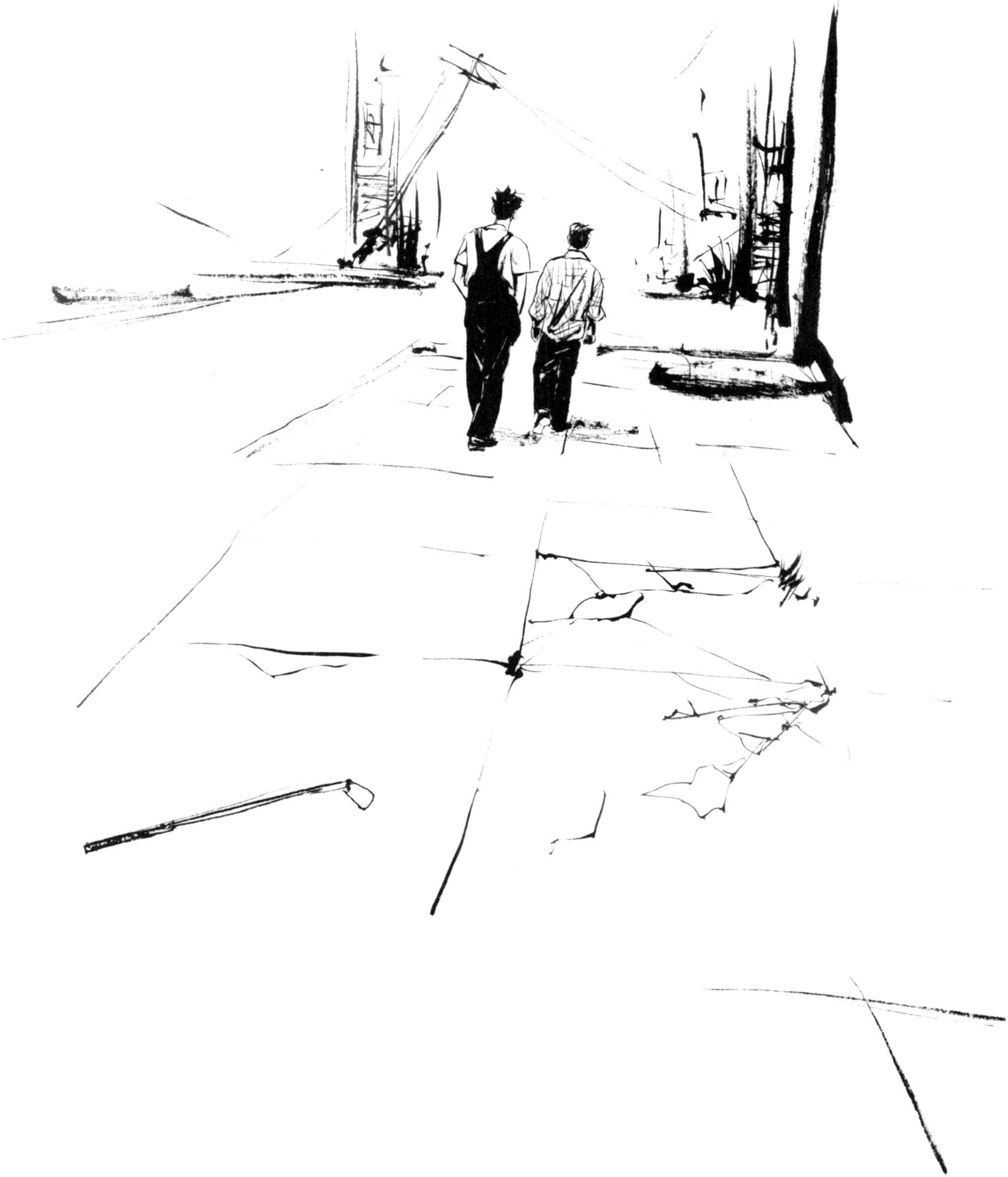

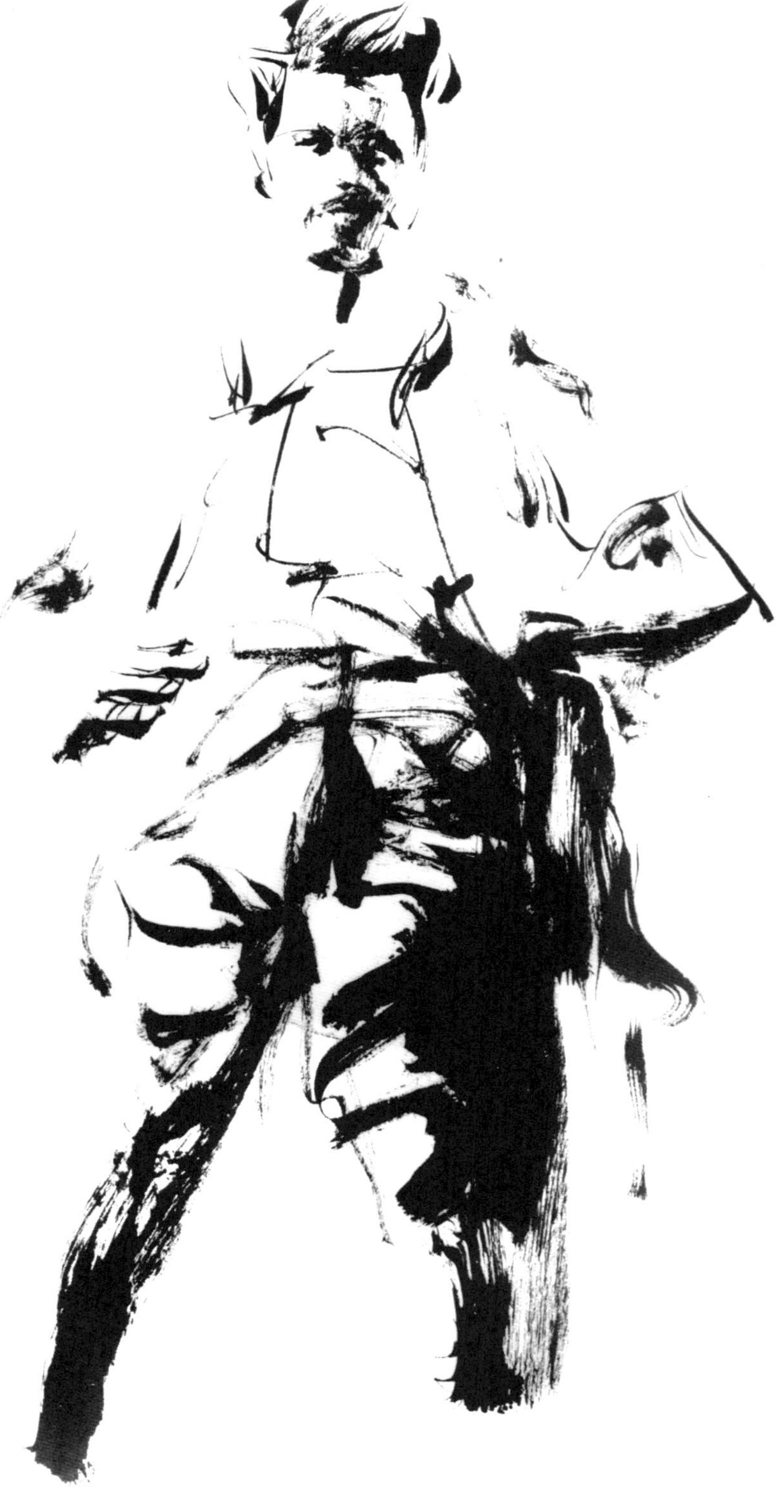

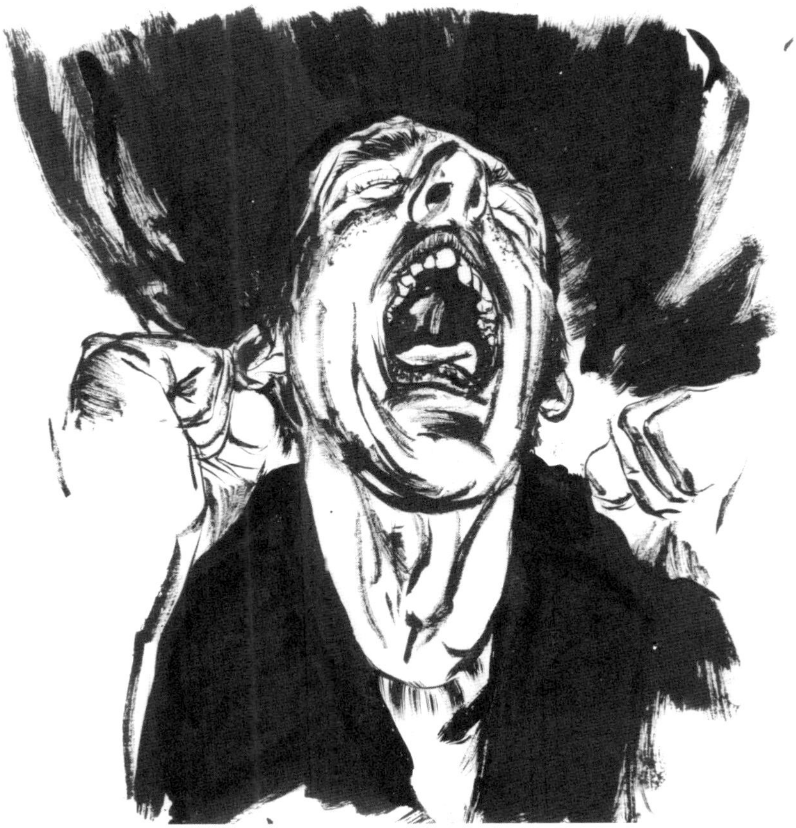

bonnie to yee de muth

pattern

4 drawings

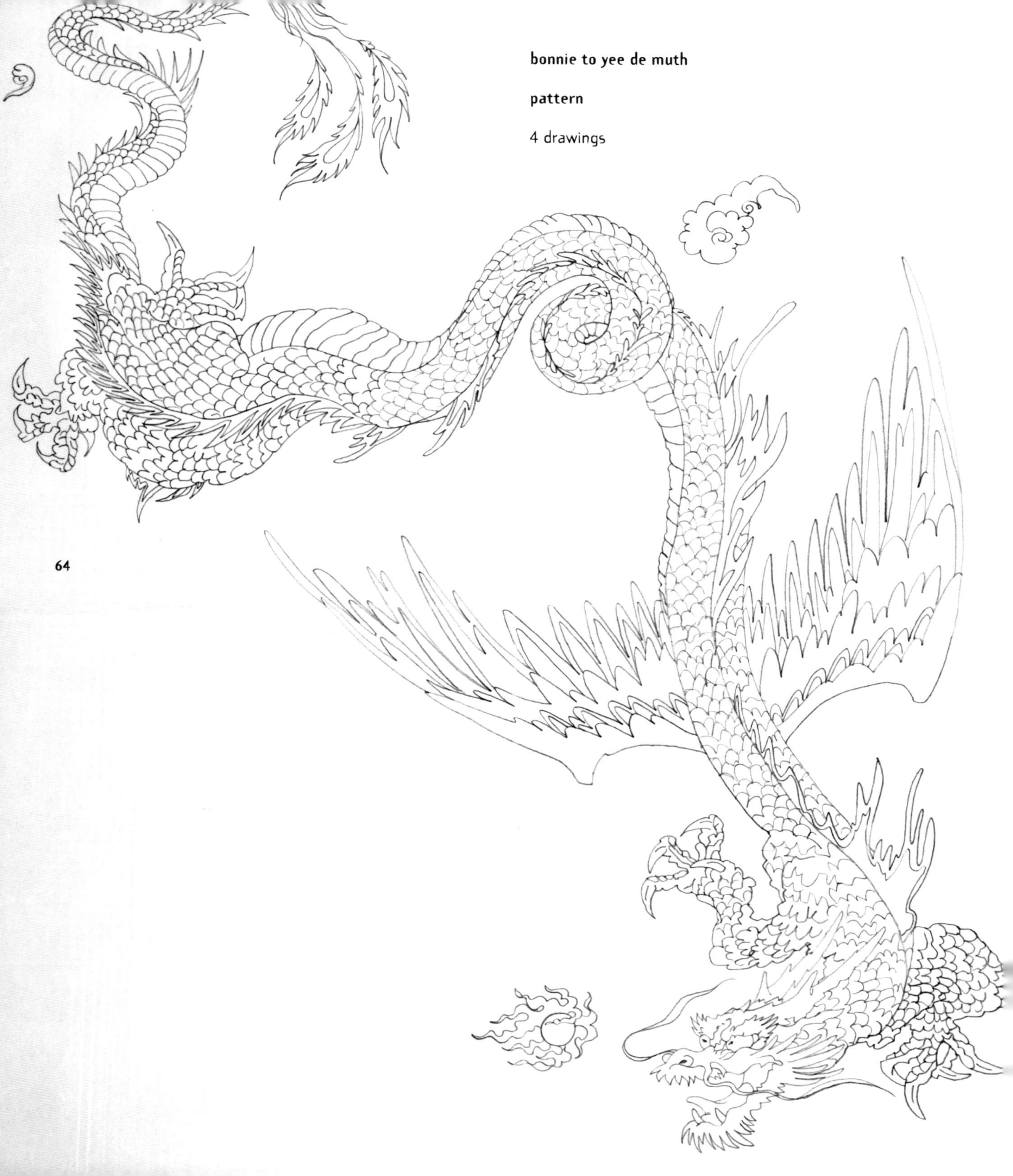

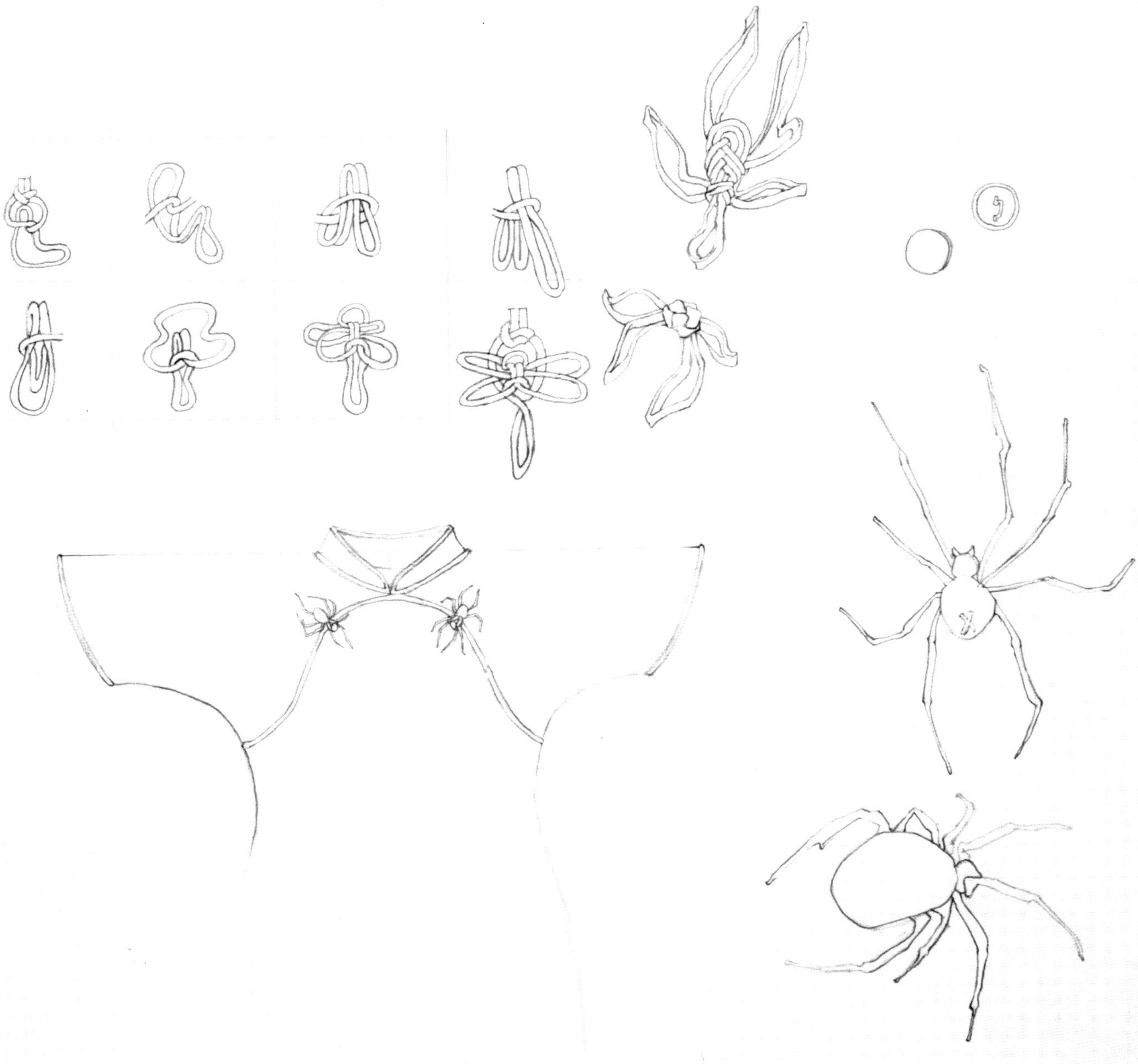

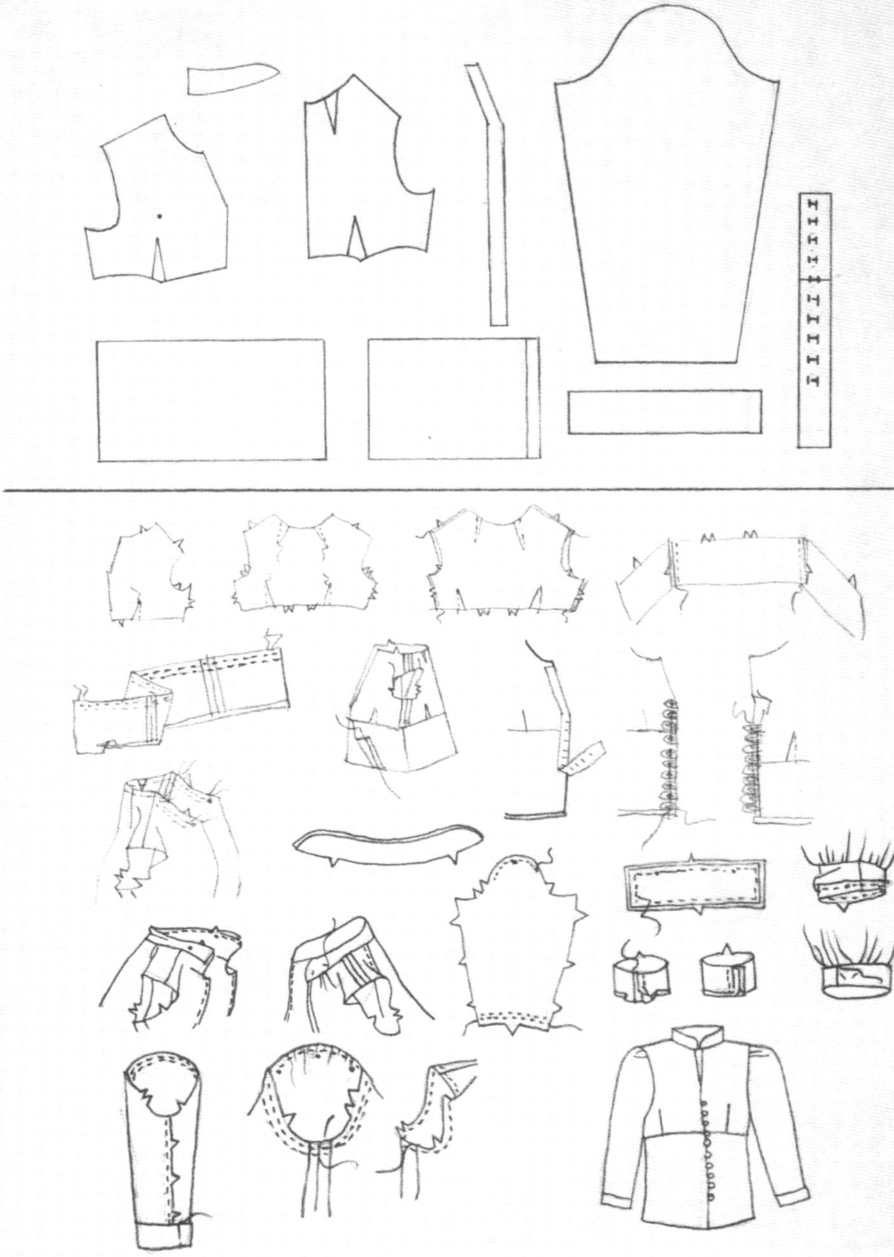

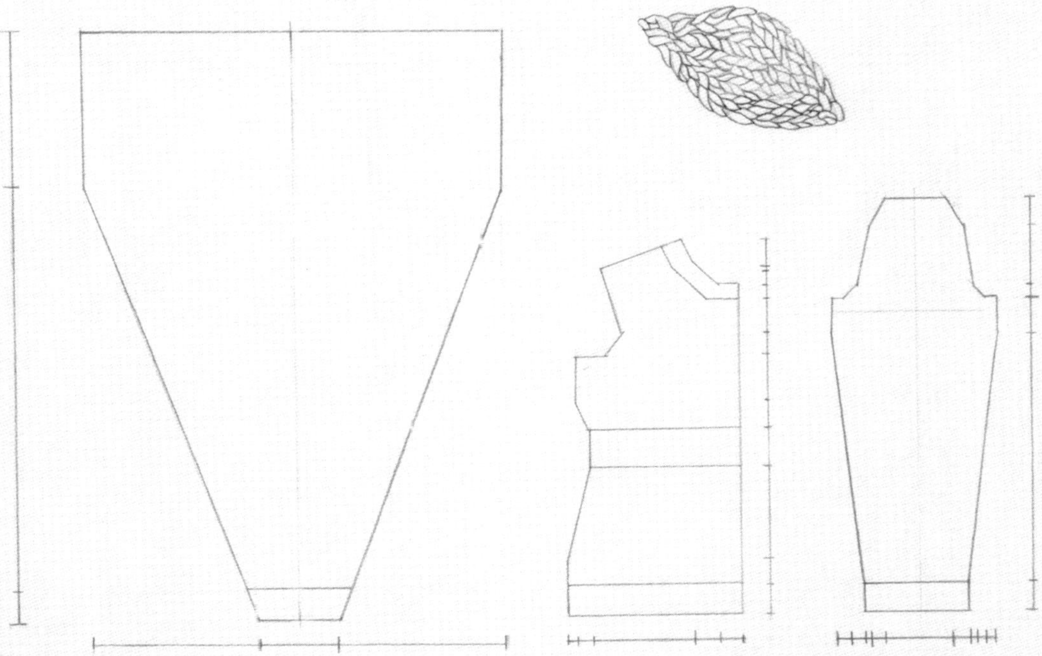

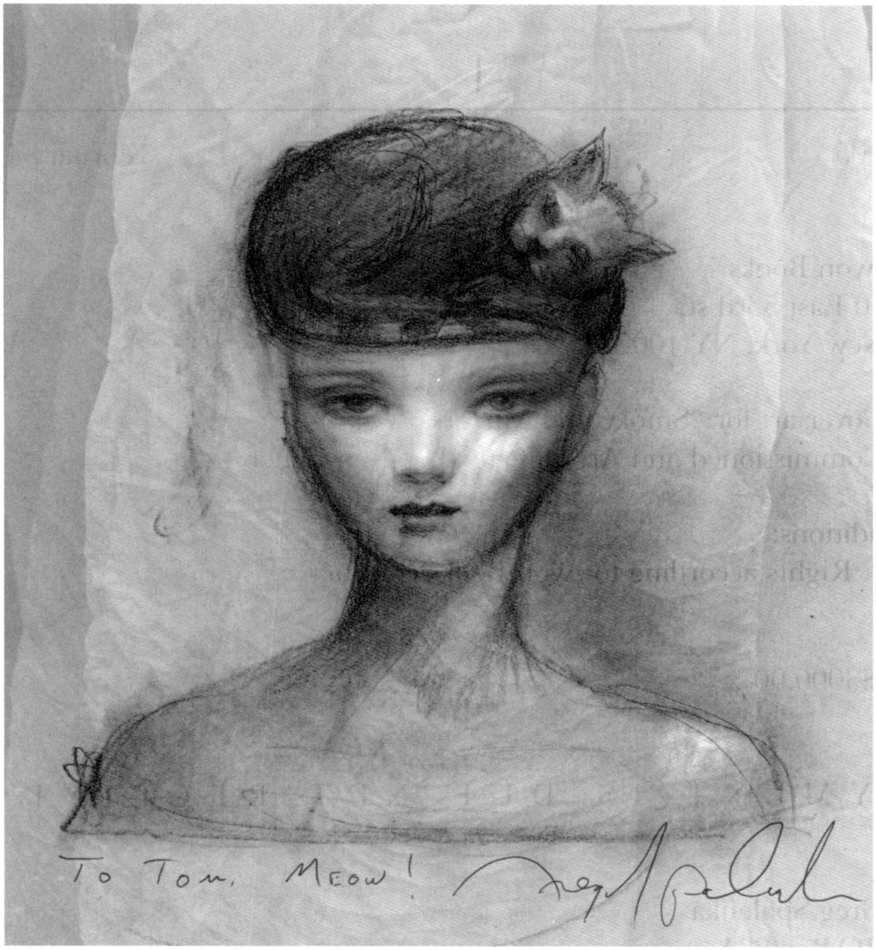
To Tom, MEOW!

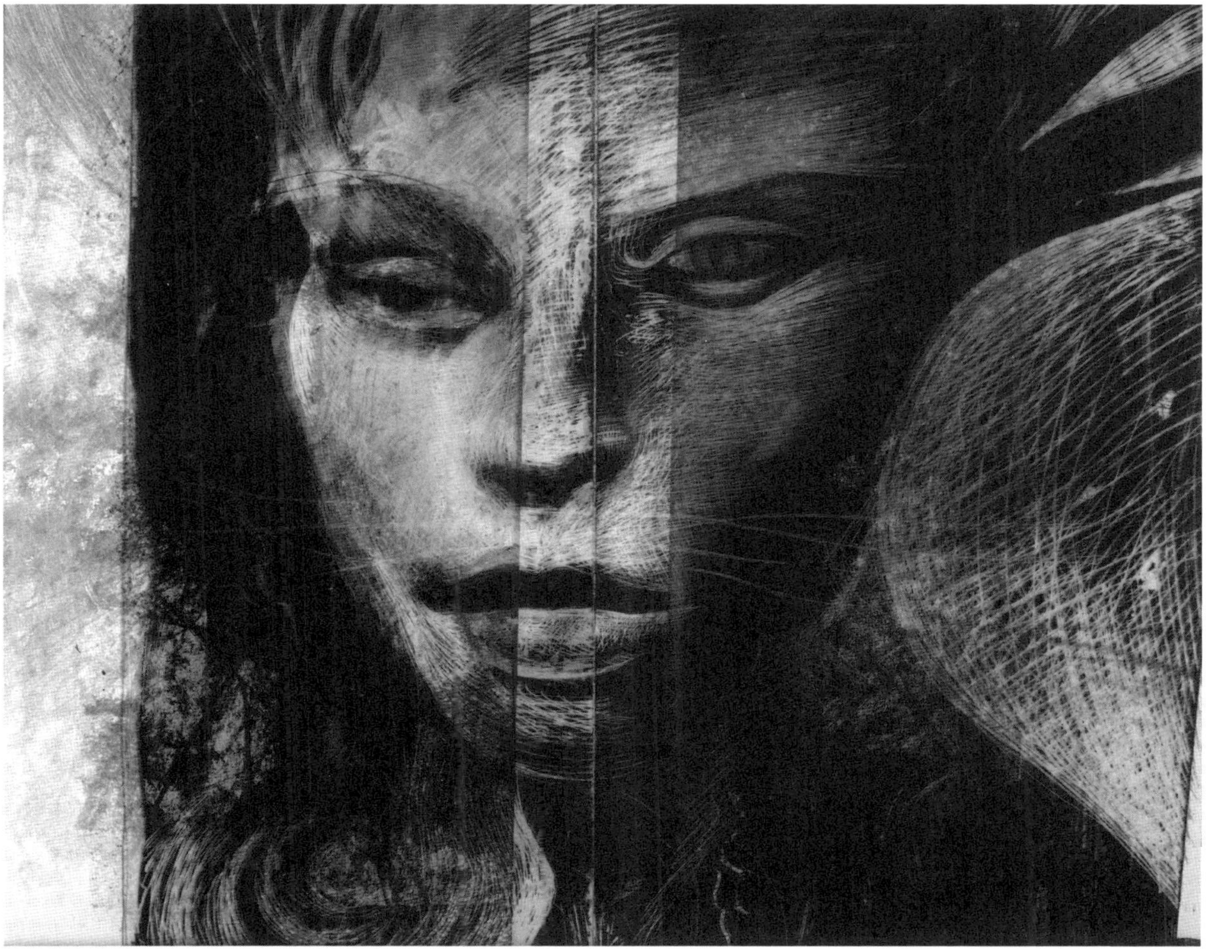

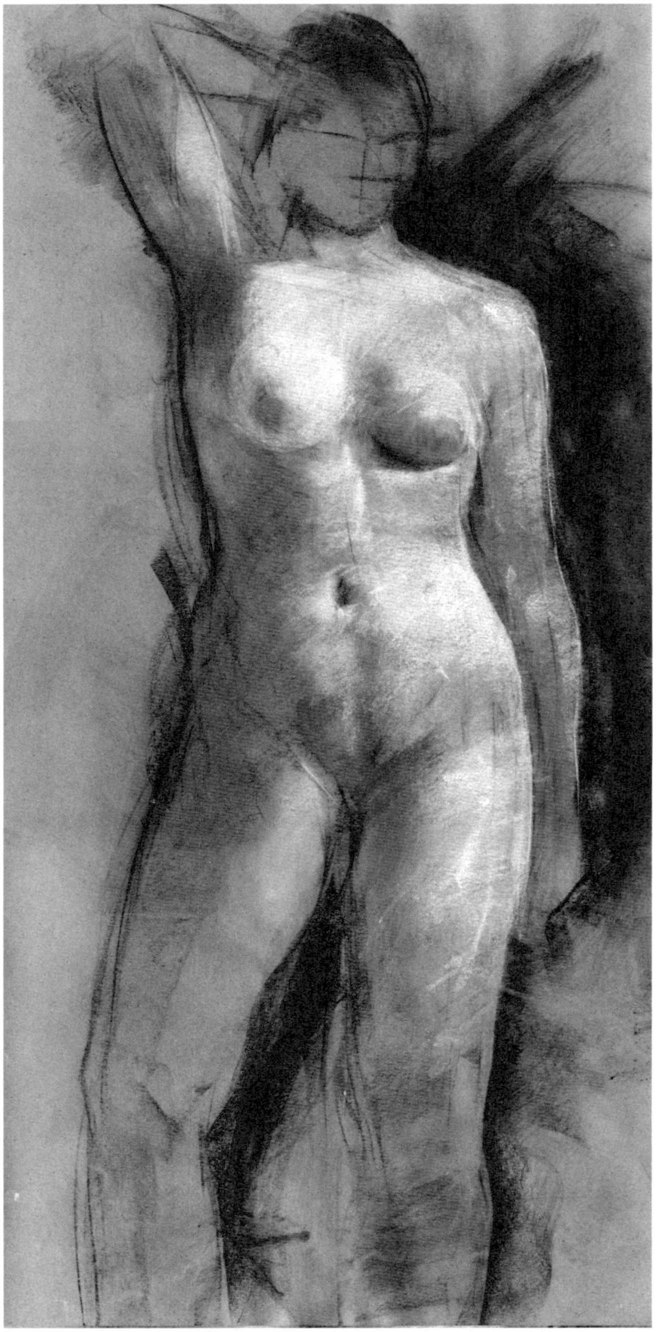

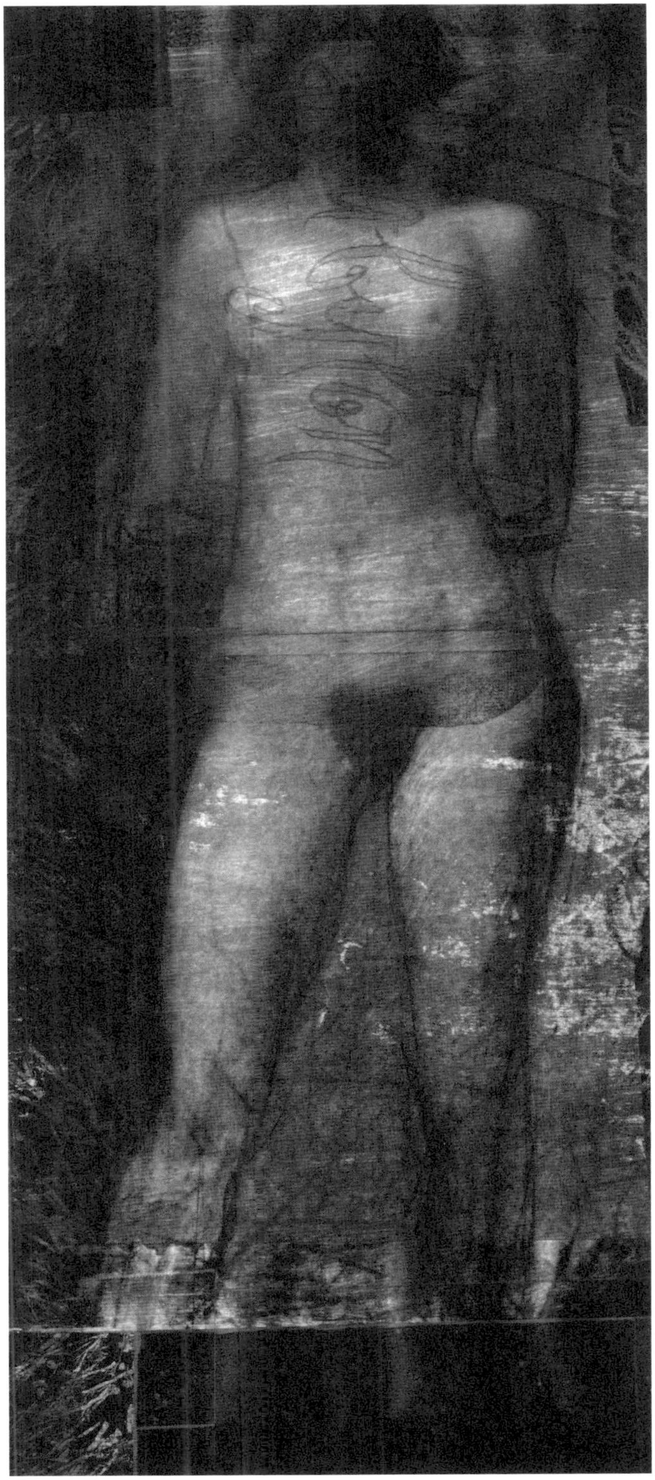

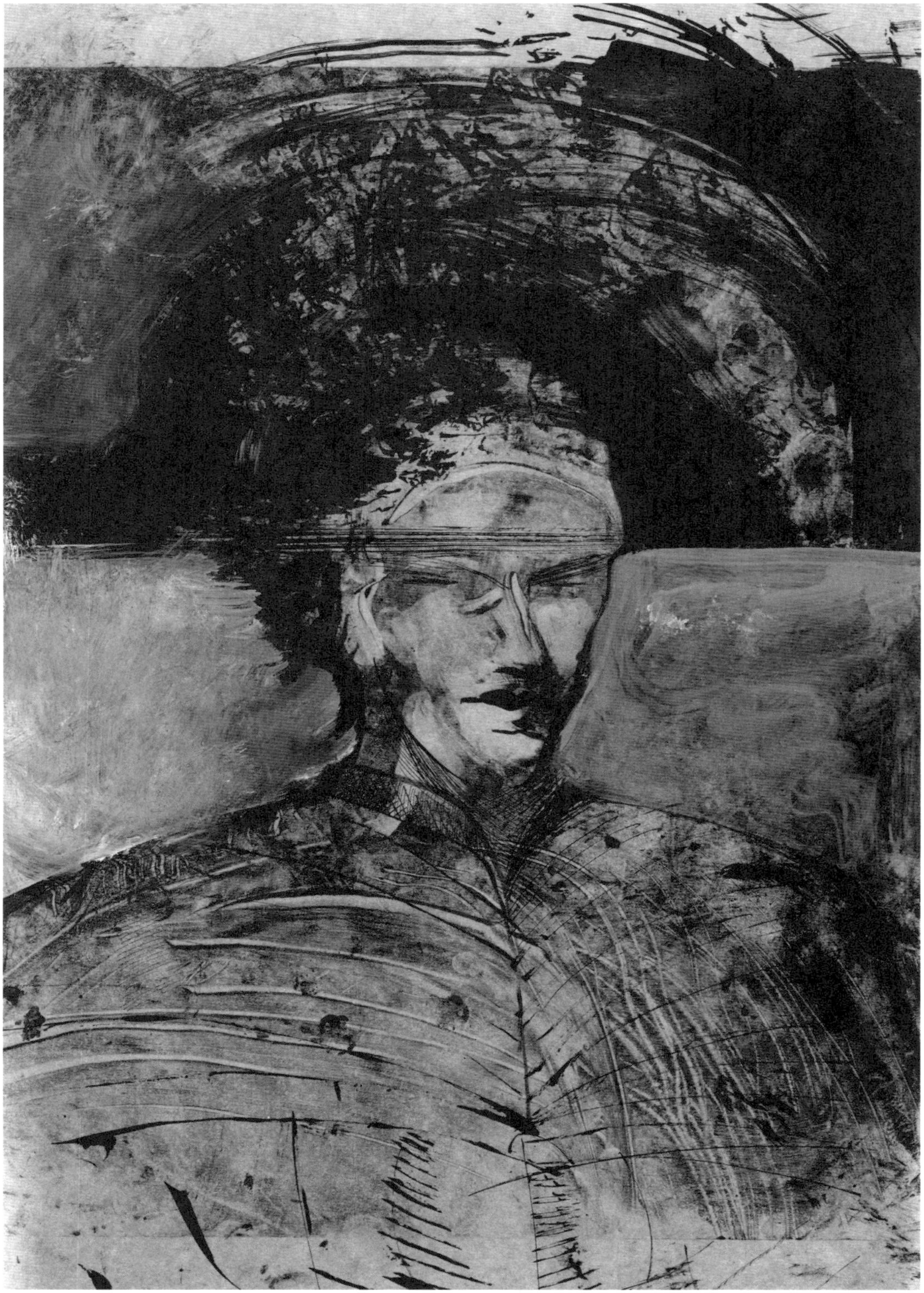

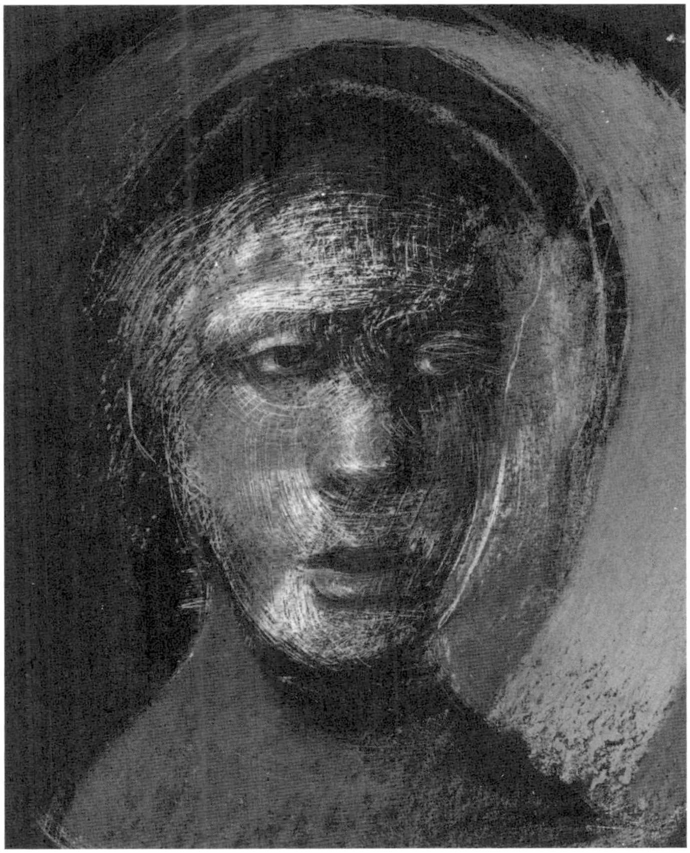

thom ang

8 drawings

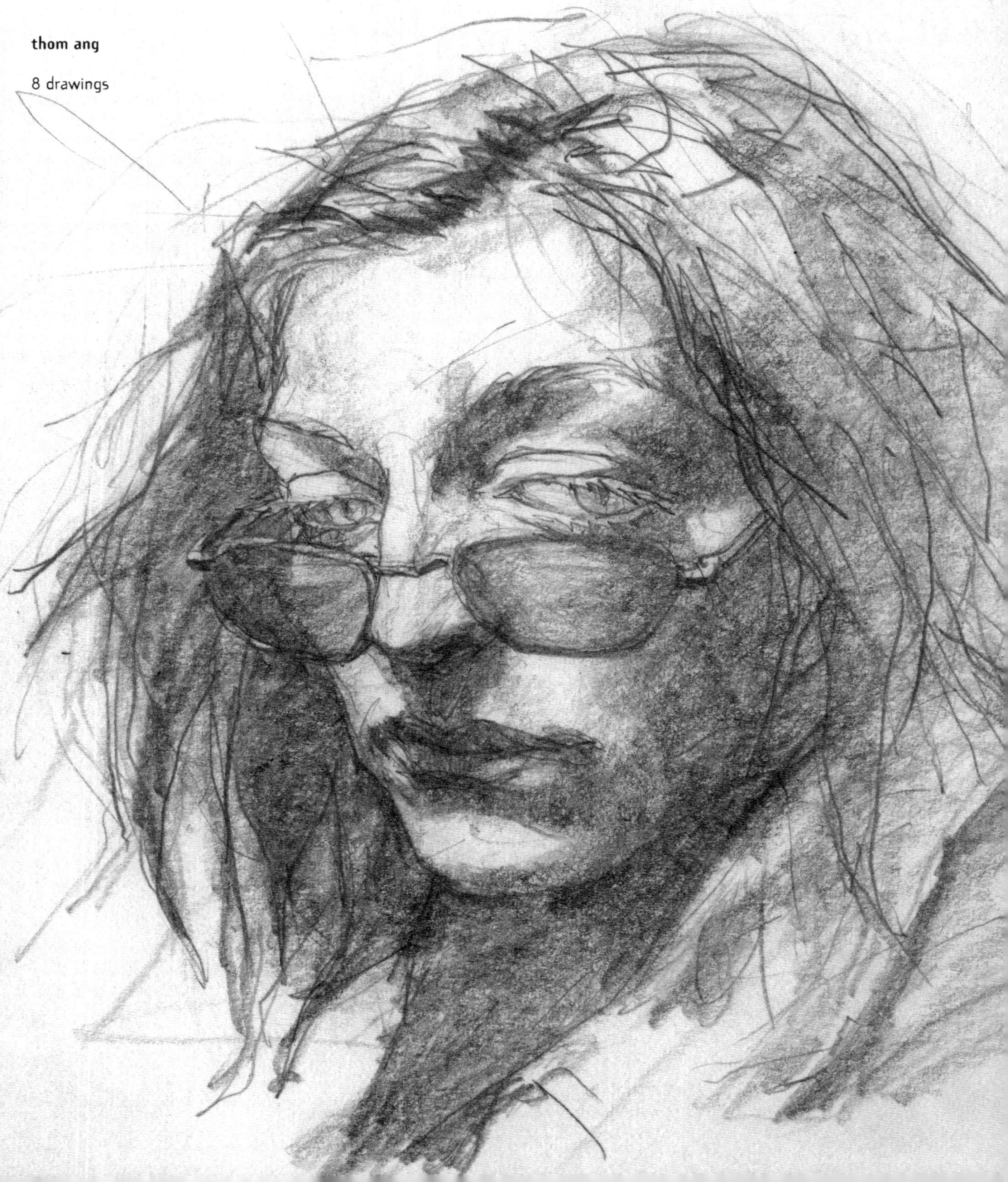

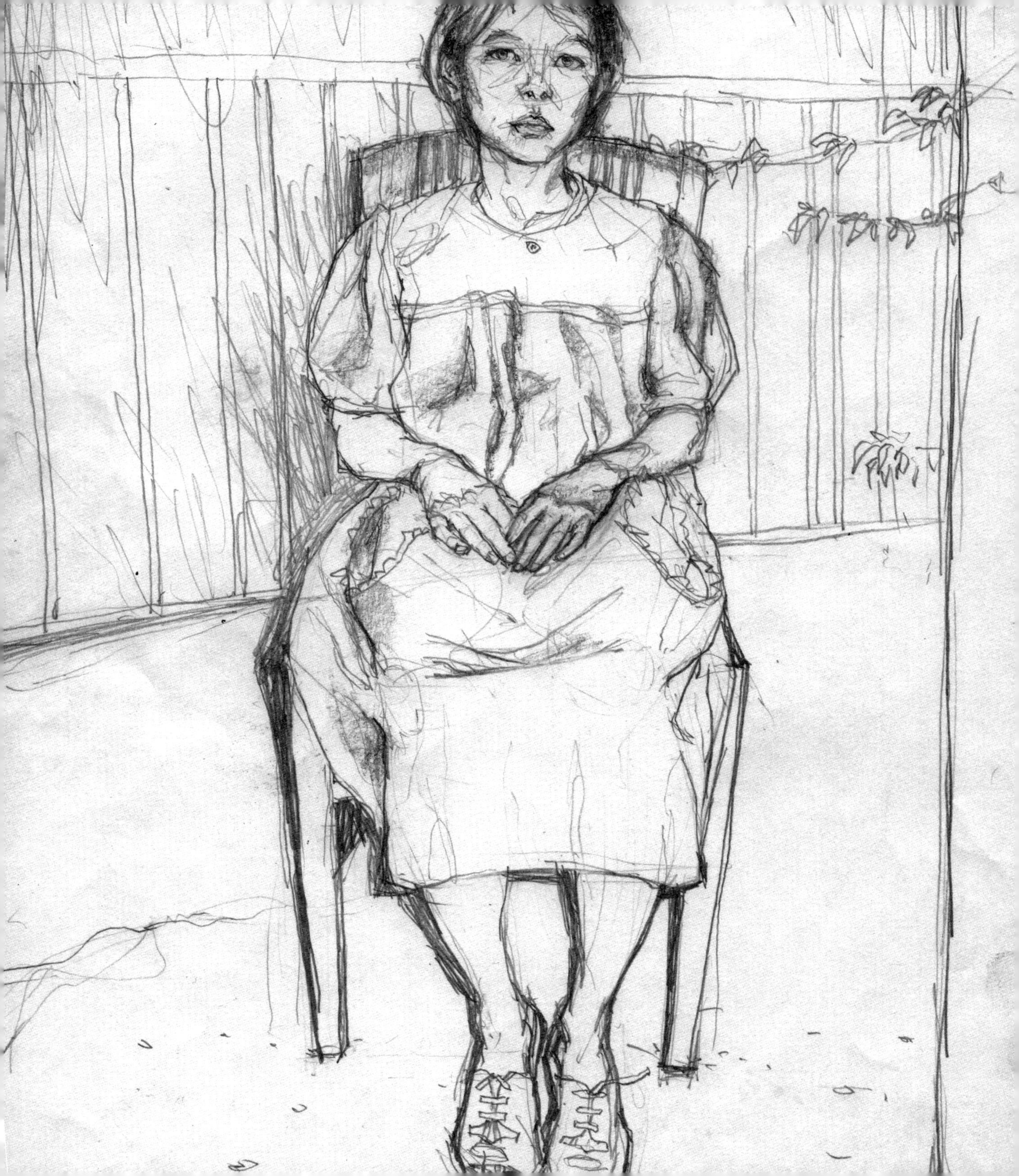

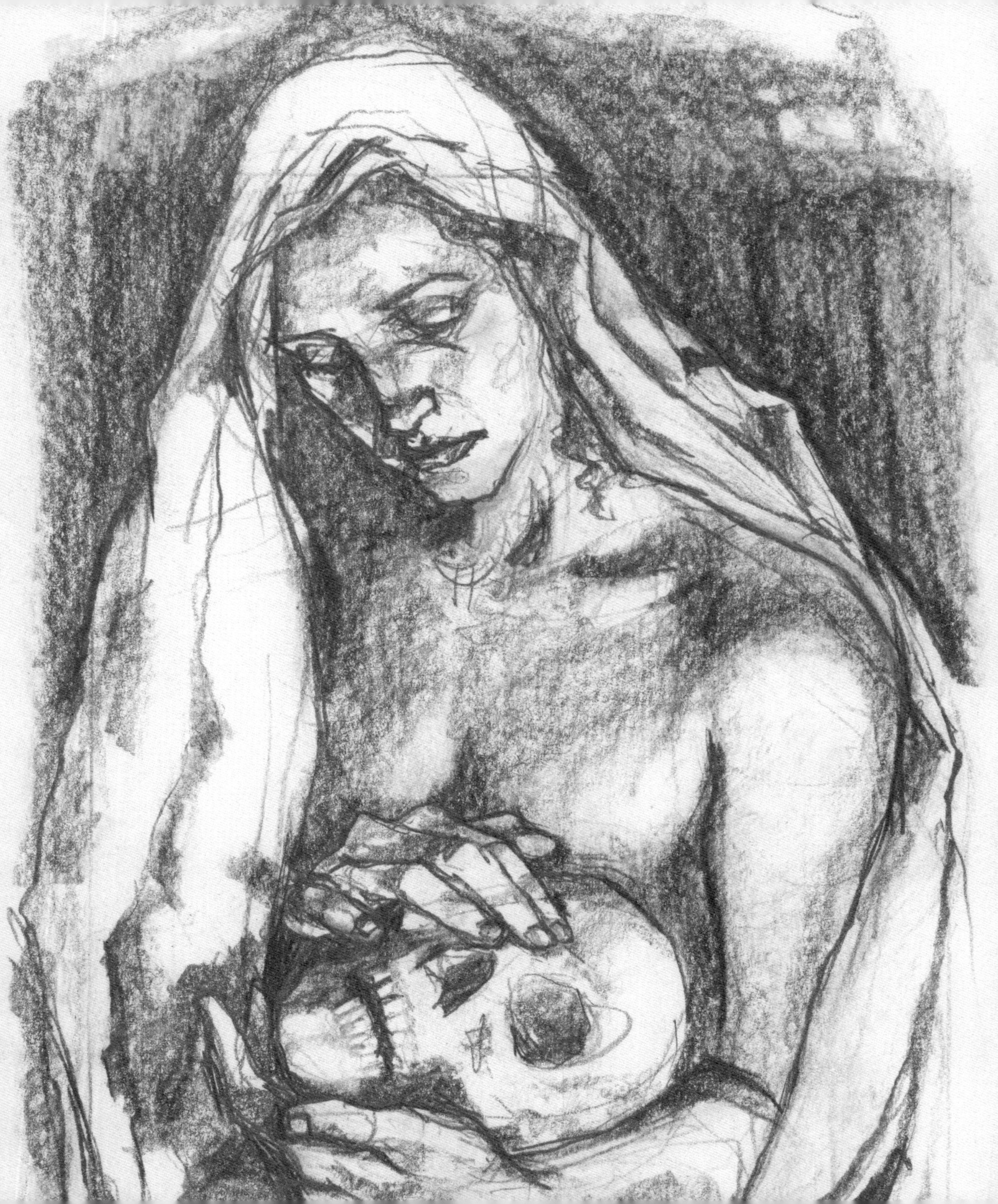

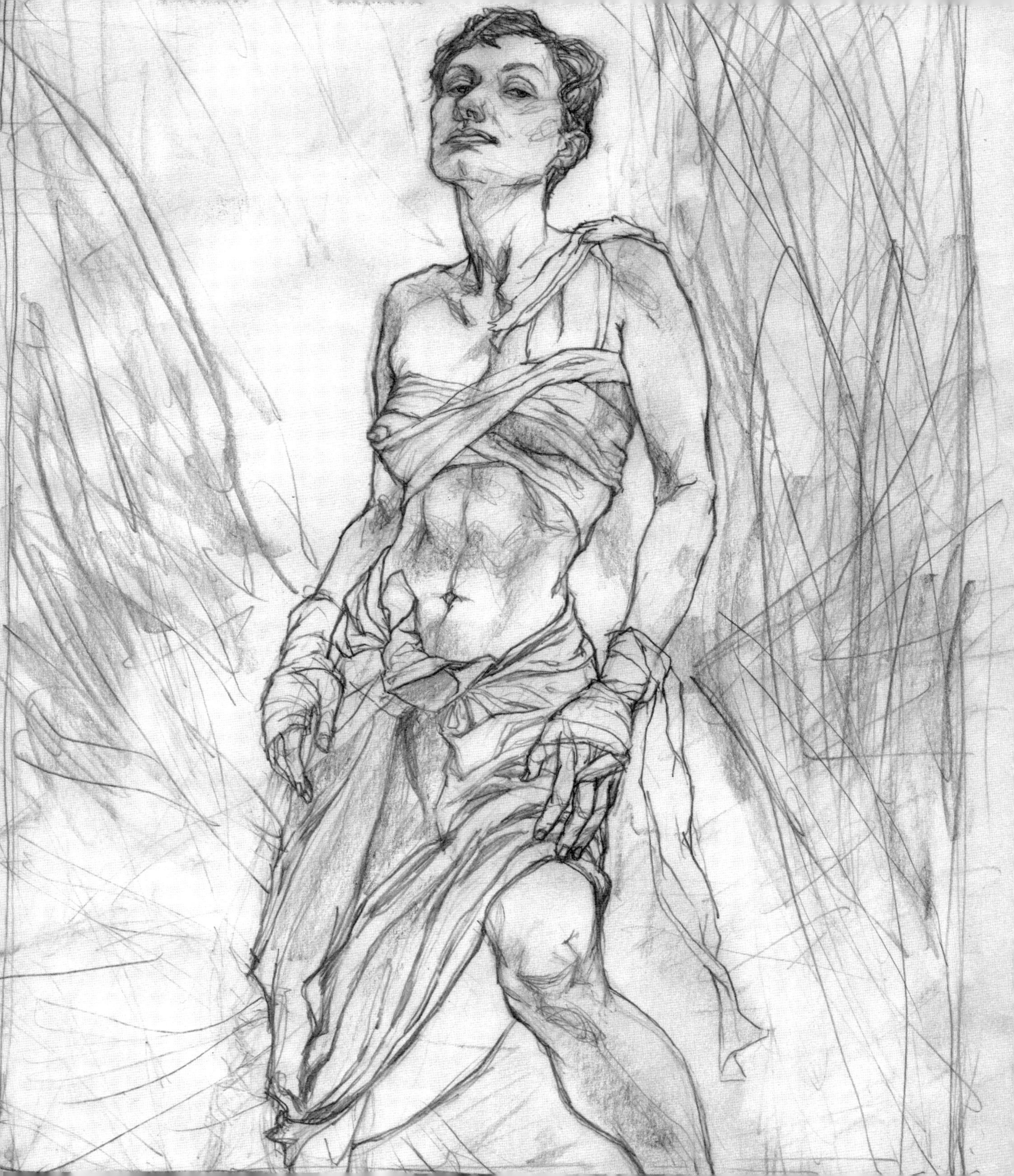

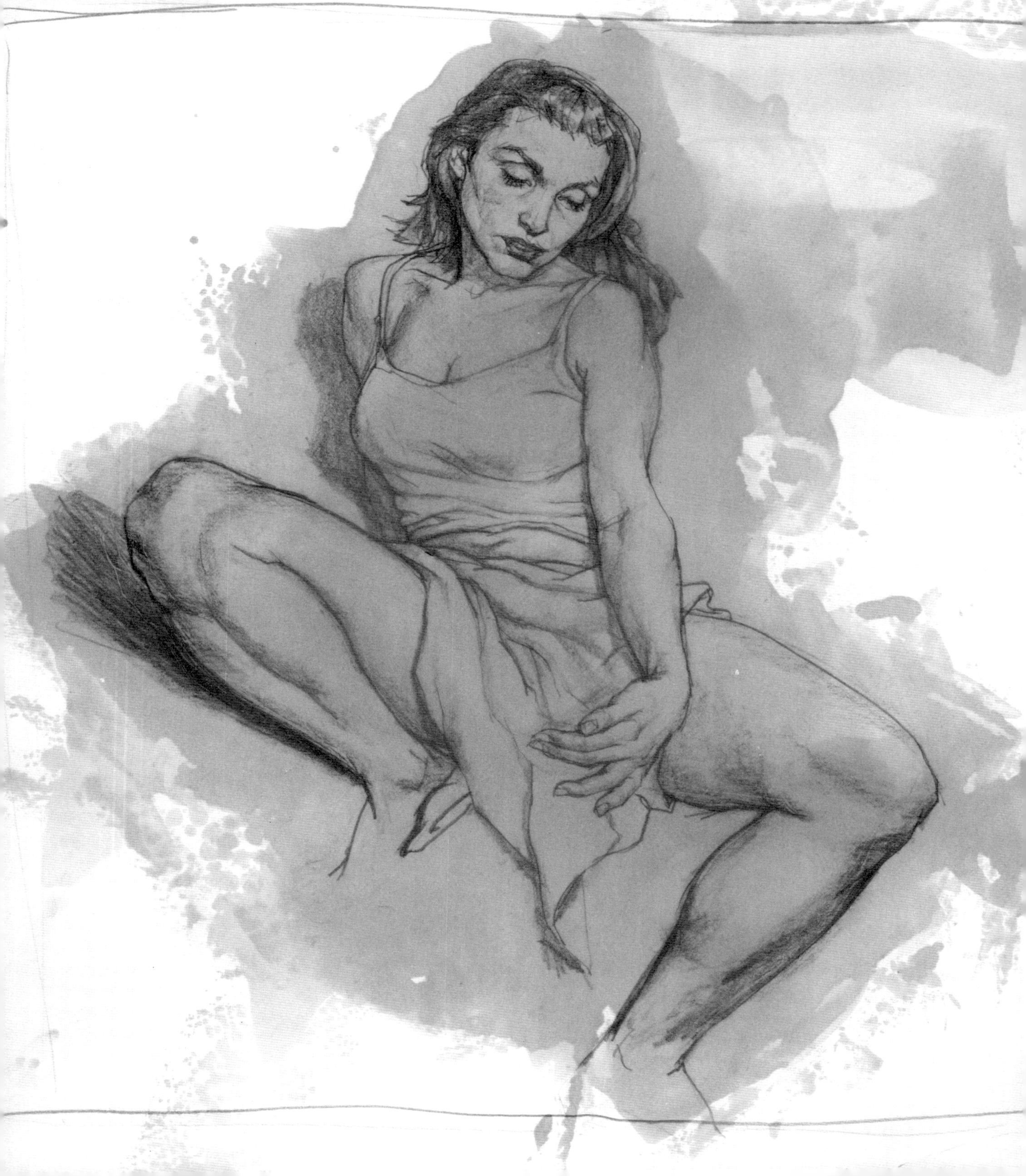

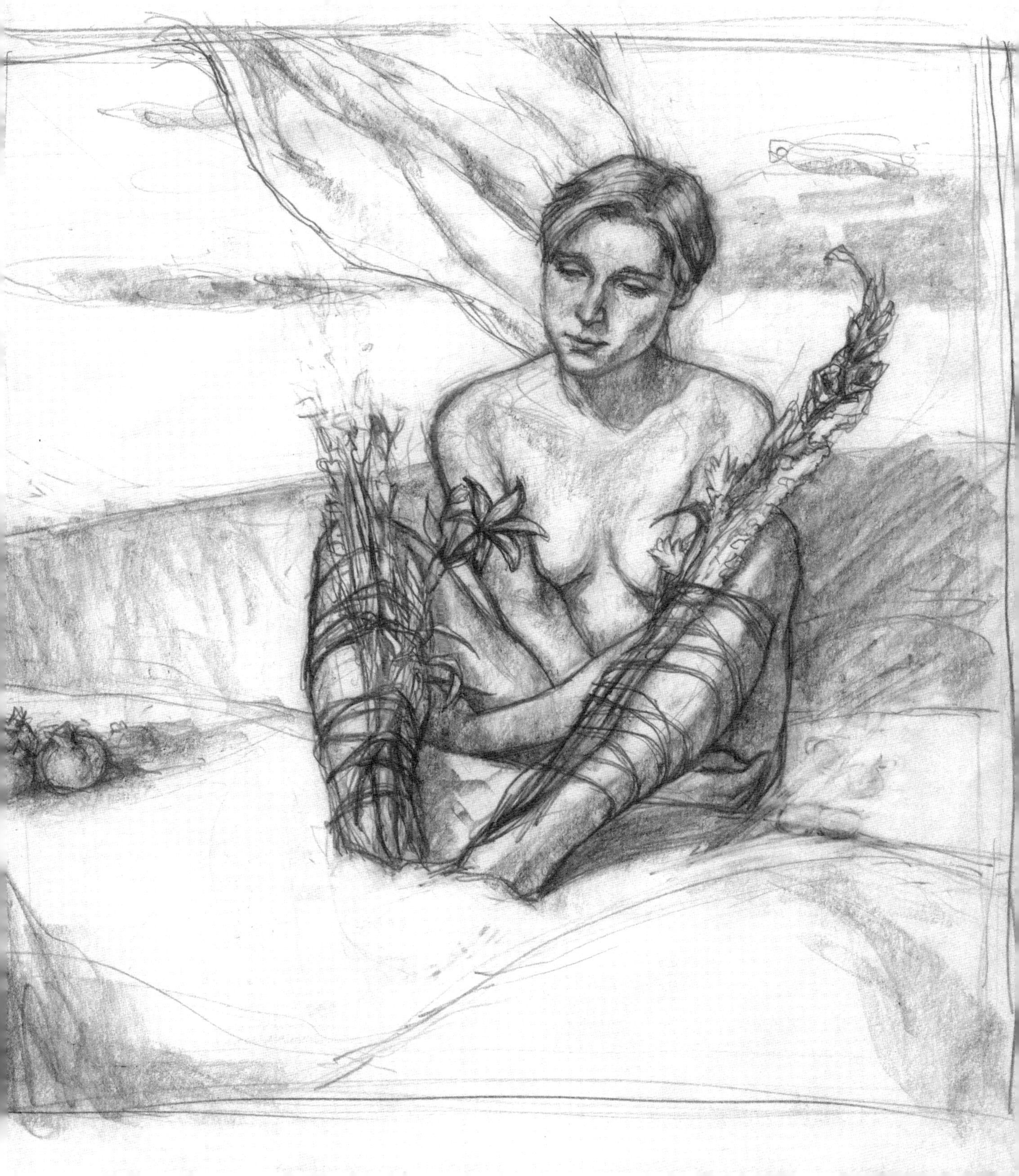

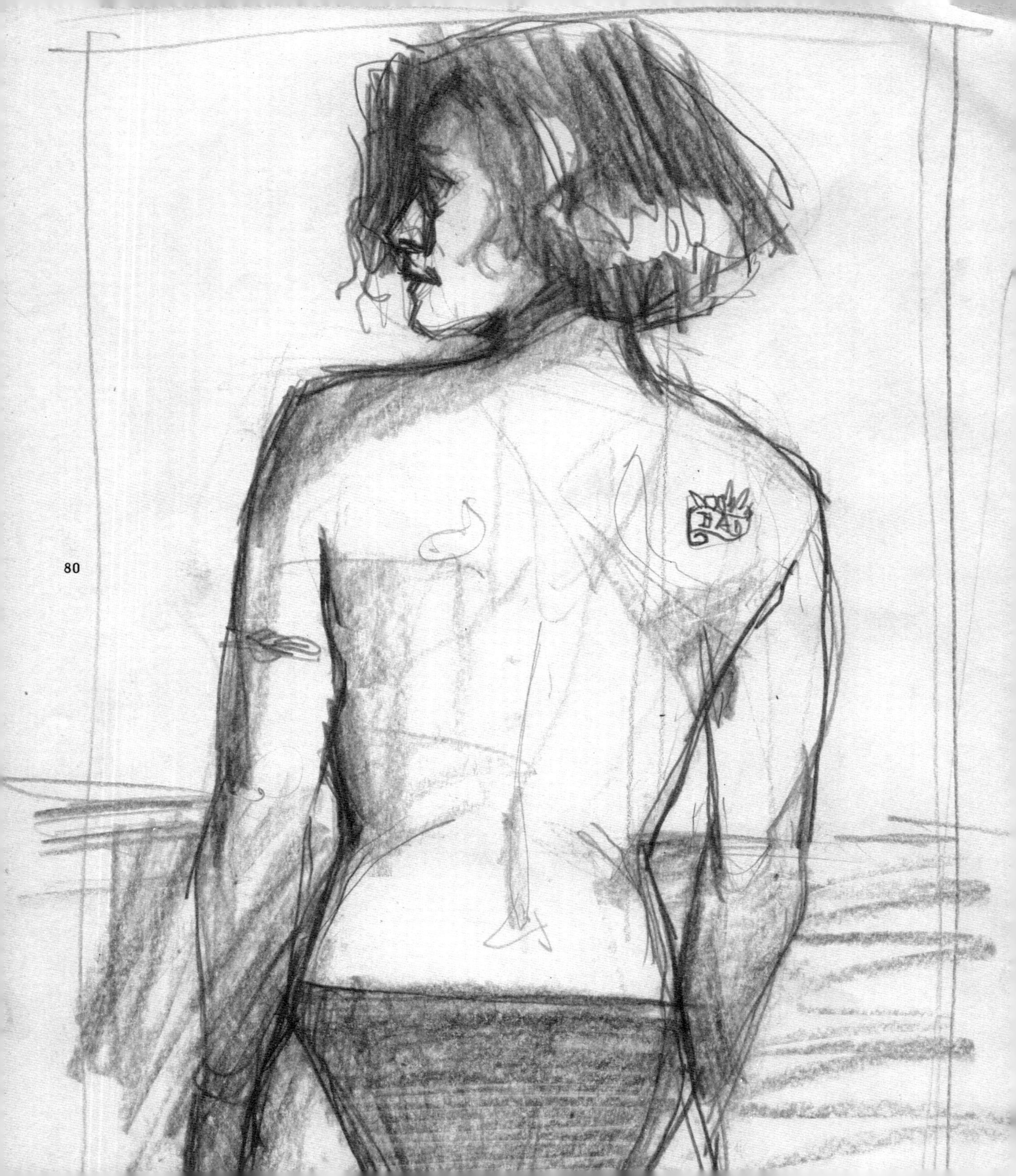

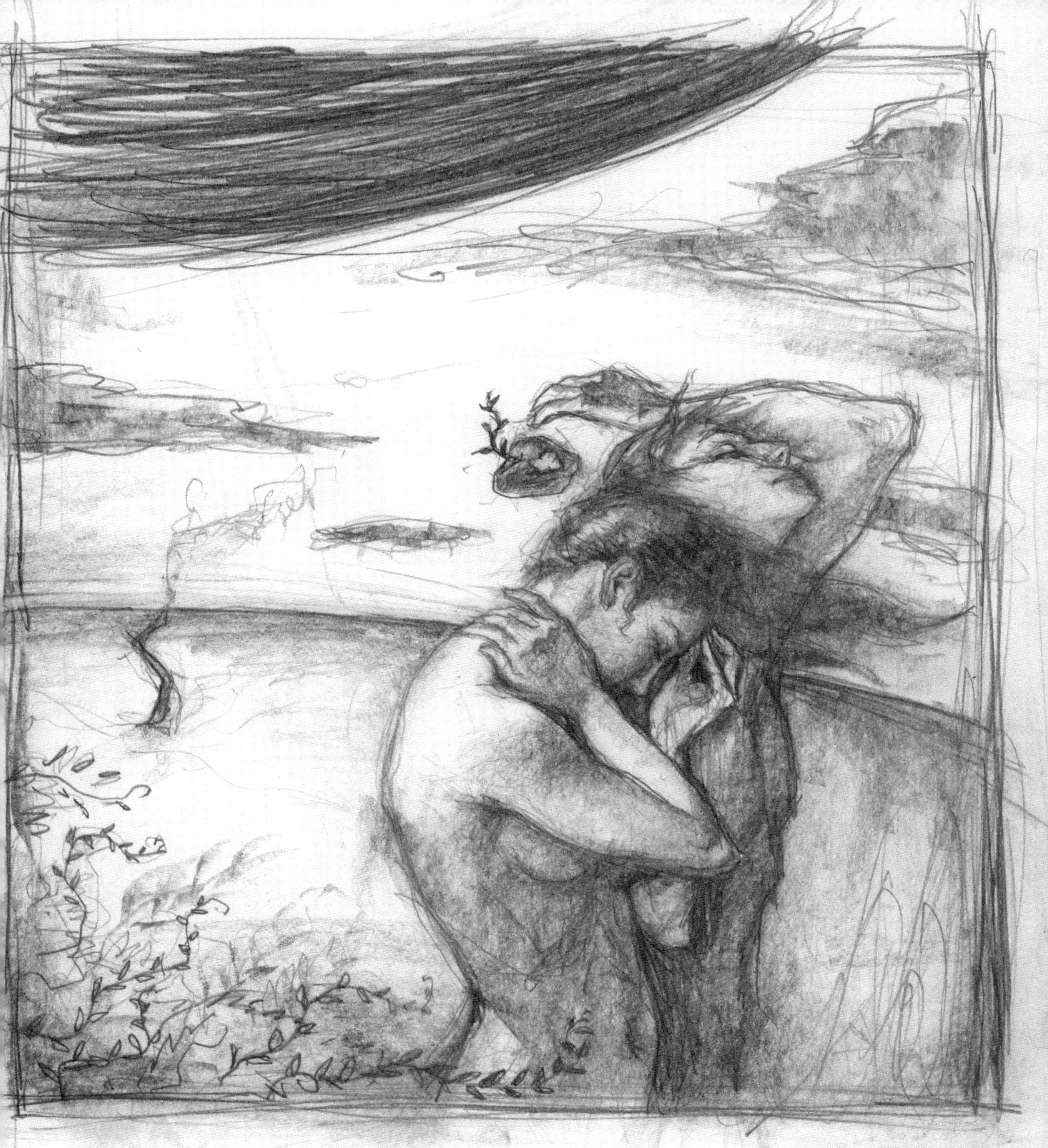

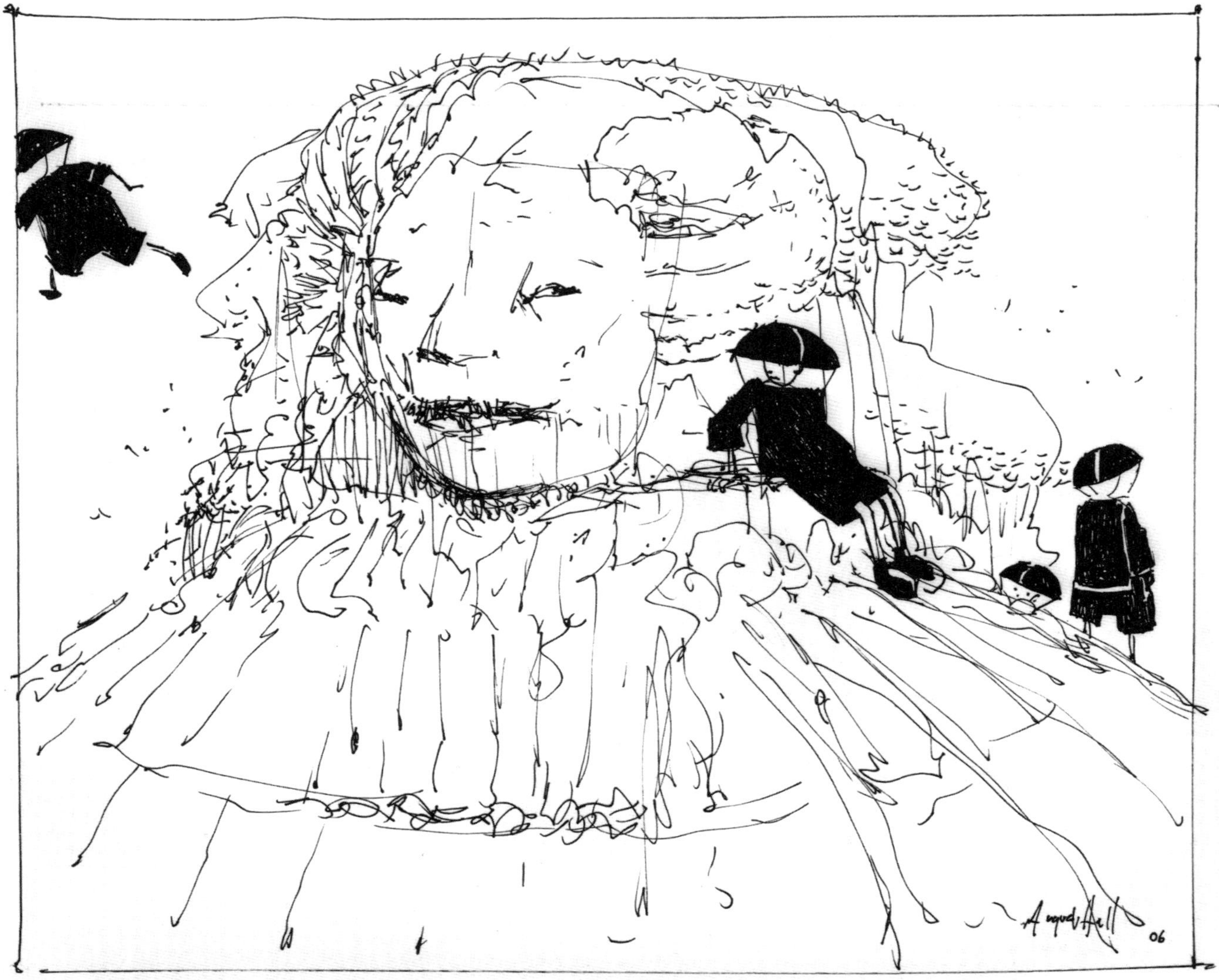

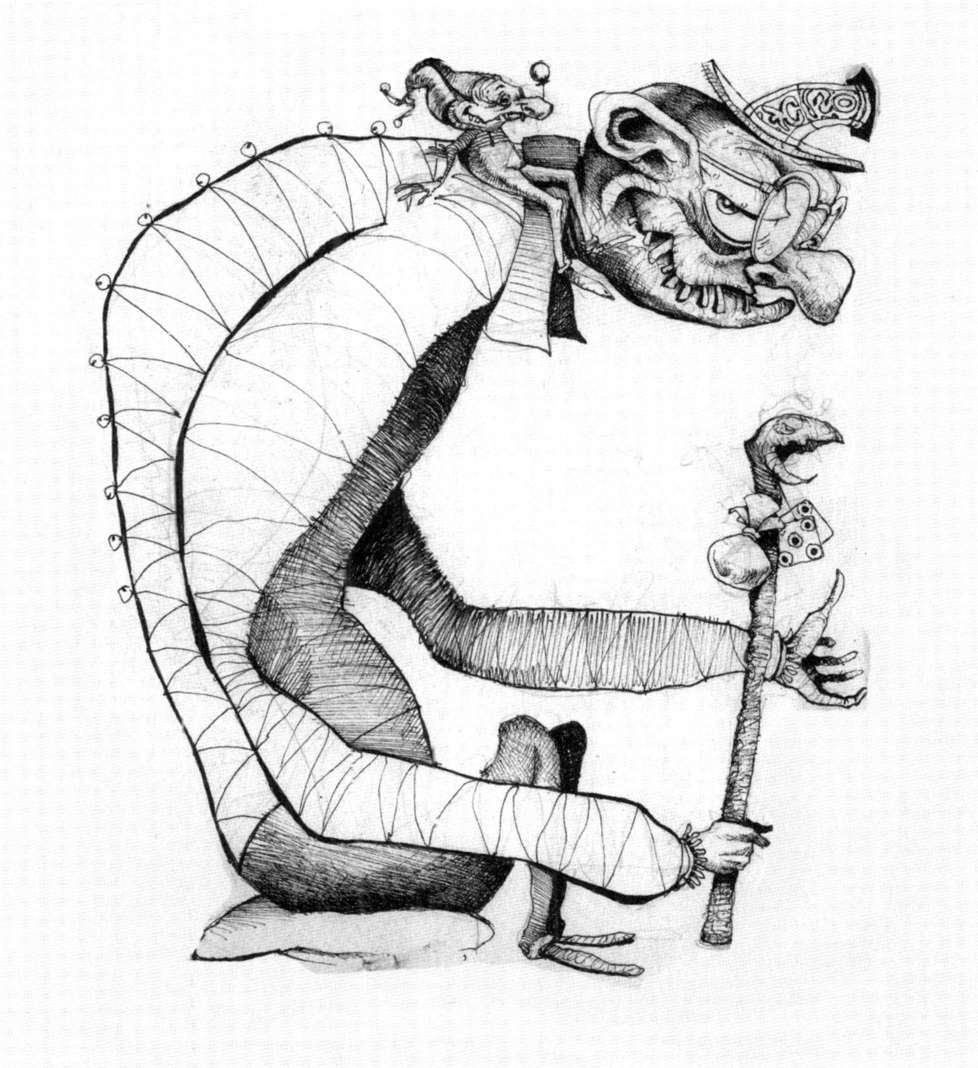

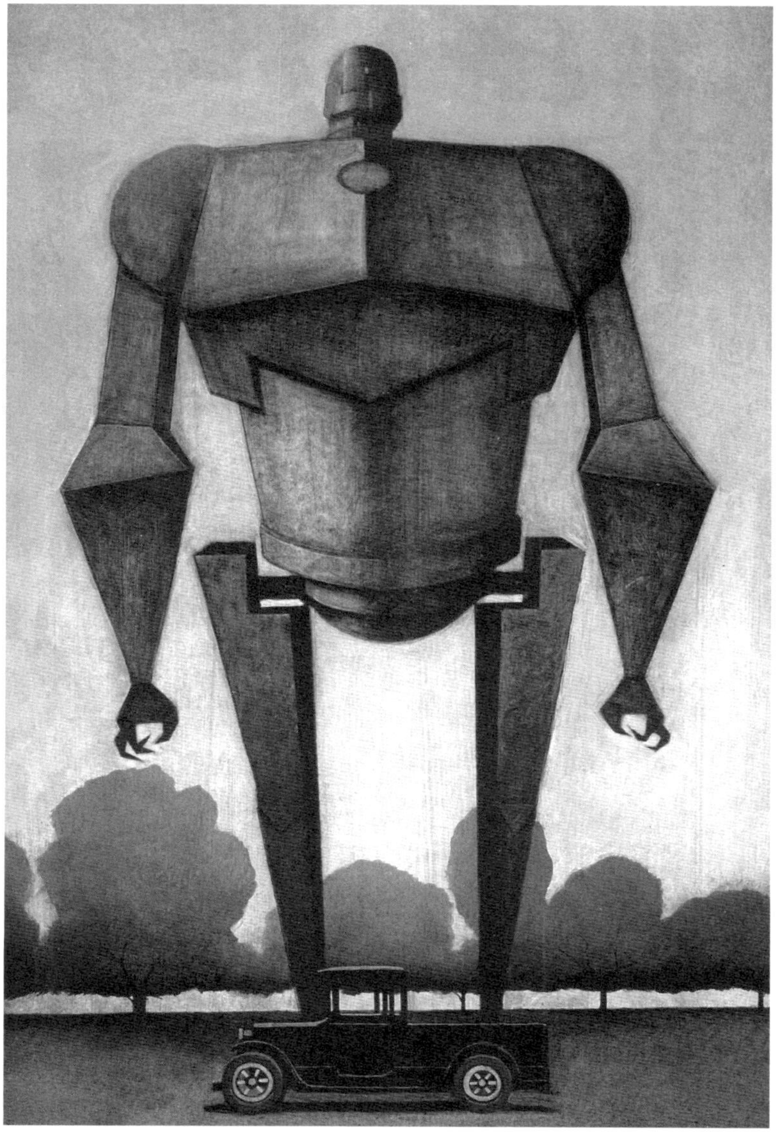

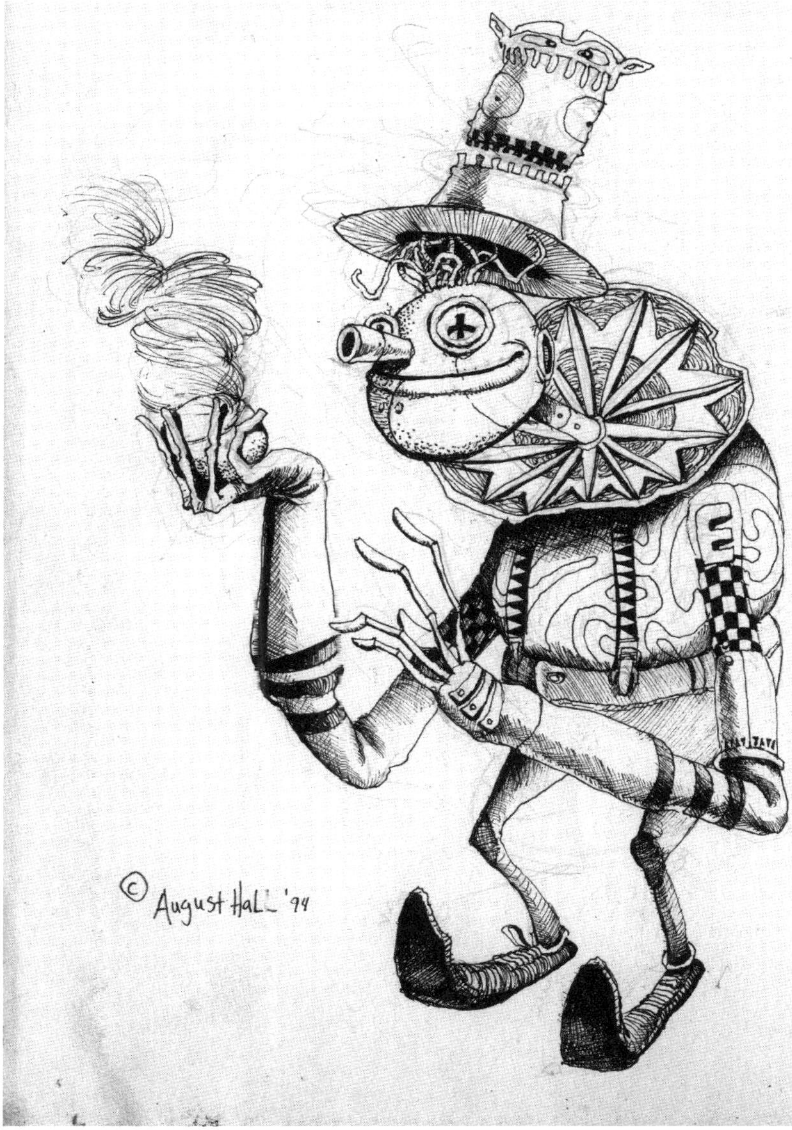
© August HaLL '94

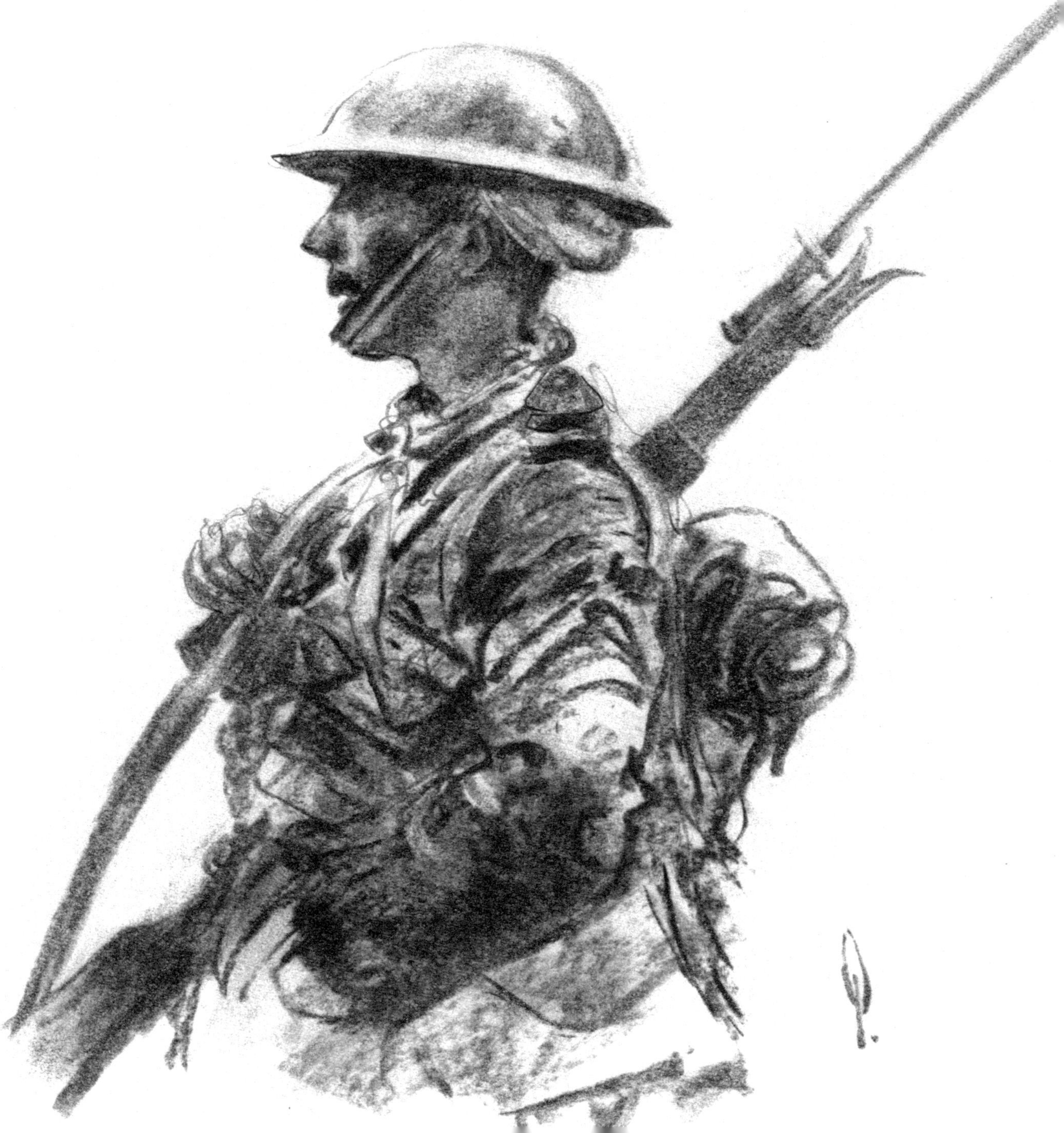

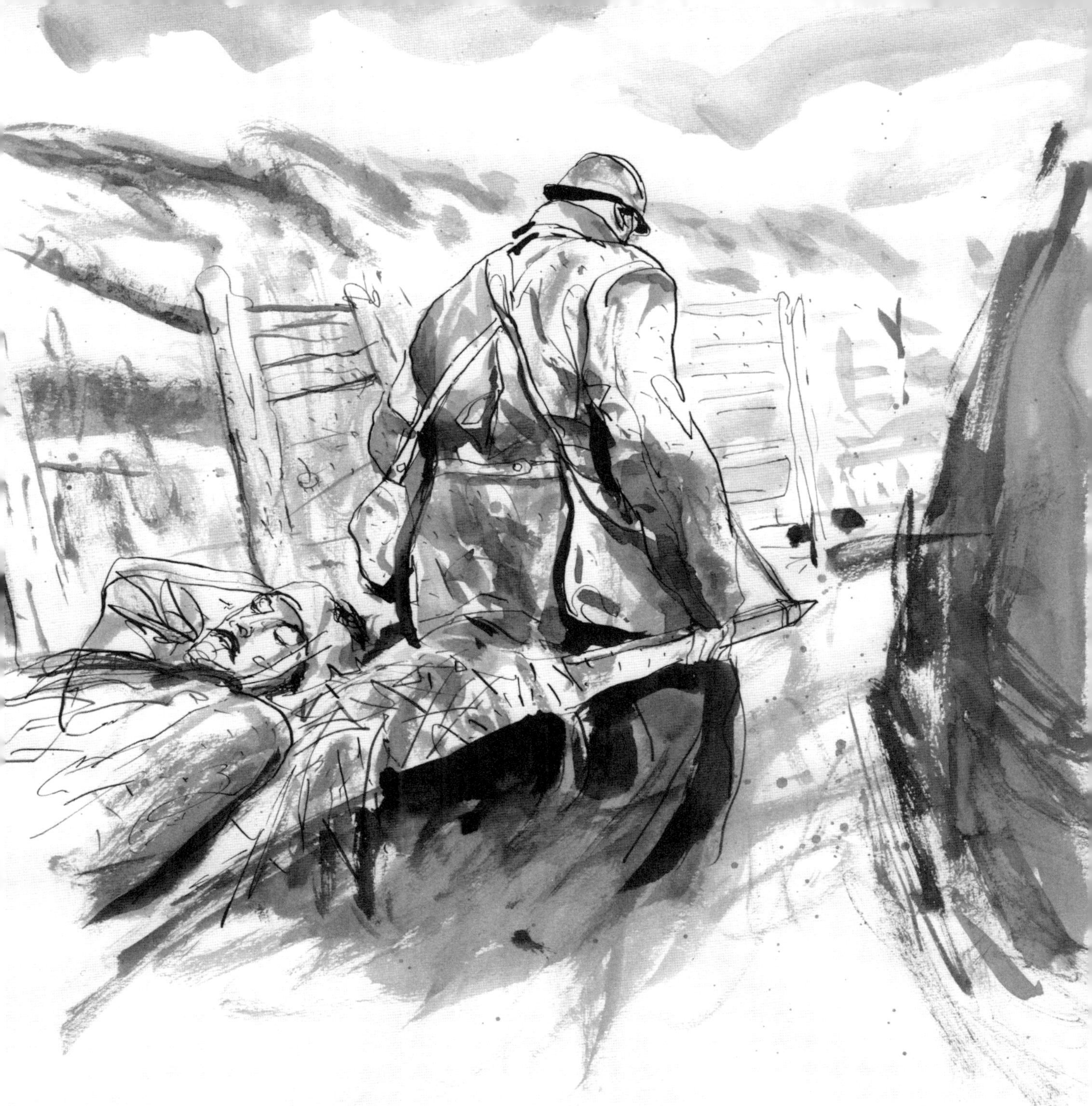

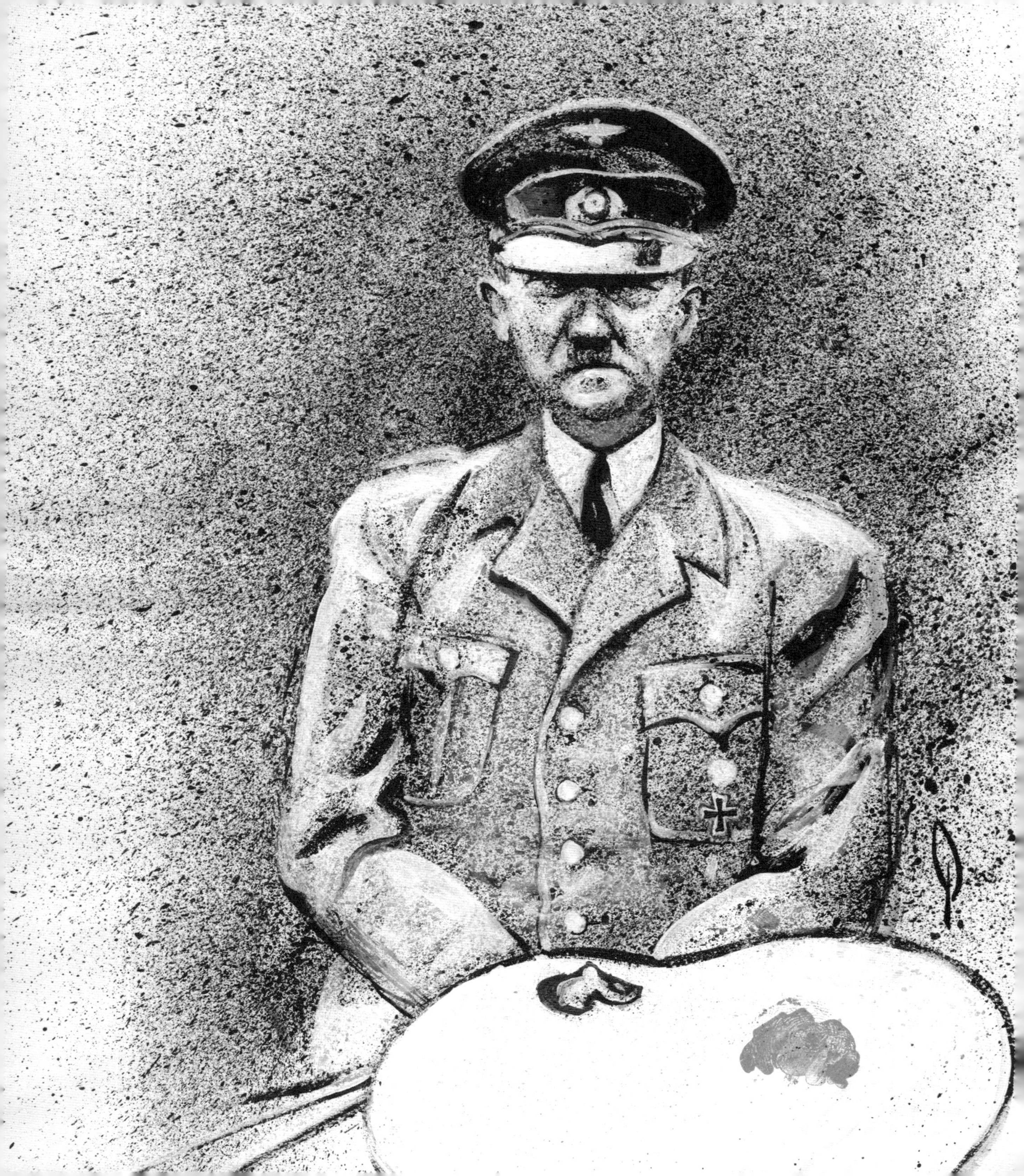

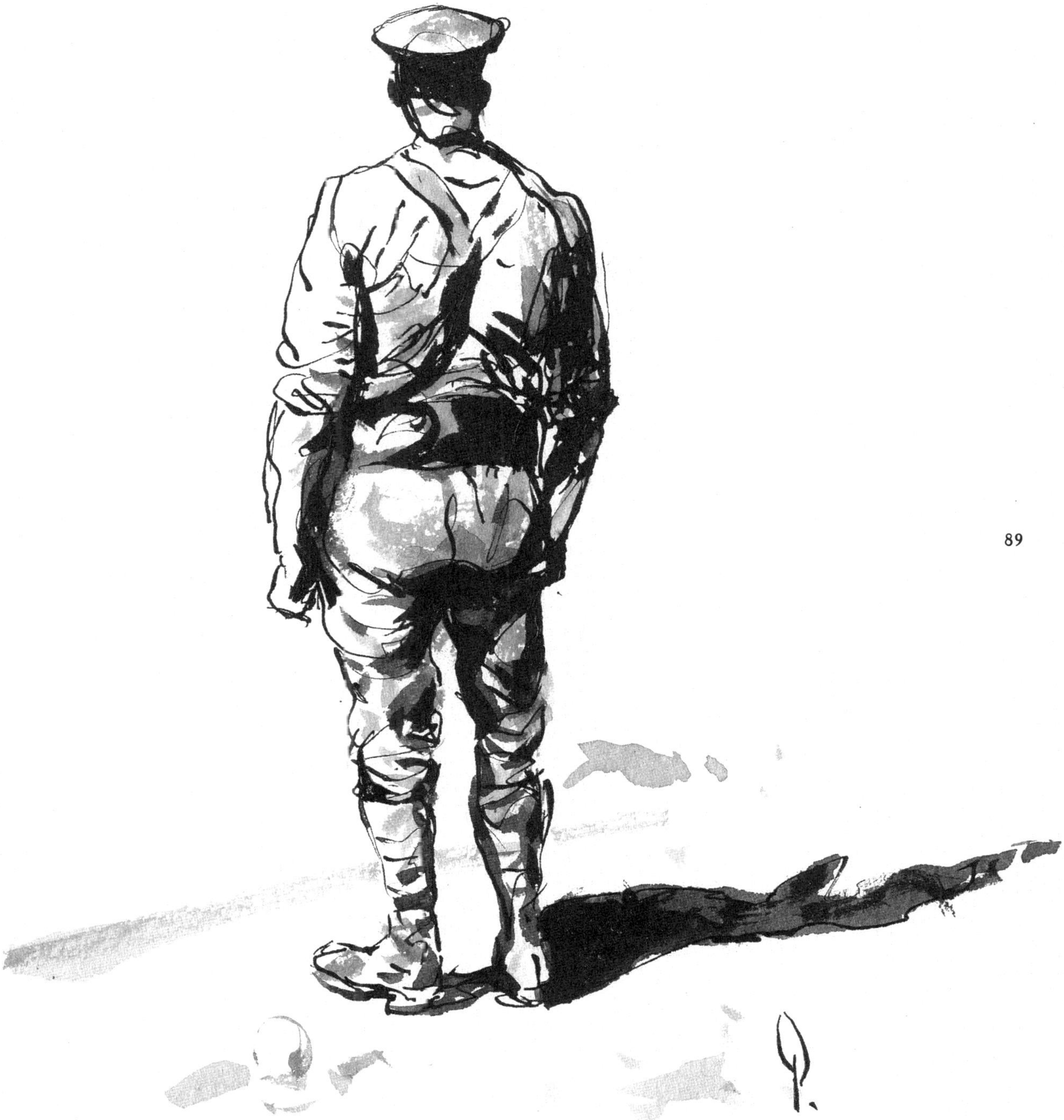

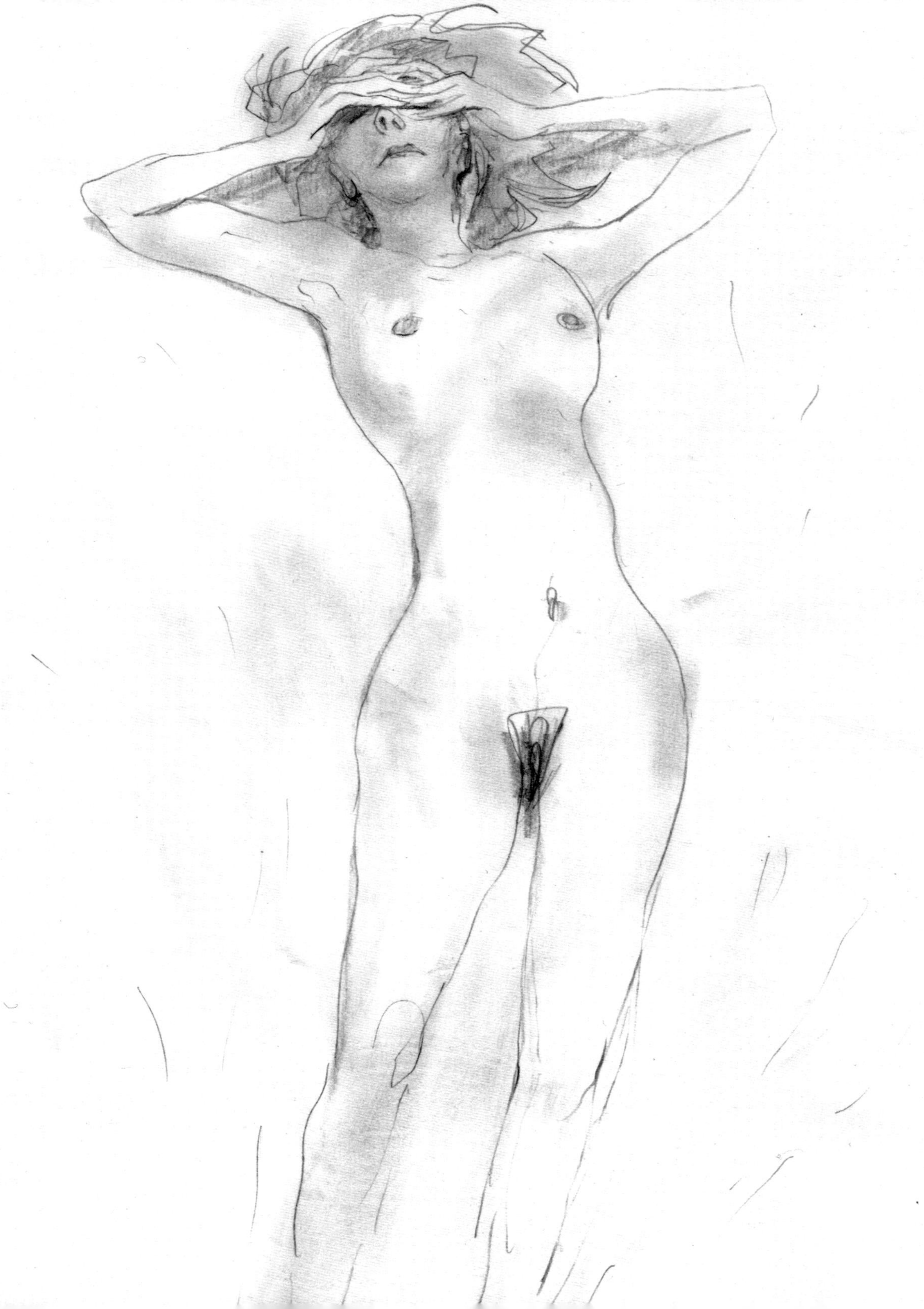

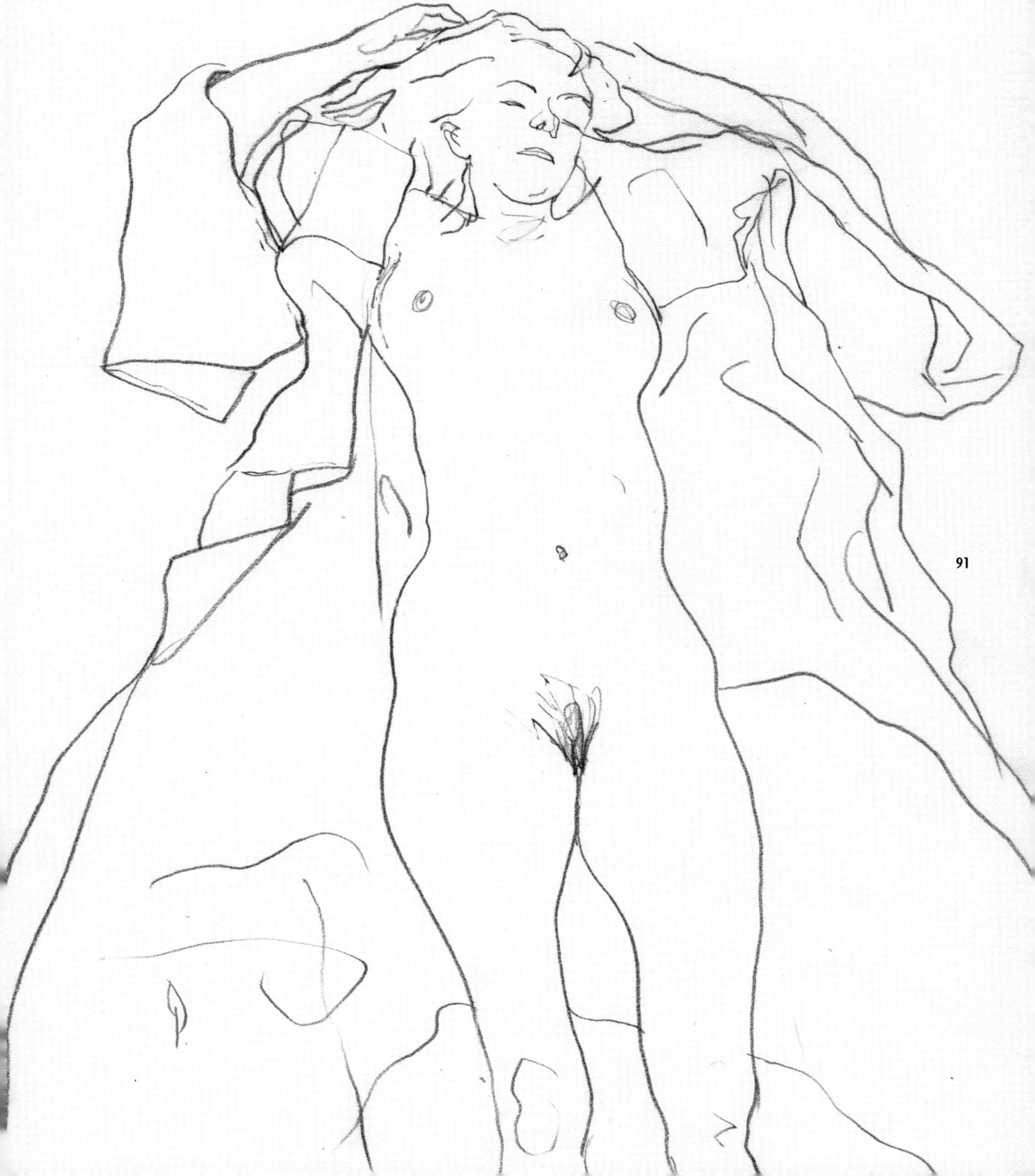

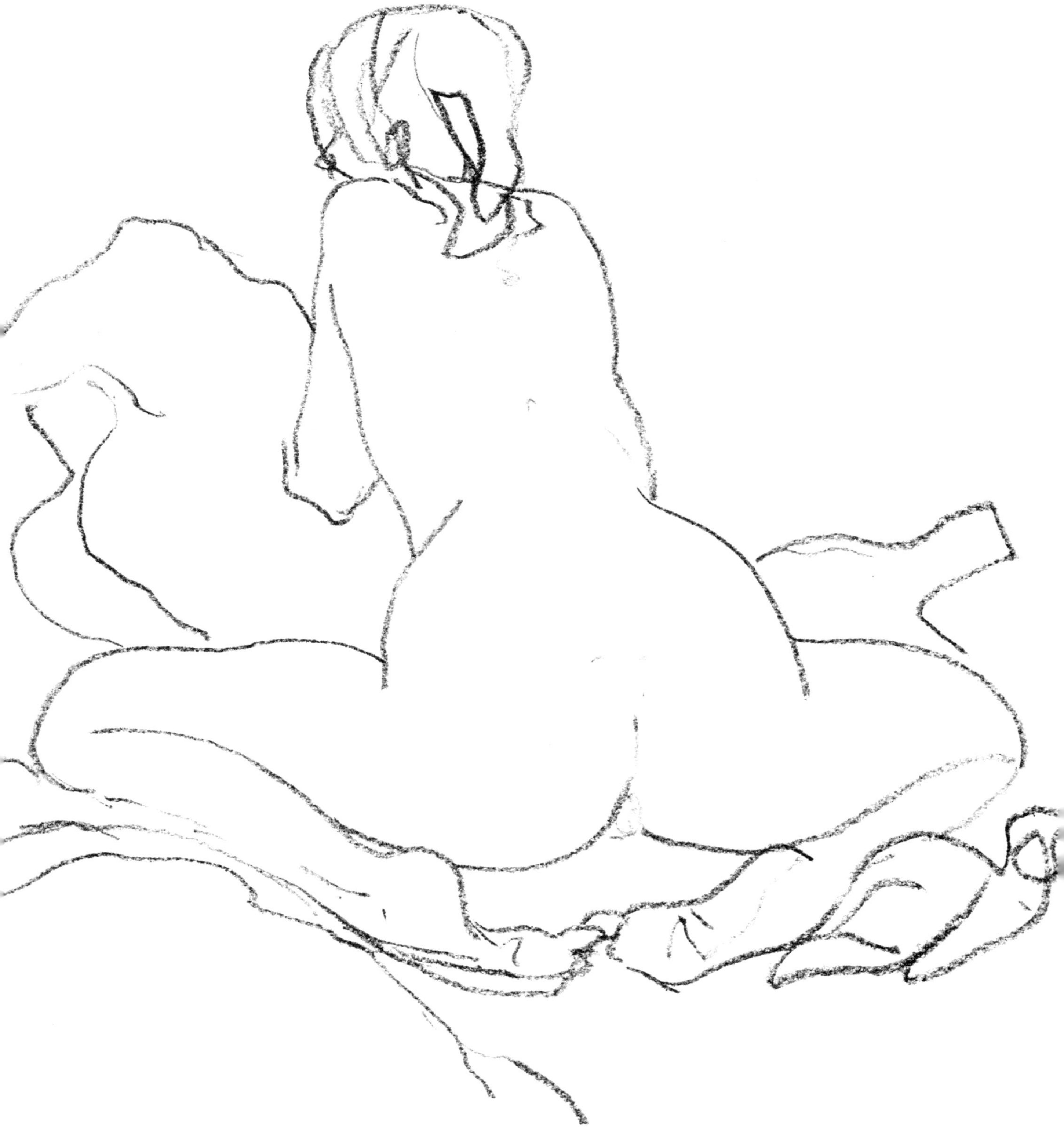

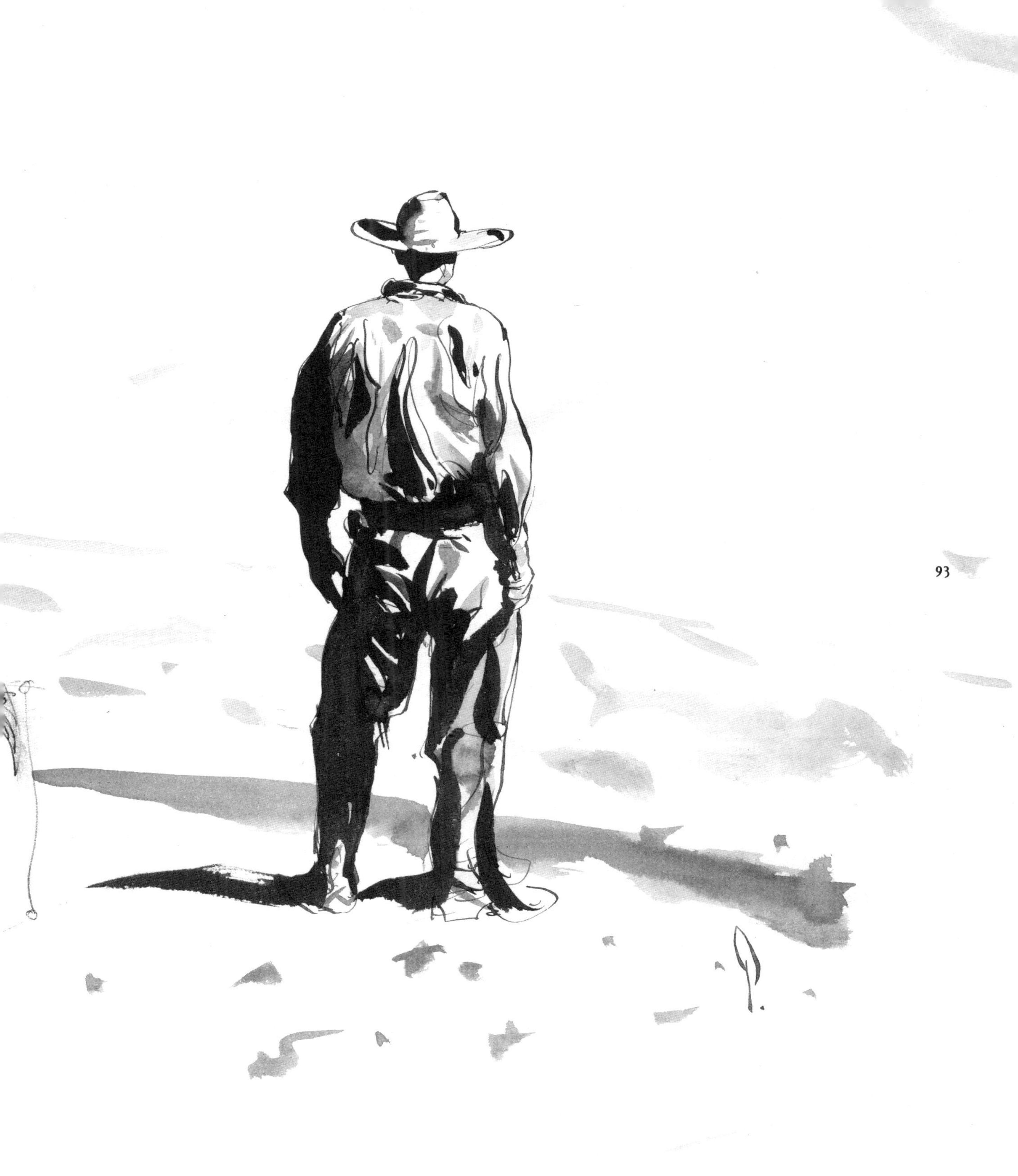

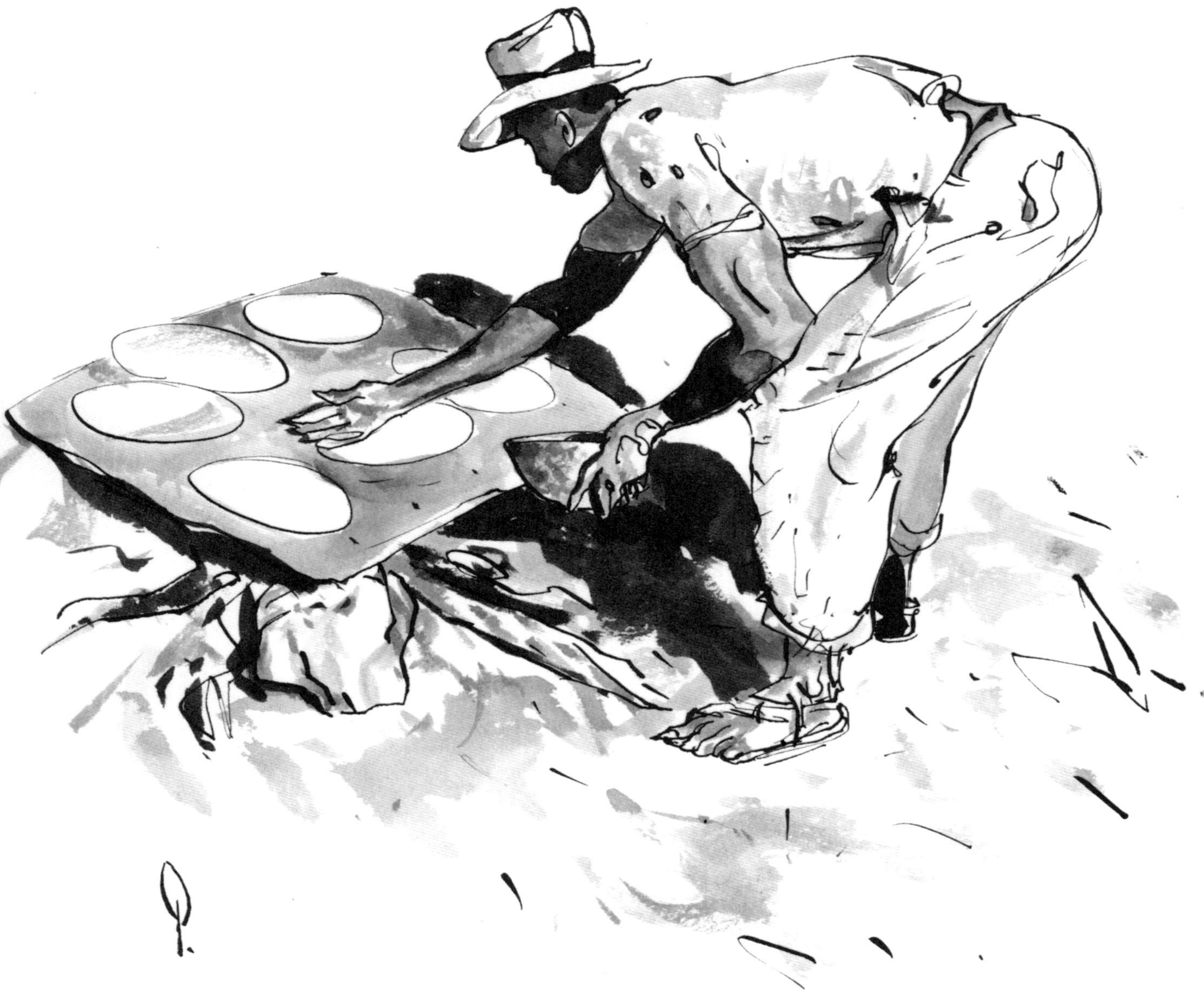

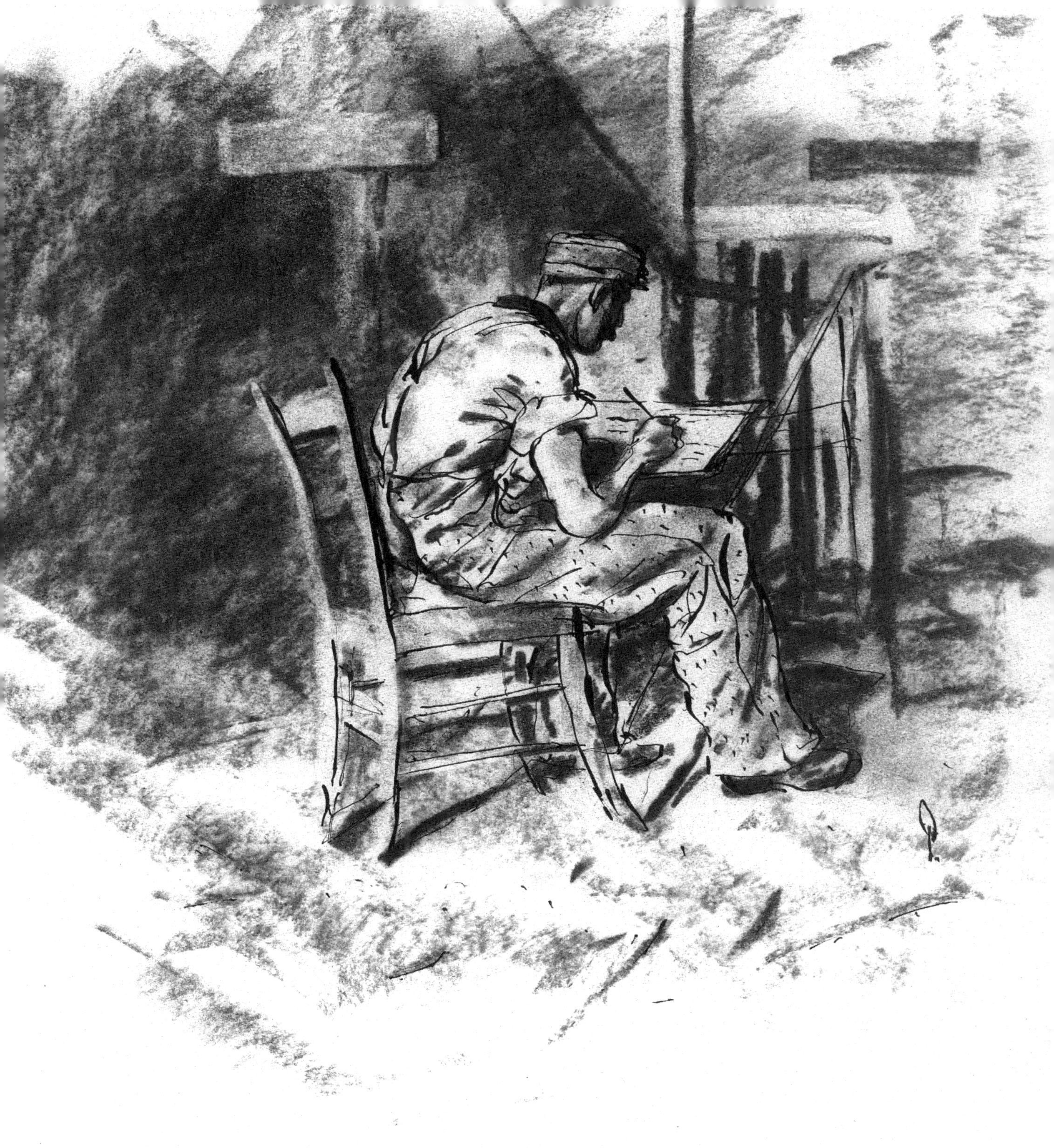

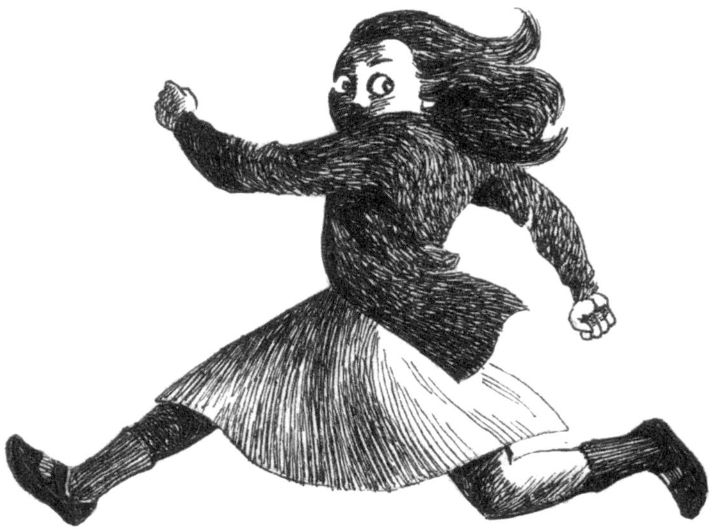

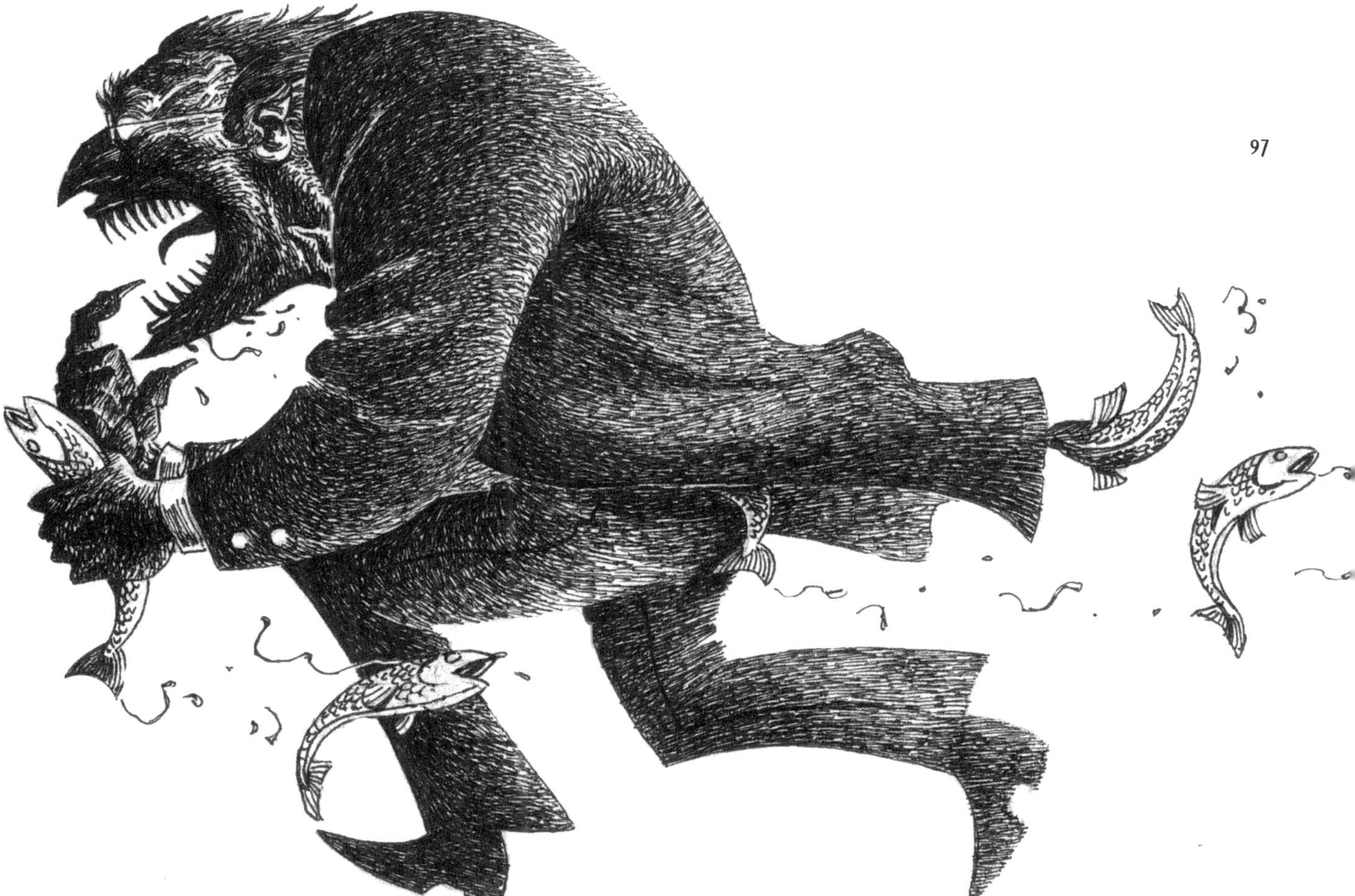

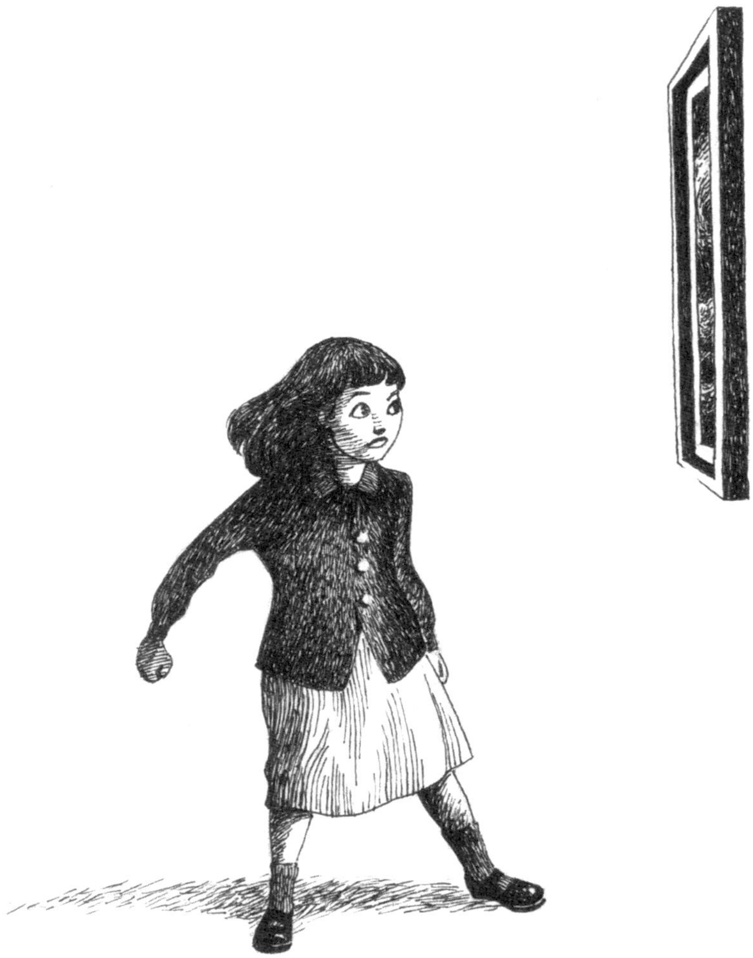

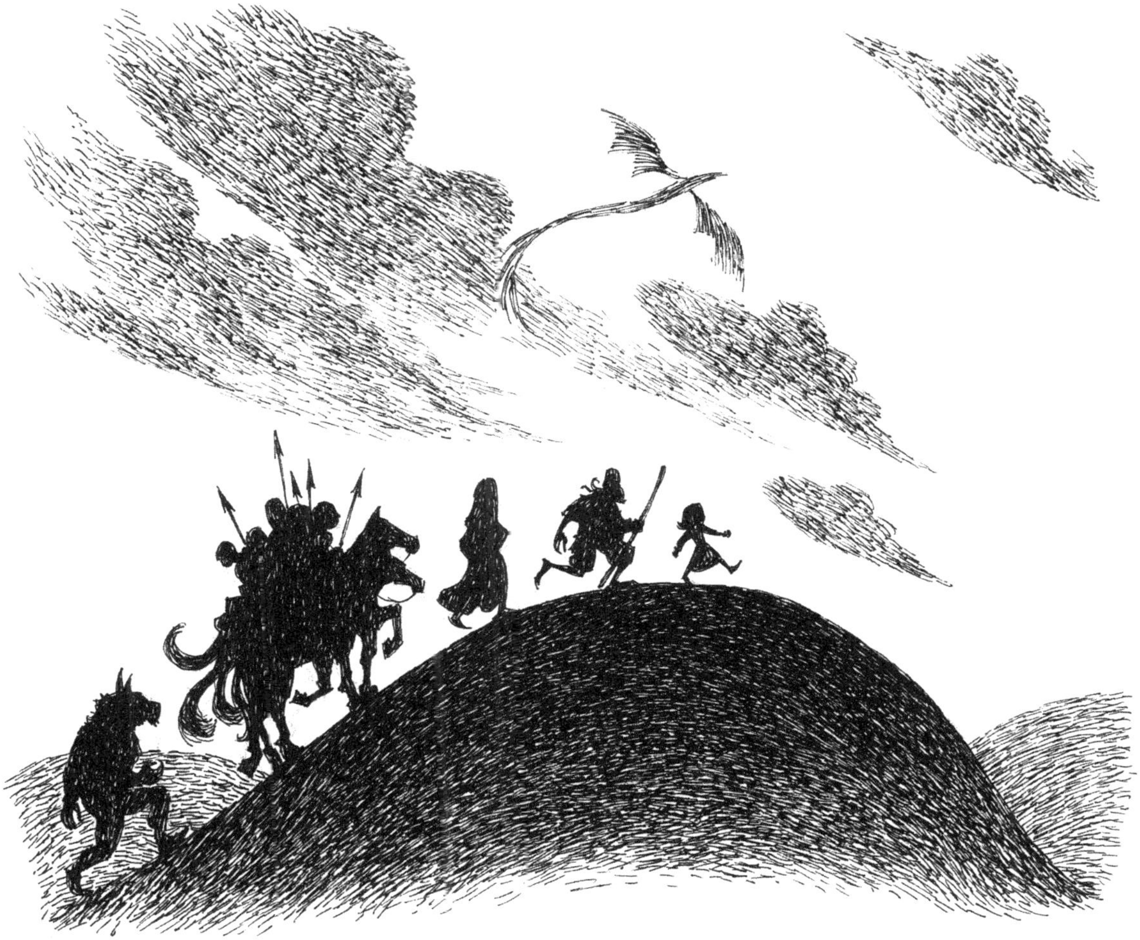

scott morse

9 drawings

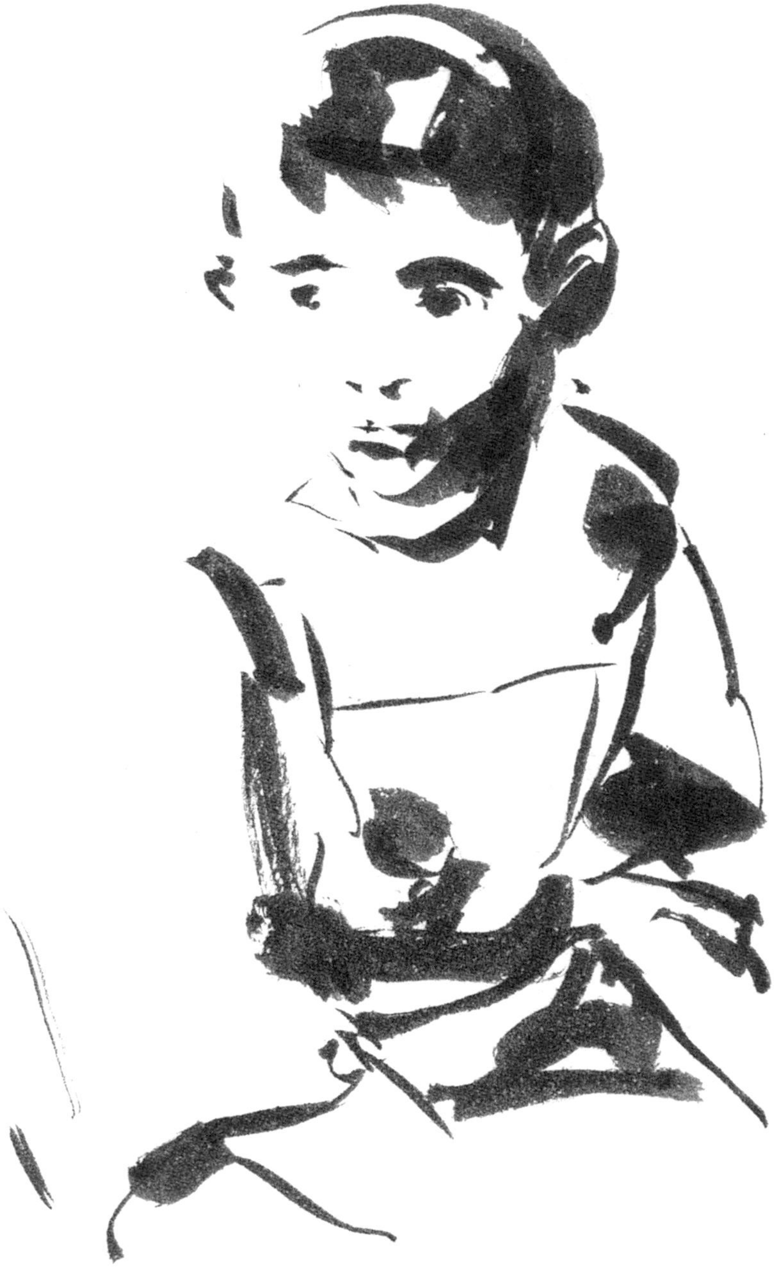

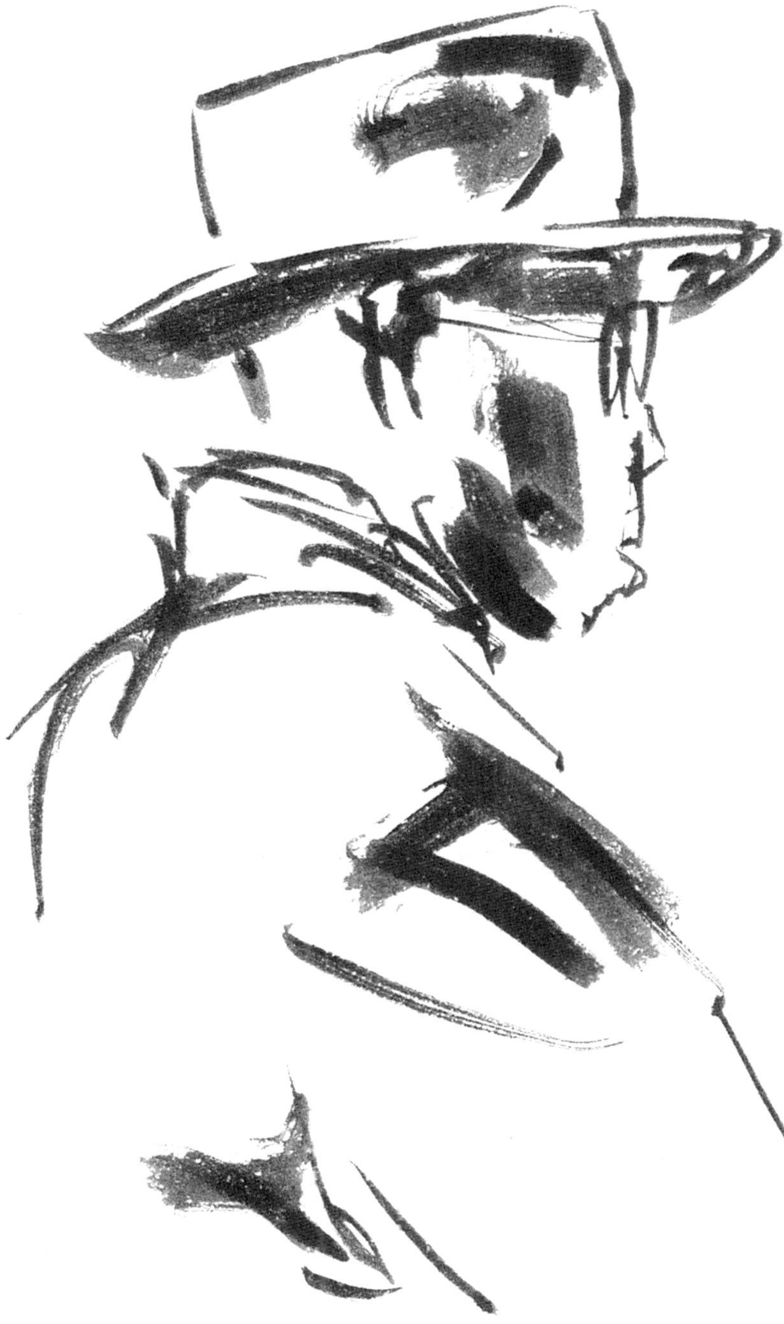

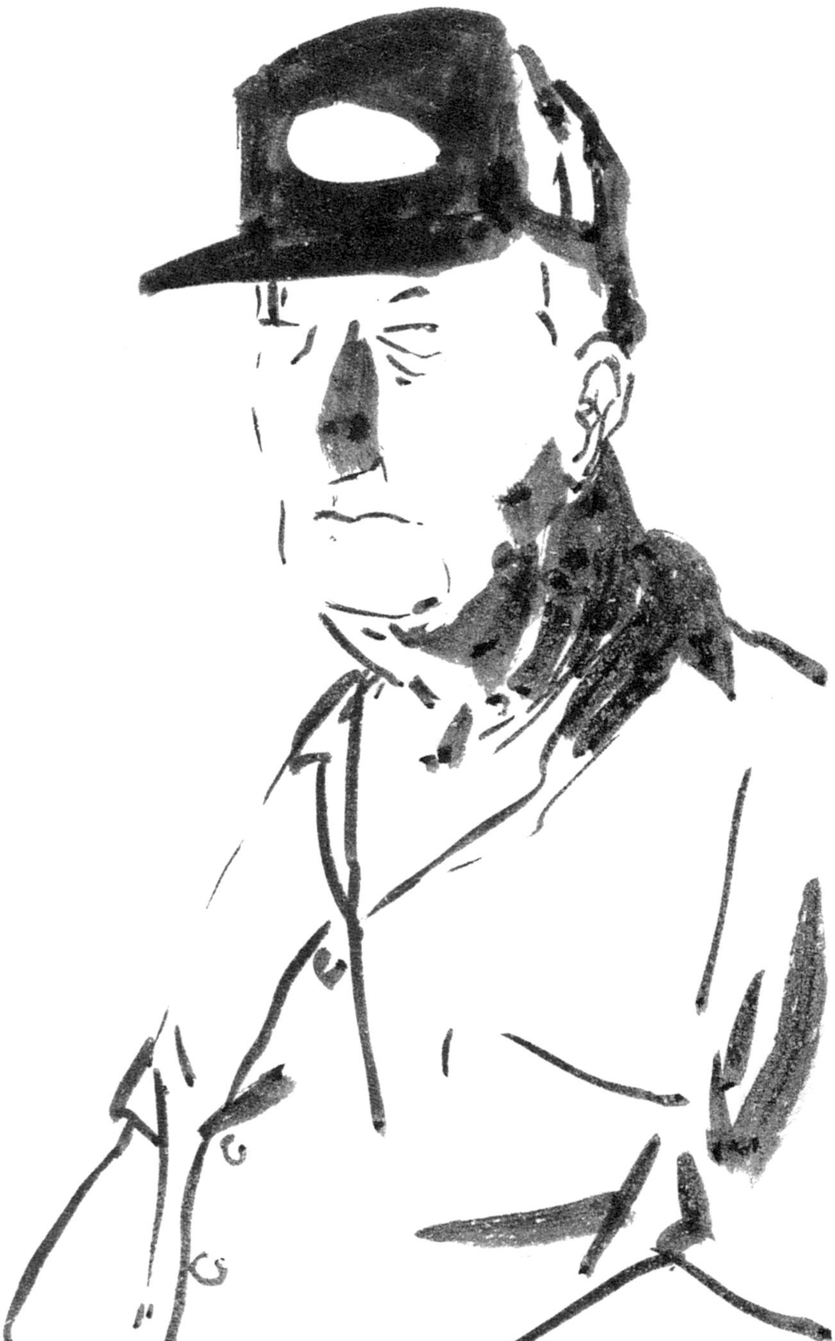

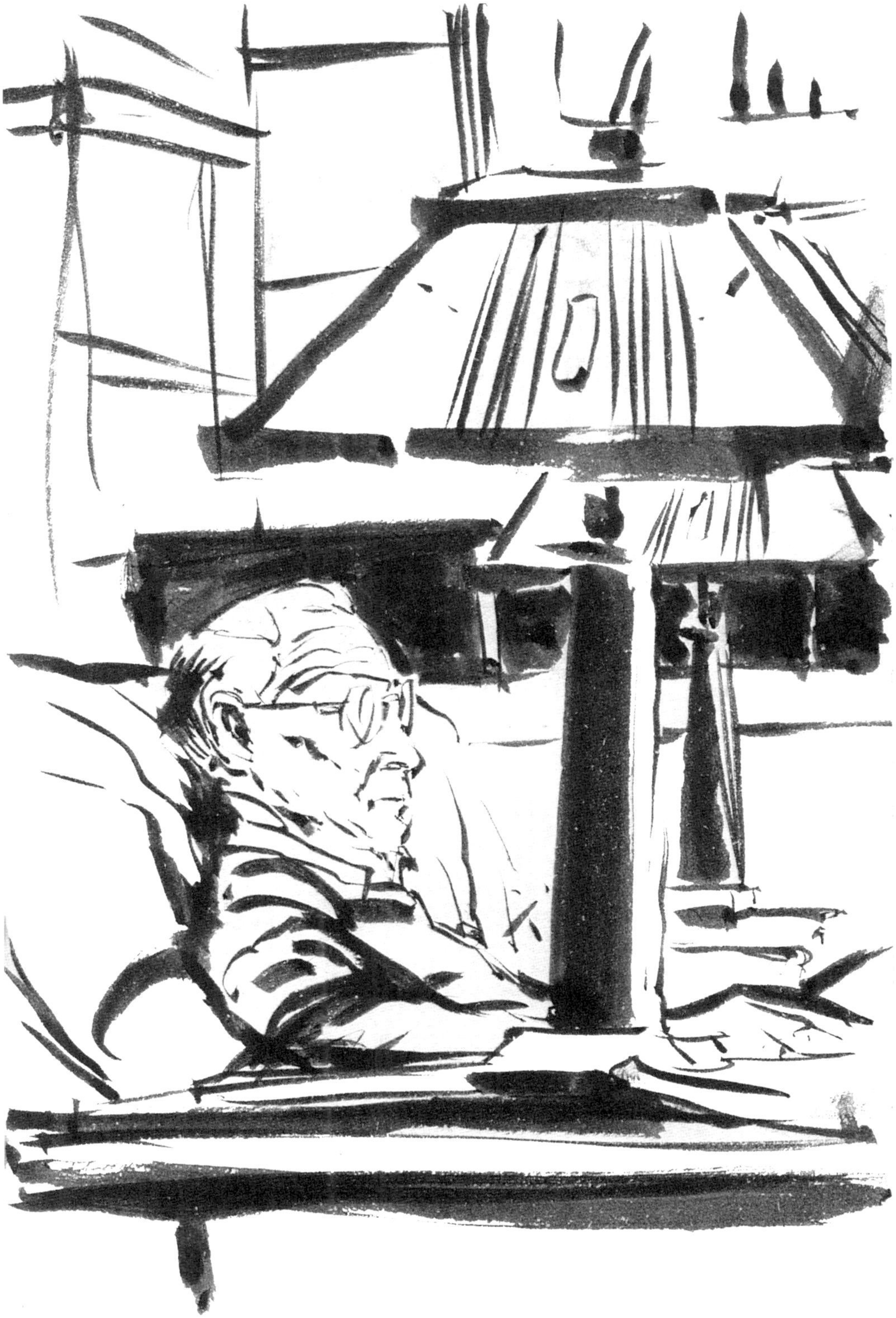

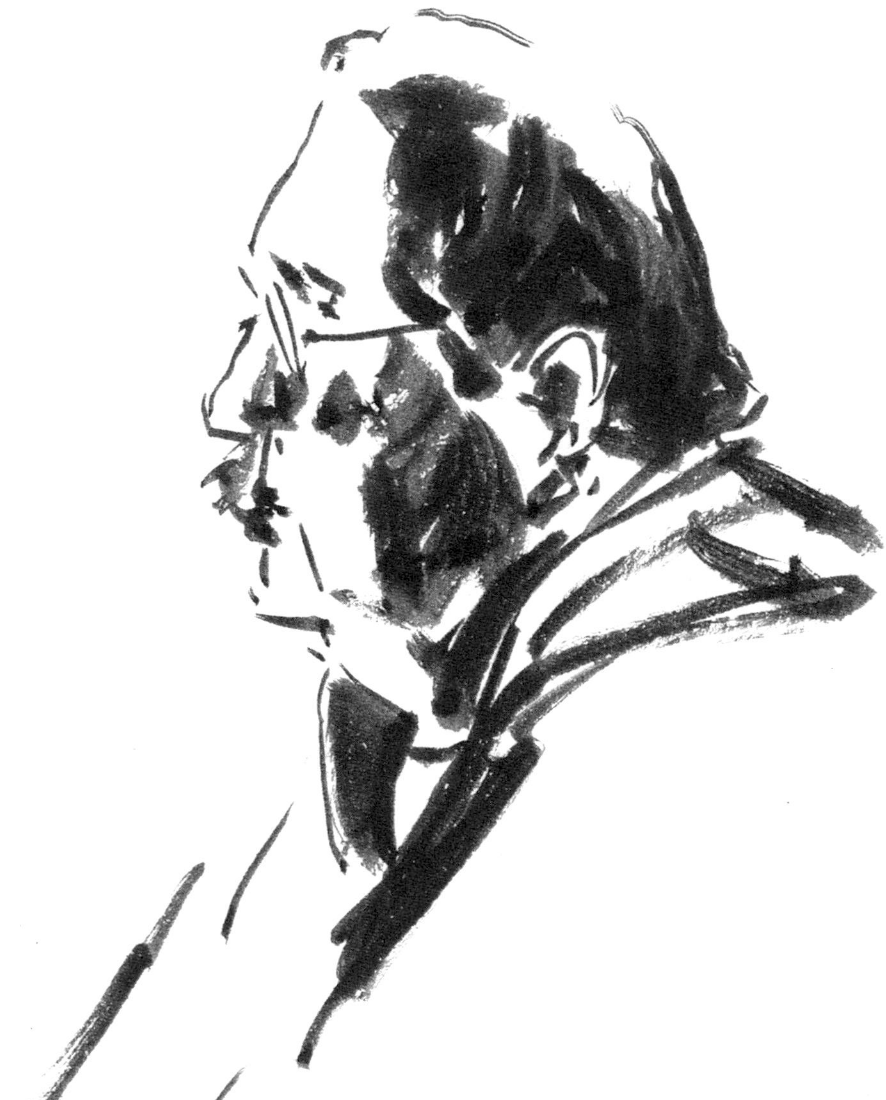

104

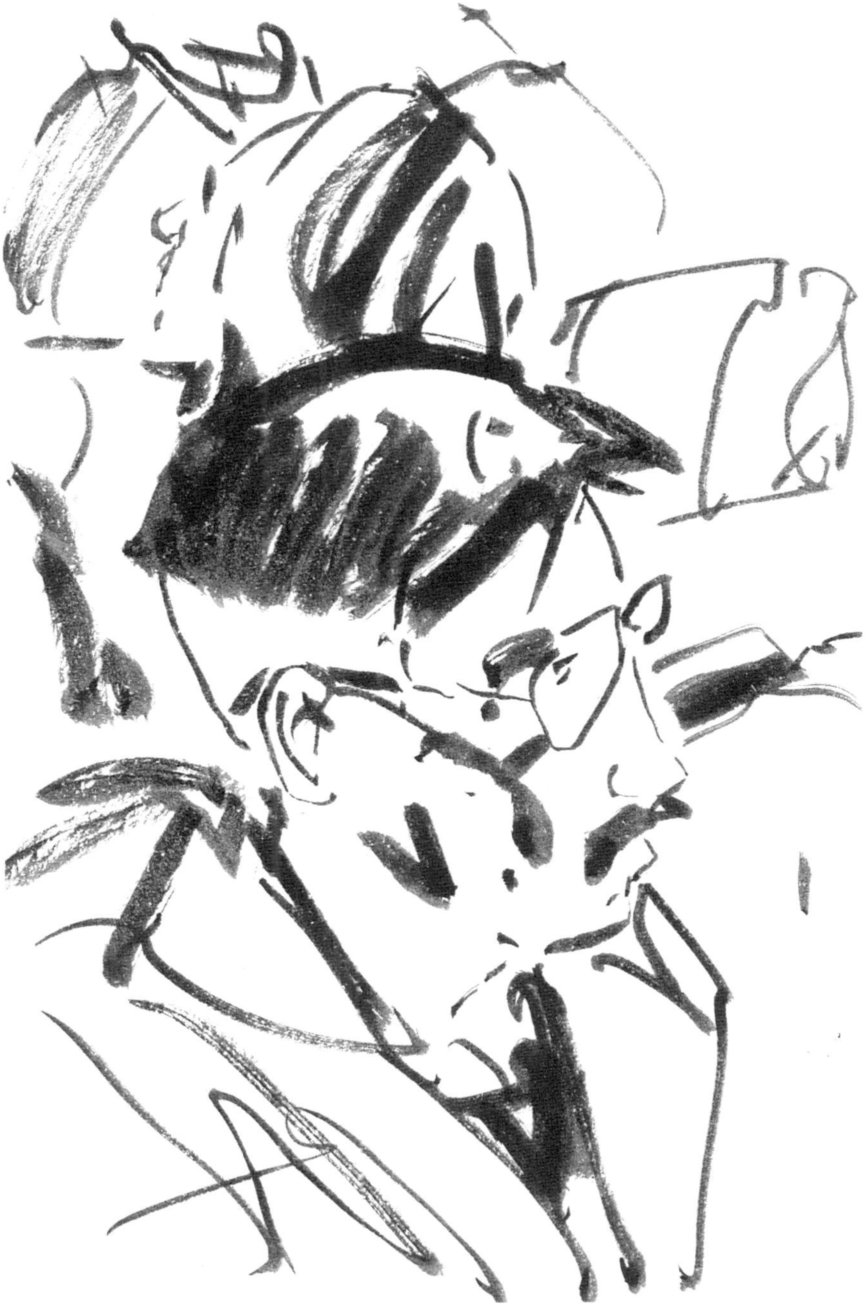

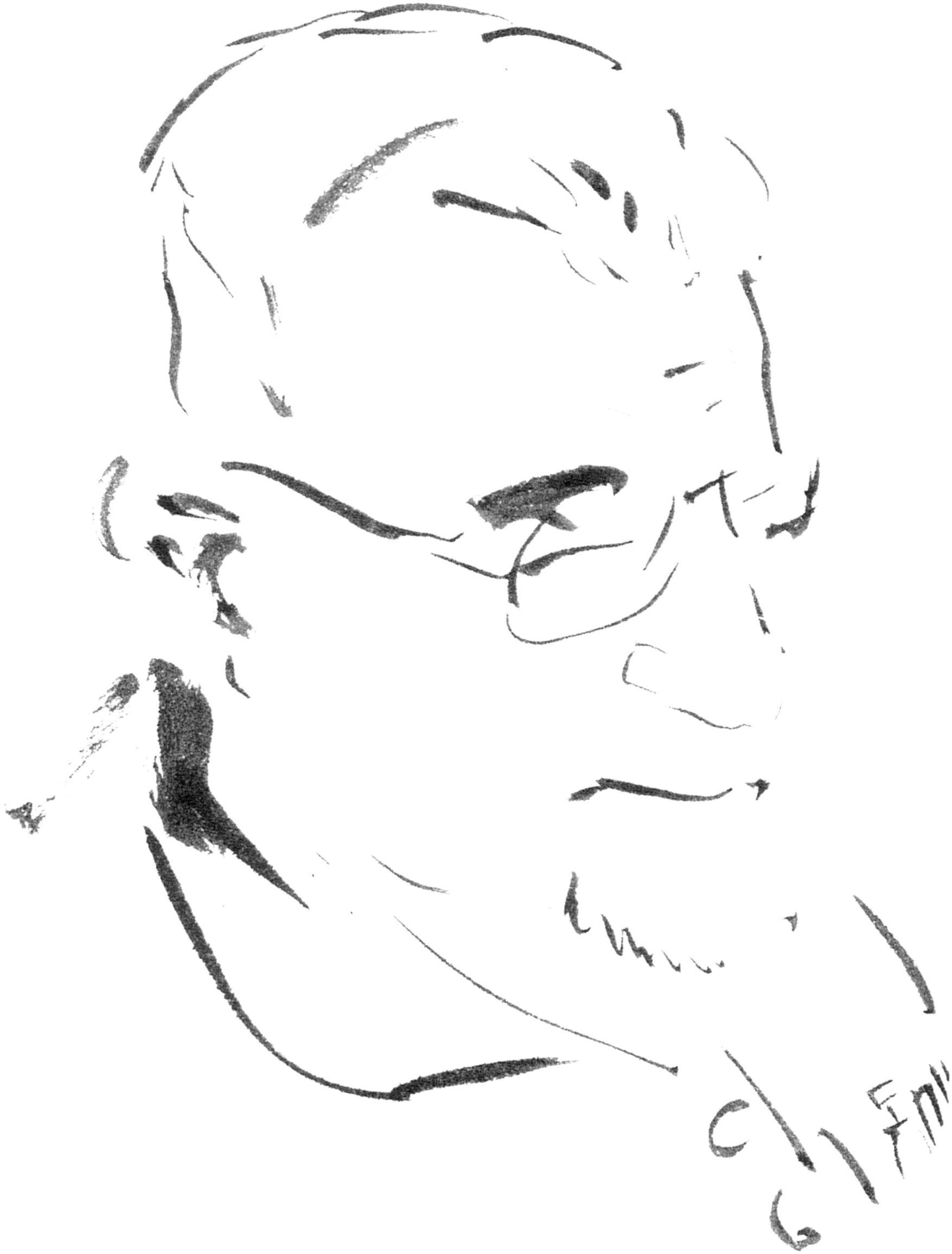

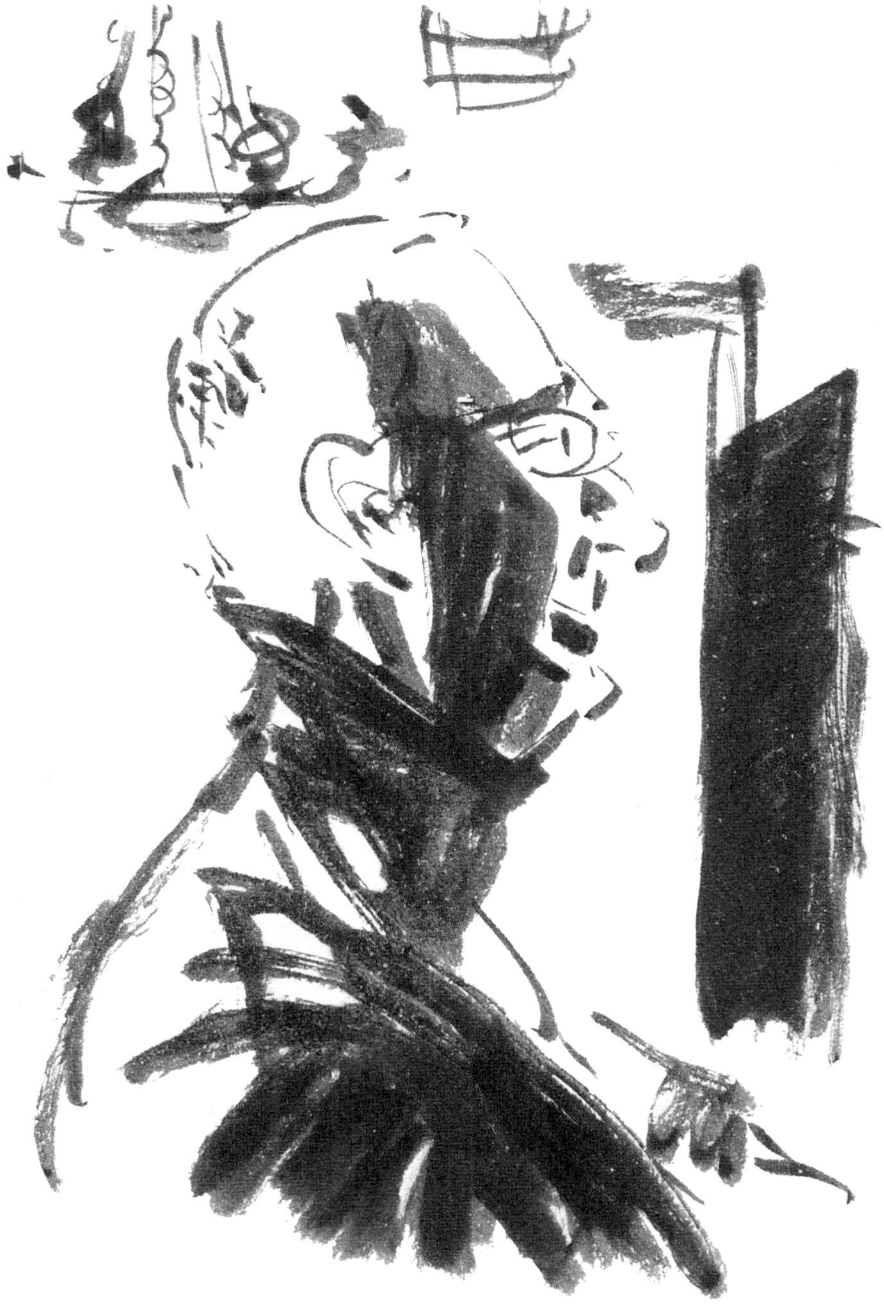

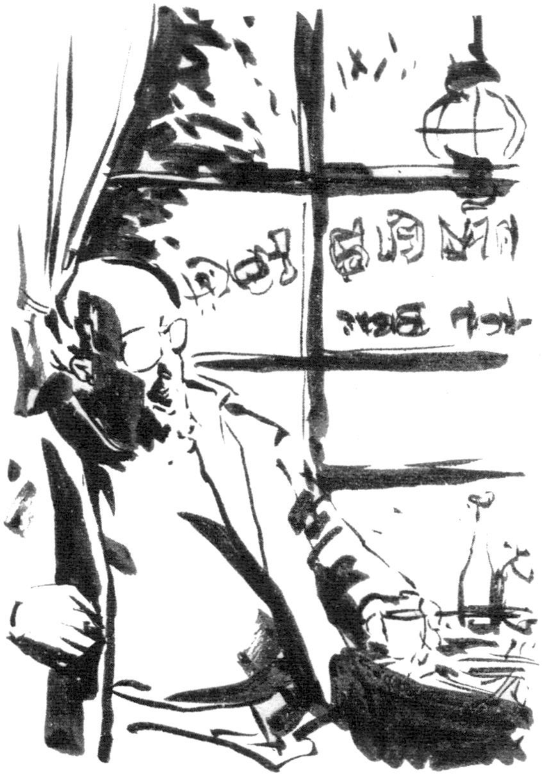

asfa presents 108 drawings, number one, 2006
published by **allen spiegel fine arts**

publisher/artists' representative:
allen spiegel fine arts
221 lobos avenue
pacific grove, ca 93950 usa
tel/fax 831.372.4672
email asfa@redshift.com
www.asfa.biz or www.allenspiegelfinearts.com

printed and bound in hong kong
through **interpress, ltd.**

design by kent williams

isbn 0-9642069-9-4
978-0-9642069-9-1